The Learning Hive

The Learning Hive

Leading Collective Innovation to Transform Education Systems

**Elizabeth Chu, Andrea Clay,
Ayeola Kinlaw, and Meghan Snyder**

Teachers College Press

Teachers College, Columbia University

Published by Teachers College Press,® 1234 Amsterdam Avenue, New York, NY 10027

Copyright © 2025 by The Trustees of Columbia University in the City of New York

Front cover design by Peter Donahue. Illustrations by Alexis Mahrus / Columbia University.

Library of Congress Cataloging-in-Publication Data is available at loc.gov

ISBN 978-0-8077-8666-6 (paper)
ISBN 978-0-8077-8667-3 (hardcover)
ISBN 978-0-8077-8286-6 (ebook)

Printed on acid-free paper
Manufactured in the United States of America

Contents

Acknowledgments

We are deeply grateful to our own Learning Hive: the Center for Public Research and Leadership (CPRL) team and our colleagues, students, peers, and partners who show us what it means to lead through learning every day. Without you, this book would not have been possible. Our hope is that you see yourselves and your work represented here.

We are especially grateful for the vision and guidance of Jim Liebman, our mentor and the founder of CPRL at Columbia University. Jim has devoted his professional life to continuous learning and to the improvement of public institutions, all in service of bettering kids' life chances. We are thankful to be a few of the many whose careers are shaped by Jim's leadership. A special thanks, also, to Kimberly Austin and Amanda Cahn, coauthors of CPRL's first Evolutionary Learning toolkit and partners in elaborating CPRL's model, and to Bryanna Willis, whose support was invaluable in completing the book. We thank as well the Learning Hives that have shared their work, time, and insights with us for this volume (the Baltimore City Public Schools improvement networks; the High Tech High Graduate School of Education and CARPE College Access Collaborative; former members of the Mississippi Department of Education and Barksdale Reading Institute; the New York City Consortium, Internationals, and Outward Bound High School District; and Partners in School Innovation).

CHAPTER 1

Miracle or Marathon?

If you work in education, you've probably heard of the "Mississippi Miracle," Mississippi's unprecedented turnaround in literacy achievement. For decades, Mississippi's literacy scores ranked among the lowest in the United States. Over the span of a single decade (2013–2022), however, Mississippi went from being ranked 49th in 4th-grade reading to 21st ("Data tools state profiles: Mississippi," n.d.). By 2024, they were ranked 9th ("Data tools state profiles: Mississippi, n.d.").

Experts across the country attribute this success to state-level policy change, in particular the 2013 Literacy-Based Promotion Act (LBPA), which requires (1) teachers to provide instruction grounded in the science of reading using evidenced-based instructional materials, (2) schools to use reading assessments to reveal student progress and need for additional support, and (3) 3rd-graders to demonstrate reading proficiency in order to advance to 4th grade (Associated Press, 2023; Hanford, 2018; B. Harris, 2019; Mississippi Literacy-Based Promotion Act, 2013; Luscombe, 2022).

The LBPA prescribed massive policy change. Educators and schools had to adopt and implement an evidence-based "science of reading" curriculum focusing on the five essential components of reading: phonemic awareness, phonics, fluency, vocabulary, and comprehension (Burk, 2020; Will, 2020), a departure from the prevailing balanced literacy approach (Hanford, 2018; Heubeck, 2023). To make this shift, Mississippi provided comprehensive professional development for administrators and preservice and inservice teachers (Burk, 2020; RMC Research Corporation, 2019), including training all teachers in Language Essentials for Teachers of Reading and Spelling (LETRS), a professional learning program on the science of reading (Schwartz, 2024). In addition, they hired and deployed dozens of literacy coaches to provide on-the-ground support to schools (Burk, 2020; Luscombe, 2022; Wicks, 2023). Schools also had to change their approach to assessment, administering a kindergarten diagnostic and universal screeners (Butler, 2024; McBride, 2021). On their surface, these shifts track top-down curricular reforms adopted by many states.

But the LBPA's policy mandates alone cannot explain Mississippi's "miracle." Other states have passed similar laws but have yet to see the same level and speed of turnaround as Mississippi (Associated Press, 2023; Schwartz, 2024). Something more happened in Mississippi, something deeper and harder to see from the outside. Not only did Mississippi change *what* educators did in schools, the state also transformed *how* educators did it—how they set strategy and aligned it to goals, how they implemented and improved, and how they shared and supported widespread, high-quality application of knowledge. In the process, Mississippi changed how it went about *deciding* what to do and how to do it.

THE MISSISSIPPI MARATHON: FROM MIRACLE TO LEARNED LEADERSHIP AND SYSTEM REDESIGN

Those deeply involved in guiding Mississippi's transformation consider it anything but a miracle, and characterize it instead as a "marathon" (Mississippi Department of Education, 2023)—one that went beyond policy mandates to changing the state school system's DNA. First came a widely shared conviction that single-digit literacy proficiency rates were unconscionable, a result of faulty system design that no longer could be tolerated. (The literacy rate was 9% in 2000; see Data Tools State Profiles: Mississippi, n.d.). Enter a broad array of actors spanning traditional divides—between public and private, research and practice, inside and outside schools, K–12 and higher education—who jointly developed a common language and goal and embarked together on a shared and continuing journey to learn how to teach all kids to read.

The Mississippi marathon of changes hypothesized, tested, and refined over time moved the state away from traditional bureaucratic methods of reform premised on a false confidence that all that needs to be known already is known. The new goal was transparent and deliberate learning about what was not yet clear: how to get better at helping *all* kids be literate. The Mississippi literacy improvement was not about a single law and set of policies that told educators and schools what to do; it required a much broader redesign effort—begun long before the law passed and extending long afterward—to incite and guide sweeping changes in how the state's system of schools, educators, and support organizations learned together how to help children read. Through this work, Mississippi created the motivation, expertise, systems, practices, community, and support networks needed to advance a vision and solutions well matched to the scale of the literacy crisis.

The marathon began over a decade before the passage of the LBPA with the launch of the Barksdale Reading Institute (BRI) in 2000. Former Netscape

CEO and philanthropist Jim Barksdale and his late wife, Sally, invested $100 million to start BRI as a public–private partnership with the Mississippi Department of Education (MDE) to address their home state's literacy crisis ("Barksdale Reading Institute," 2010; Wilson, 2000). From the outset, BRI set out to take a systems-oriented, experimentalist approach to transforming literacy instruction in schools, testing, evaluating, adapting, and scaling interventions that proved successful. As Jim Barksdale states:

> One of the things I learned in business is that one of the best ways to learn how to do something new is to try different methods. Find the ones that work and move towards them and the ones that don't work—the ideas or the programs or just the overall concept—if it doesn't work, don't be too proud. Quit it. (Barksdale Reading Institute, n.d.)

From the outset, BRI's problem orientation was clear. It was not that the Institute had to discover an evidence-based method for teaching literacy. On this, the research already was unambiguous, particularly after the release in 2000 of the National Reading Panel's germinal report: *Teaching Children to Read: An Evidence-Based Assessment of the Scientific Research Literature on Reading and Its Implications for Reading Instruction*. The problem that had yet to be solved was how to transform the way an entire state's system of public schools teaches literacy, making sure all schools consistently use the most effective evidence-based practices available.

Eschewing traditional bureaucratic methods of achieving system transformation by mandating behavior change and holding educators and schools accountable for complying with prescribed policy, BRI set about discovering how to achieve consistent implementation of effective evidence-based reading instruction at scale, acting as the "engine for reading expertise in the state" and as the research and design shop for policies that only later were codified in the LBPA (Reading Universe, 2023). Over the course of its first decade, BRI experimented with a number of implementation and scaling models, modifying and expanding its overall theory of change based on collected data. For example, from a 2006–2009 pilot of demonstration classrooms in some of the lowest performing elementary schools in the state, BRI learned alongside teaching staff how to structure and deliver literacy instruction to make significant gains in student literacy learning—developing instructional and intervention strategies while addressing operational questions, such as the time required for a classroom literacy block (McBride, 2021). During this time, BRI also learned—and forthrightly acknowledged what the developers of so many promising innovations never discover or admit—that, as effective as its model initially was, it did not know *precisely how* the model worked because its first efforts failed to "expand practice beyond the demonstration site itself" (McBride, 2021, p. 15). Only through more experimentation did BRI discover that its scaling strategy had to focus more on coaching and building district and school leaders' knowledge and buy-in for effective implementation of the evidence-based literacy blocks that had performed so well under demonstration conditions (McBride, 2021).

BRI's systems-change approach generated the additional insight that scaling up effective literacy instruction would mean addressing factors outside the walls of a classroom and the boundaries of a school. Recognizing the steep cost of retraining teachers who had not had science of reading training in their educator preparation programs, BRI partnered with MDE and universities to test methods for improving preservice training (Hanford, 2018). Initial approaches (e.g., funding salaries of faculty members who were to implement and spread the use of science of reading coursework) made little difference, so they employed other strategies, such as training faculty and altering preservice exam requirements, to greater effect (Burk, 2020). In one of many interviews conducted with educators and leaders between 2020 and 2025 for this volume, BRI's Kelly Butler summarized their early efforts: "We were able to be nimble and try things long enough to see what conditions they might work under and if we felt like conditions weren't going to change and we weren't going to be successful. In any definition of bureaucracy, you will not find the word nimble, and I think that's a part of systems change."

The LBPA captured the fruits of this R&D phase, operationalizing the explicit body of knowledge that practitioners, researchers, and administrators had developed over the prior decade. After the LBPA passed, experimentation continued, using the law as a framework that guided decisionmaking, collaboration, problem-solving, and improvement, rather than as the source of mandates. Instead of communicating practice standards and systems via prescriptive rules, the state enabled their widespread, contextually-appropriate application through a number of supports, from state-provided professional development, to regional trainings, to school-based coaches focused on the lowest performing schools. These coaches upskill teachers and administrators, support implementation, and serve as a feedback mechanism to the state about what is working and what needs to be changed.

The department itself is responsible for pursuing learning and improvement in system design, support, and culture in parallel with improvements in classrooms and schools. The focus is not on compliance with policy, but on improving quality—how well teachers are trained, how well teachers are supported, how well teachers learn, and how well teachers teach. The MDE shed its former role as a regulator focused on compliance and recreated itself as a quality support and facilitator of improvement. In former MDE Literacy Director Kymyona Burk's words,

> It really changed the perception of the agency, from an auditing arm, where the department's role is to come out to your school because something's happened, to more of a support for schools and districts. Before, the state was seen as just giving you the standards and being responsible for state tests. But this effort was complete—and just different. There was a different department, different feel. Our support went beyond checking on the implementation of the policies that we adopted. It was all of the other nuances as to how we supported and engaged with educators and stakeholders that I think has made it all come together like it has.

Take a striking example that illustrates the state's focus on *quality* support from the earliest implementation of the LBPA. After the LBPA passed, MDE, in partnership with BRI, set out to hire 75 coaches statewide to support implementation of science of reading curriculum in schools with the lowest 3rd-grade reading scores (Heubeck, 2023). Over 600 individuals applied for the job, but MDE determined that only 24 met its quality criteria—and only those few were hired (Heubeck, 2023). As Tenette Smith, executive director of elementary education and reading at MDE, explained: "They were looking for quality over quantity. That only 24 were selected showed us we had a lot of ground to cover" (Heubeck, 2023). The state has continued to expand its coaching capacity, while maintaining its emphasis on quality over quantity in its selection process. As of the 2022–2023 school year, the state had 52 coaches serving 86 public schools (Heubeck, 2023).

Crucial to Mississippi's success was the way BRI, and then the LBPA and the MDE in implementing it, changed how the state views problems: Not as something to be hidden or ignored but as an opportunity to discover and apply improved strategies and interventions through democratic learning processes integrated into the system's daily work. The LBPA's mandated screeners and criteria for promoting students to 4th grade, along with practices spread through the act's implementation, such as informal daily assessments and data-informed coaching cycles, supported this shift (Heubeck, 2023). Schools across the state use screening and intervention to identify and address reading problems early, often in collaboration with parents and caregivers. When students do not learn at expected rates, schools and teachers see that information as both prompting a responsibility and providing an opportunity to adjust their strategy and improve their practice. For example, leading up to the end of 3rd grade, schools assess students' reading levels and use interventions, including tutoring and summer literacy camps, to support students who are not yet proficient (Associated Press, 2023). If students do not demonstrate reading levels required for 4th-grade promotion, they are assigned to a highly effective teacher, and teachers, coaches, and parents/guardians come together to diagnose the challenges and create an Individual Reading Plan (IRP) to meet that individual student's needs through focused literacy instruction and intervention (Collins, 2022; Heubeck, 2023). Educators and families understand IRPs not as punitive measures but as supportive ones, manifesting, in turn, a systemwide "expectation of shared responsibility for literacy," a shift from command and compliance to collaborative problem solving, and a focus on continued, systemic improvement (Mississippi Department of Education, n.d.). This shift has had a measurable effect on student outcomes: a 2023 study found that 3 years after retention and IRP intervention, retained students outperformed their peers by 1.2 standard deviations with no impact on student absenteeism or special education referral (Collins, 2023). In other words, rethinking the way they understood problems ultimately drove higher quality of instruction and stronger outcomes.

Mississippi's efforts have paid off. Despite being the poorest state in the nation and ranking among the lowest with respect to per pupil funding and education spending, its 4th grade proficiency rates have increased by almost 20 percentage points since the marathon's start in 2000, pushing the state just above the national average (Data tools state profiles: Mississippi, n.d.). Although all student groups have improved, historically marginalized students have seen the greatest gains. After adjusting for sociodemographic and other background characteristics, Mississippi ranks near the top of the nation in 4th grade literacy performance on the National Assessment for Educational Progress (NAEP), a turnaround from its near-bottom performance in 2002 (Barnum, 2023; Blagg et al., 2020). Over that period, proficiency rates for Black students and low-income students more than doubled (Data tools state profiles: Mississippi, n.d.).

THE LEARNING HIVE: EQUITY-ADVANCING SYSTEM DESIGN AND LEADERSHIP

Trust in public schooling is at an all-time low (Saad, 2023), and after decades of data suggesting failure to serve our most vulnerable students, this lack of confidence is not unfounded. But our public schools are too important to abandon. At their best, they provide fulfilling, joyful, and transformative learning experiences for children from all backgrounds. They contribute to civic strength, providing young people and their communities with opportunities and skills to participate in democracy and forge bonds across lines of difference. And they are sites of community strength, serving as anchors for human connection in an increasingly isolated and isolating world.

To realize this promise, schools need to change. As in Mississippi—and other states, districts, and schools like it—we have to rewire how institutions, organizations, schools, and individuals learn, make decisions, adapt, and grow. In a quickly evolving world, we need a model for public schooling that is more dynamic, that draws in more voices, that experiments and seeks constant improvement. And we need leaders with the vision to drive this change. There is already evidence that such a model produces results.

Mississippi is one of many school systems and school support organizations that employ similar policies, strategies, programming, and materials, to far different effects. It is tragic when a promising strategy successful in one context is implemented in another without regard to contextual differences and needs; disappointing outcomes are almost inevitable and strategies that could make a real difference for students are abandoned. The central system design and leadership challenge, therefore, is how to ensure high-quality choices about what strategies to implement when and where, and then how to ensure strategies' high-quality implementation at scale. This challenge is one of equity, as it largely accounts for systematic variability in the quality of service provision and thus in the extent to which the needs of different students are met.

Delivering consistently high-quality service doesn't mean delivering uniform service. In complex systems that inevitably differ one from the next, quality service is highly dependent on context—demanding different substantive strategies for different communities, schools, classrooms, families, and students, and different ways of implementing those strategies. Therefore, it is only by improving governance (how we identify, choose among, and implement strategies) and democracy (how fully we enable implementing employees and affected populations to drive those choices) that we can assure that public school systems effectively align different policies to the different contexts in which they operate.

The lesson we draw from the Mississippi miracle: When systems work together with their constituencies to get better every day in how they choose, implement, observe, and improve policies suited to their diverse children and communities, they make progress toward equity. Further, each increment of progress validates and sustains the structures, practices, and mindsets that enable systems to adapt effectively to an uncertain and quickly changing world.

This shift in focus, from policy to governance, from *what* you do to *how* to choose, implement, and improve what you do, begins with leaders. Leaders in these systems think and operate in a new way. They equip and expect everyone in the system—including themselves—to pursue, in a coordinated manner, answers to one core question: "How do we get better all the time?"

This coordinated pursuit is key to implementing high-quality services at scale, and it has a name: Evolutionary Learning (EL). Leaders of transformed systems move away from the inflexible bureaucratic approaches so common in education and shape their organizations into dynamic hives of experimentation where daily operations are treated as ongoing opportunities for collaborative learning and improvement. This requires fundamental changes in how leaders enable organizational actors—students, families, ground-level staff (e.g., teachers, paraprofessionals, counselors, bus drivers), and administrators—to make decisions, access the expertise of community members, approach learning and measurement, spread and scale knowledge, and define success. Rejecting the myth of the complete leader—the idea that those in charge hold answers to and expertise in all of the organization's problems—leaders function as "learners in chief," both by orchestrating learning across the system and by actively participating in it, submitting their own leadership strategy and system design to the same scrutiny they apply to the activities and processes of others. Through this work, leaders build organizations that are able to adjust and tailor practice to meet the needs of different people, contexts, and moments— and, as a result, deliver more effective learning experiences to more students more often.

We often compare EL-driven systems to beehives, which, like active, healthy schools and organizations, look and sound busy—even agitated to the point of seeming disorganized—to an outsider. But amidst this apparent disarray, bee colonies function as democratic and integrated communities in which each bee has a substantive role in decision-making that allows the collective to adapt and build a dynamic survival strategy in a changing environment (Seeley, 2011).

Our Evolutionary Learning framework is grounded in exactly these principles, which we can cast as four core drivers of effective system design.

- *Build a hive:* Cultivate systems that draw in all system actors— those the system employs and those it serves—to engage in robust vision-setting, strategy development, and learning.
- *Swarm problems, innovate, and pollinate learning:* Democratize and streamline the generation, consolidation, capture,

sharing, and application of knowledge to solve problems and innovate.

- *Harvest data to monitor and improve:* Measure process and outcomes across the system to identify what works, for whom, under what conditions.
- *Lead the Learning Hive:* Propel innovation, enable participatory decision-making and collaboration, and serve as learners in chief.

Four cross-cutting concepts shape the operationalization of each driver. The first is *equity*, which means meeting the needs of each student, especially students of color, experiencing poverty, or otherwise traditionally underserved. This lens is built on what Sabel et al. (2011, p. 84) describe as a shift from a traditional conception of "fairness" or "equality" as "treating all in the same way" to, instead, "an understanding of equality as an obligation to give due regard to the needs of each and so enable all to flourish." In systems that outperform their peers, like Mississippi's, leaders' and their systems' conceptions of equity move away from assuring uniform inputs and instead focus on adapting strategy and services to meet the specific needs of each child and community as a matter of course. That shift is at the root of any "miracle" improvement in outcomes: Attention to providing service that met the needs of every child improved individual student outcomes and, over time, decreased the variation in outcomes among children, schools, and districts with different backgrounds, contexts, and needs.

The second concept is *governance*, which refers to how public school systems and other organizations go about deciding what substantive policies to implement in given circumstances and how to implement those policies and improve them over time. Governance defines the "how" of an organization's practice—how organizations and systems set goals, motivate actors to meet those goals, design strategies, engage stakeholders, measure progress, and respond to evidence of success and failure.

The third key idea is *democracy*—or described differently, politics—which defines how and to what extent public systems enable their client populations, ground-level staff, and other stakeholders to participate meaningfully in making, carrying out, evaluating, and improving substantive decisions. Because public schools are public institutions, their approach to democracy is particularly salient to their success and that of our society.

The final overall concept is *policy*, which we intentionally put last, though it is often considered first in education circles. Policy refers to the laws, rules, strategies, standards, guidance, and accepted practices that create expectations and shape how public systems execute their work. Policy captures *what* systems aim to do at any given moment—and what they strive to choose well and improve continuously through the operation of the other three lenses.

Key Terms

- *Equity*: Meeting the needs of each student, enabling all to thrive.
- *Governance:* How public school systems and other organizations go about deciding what substantive policies to implement in given circumstances and how to implement those policies and improve them over time in order to reach stated and unstated goals.
- *Democracy:* How and to what extent public systems enable their client populations, ground-level staff, and other interested parties to participate meaningfully in making, carrying out, evaluating, and improving substantive decisions.
- *Policy:* Laws, rules, strategies, standards, guidance, and accepted practices that create expectations and shape how public systems execute their work.

In this book, we make the case that what distinguishes EL learning hives is leaders' attention to the alignment of system context and goals, on the one hand, and governance and democracy, on the other. We ask:

- What if instead of searching for the right policy for *all* contexts, we search for good ways to identify and improve policies for *each* context?
- What if instead of constant triage to address challenges, we alter our organizational structures so that we can get to and address the roots of these challenges?
- And what if instead of relying on central leaders to have all the answers, we engage everyone—system and local leaders, frontline staff, students, families, communities—in embracing uncertainty as they learn together?

Making these shifts requires a commitment to customization instead of to one-size-fits-all policies and practices. Actors must employ an experimentalist governance approach that motivates ongoing system improvement. Organized as a hive (see Figure 1.1), a wide cohort of stakeholders—including students, families, teachers, counselors, and other ground-level

Figure 1.1. The Learning Hive (adapted from Aghina et al., 2018)

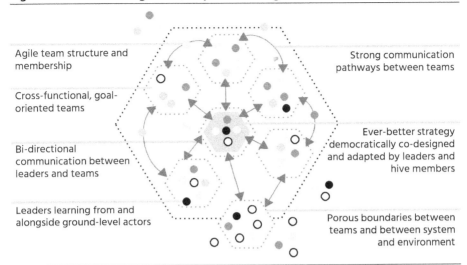

Agile team structure and membership

Cross-functional, goal-oriented teams

Bi-directional communication between leaders and teams

Leaders learning from and alongside ground-level actors

Strong communication pathways between teams

Ever-better strategy democratically co-designed and adapted by leaders and hive members

Porous boundaries between teams and between system and environment

staff—participate in and contribute to learning and decision-making, ensuring system learning is rich and responsive to local context and needs.

WHAT'S AHEAD

This book guides emerging, aspiring, and established leaders as they rewire systems to engage in systematic learning and experimentation in pursuit of all students thriving. These systems intentionally attune policy and its implementation to differences that exist from student to student, classroom to classroom, school to school, system to system. Throughout this book, we draw from nearly a decade and a half of research at the Center for Public Research and Leadership (CPRL) at Columbia University, including dozens of interviews with and observations of the Evolutionary Learning hives profiled in each chapter. Reflecting the interdisciplinary nature of problem-solving in public education, we also draw insights, examples, and tools from a range of disciplines outside of education—business, law, healthcare, climate science, and public policy.

In Chapter 2, we lay out in greater detail the hypothesis that educational inequity stems from a fundamental mismatch between school systems' contexts and goals and their governance and democracy. School systems are complex organizations operating in unstable conditions aiming to provide equitable service to students and communities with diverse needs. Yet most school systems rely on entrenched and outmoded approaches to governance and democracy designed to perform in entirely different circumstances, where conditions are stable, needs homogeneous, and outcomes predictable. We provide a number of examples of systems that have tried valiantly to pursue and fallen short of achieving equity at scale, held back by bureaucratic, managerialist, professionalist, and craft models of governance.

In Chapter 3, we introduce Evolutionary Learning, our alternative to the governance models outlined in Chapter 2. A novel form of public institutional research, problem-solving, governance, and democratic participation, Evolutionary Learning offers a disciplined approach to organizational learning and improvement. That discipline, with its complementary set of concepts and tools, motivates and enables individuals and organizations to structure all aspects of everyday activity as carefully observed tests; from these, they can learn rapidly and constantly how to improve their theory of action and its implementation and to maximize its impact. Central to the framework is a theory and practical mode of democracy that puts consequential participation by the frontline staff who implement organizational strategies and the people and communities affected by them at the heart of the strategies' design and improvement.

In Chapter 4, we explore how learning organizations build and organize their hives. We describe the structures, routines, practices, and culture needed to ensure that Evolutionary Learning hives make "learning the work" (Fullan, 2020). Hives orient all activity around a shared, evolving strategy and learning approach, making permeable the boundaries between those leading, those implementing, and those served. As routine daily work and problem-solving become the grist for local and system-level improvement, hives widen and make porous their boundaries, thinking more expansively about who needs to be engaged if the system is to develop and improve strategy and practice that works for every child. A commitment to cultivating a culture grounded in concrete collaborative problem-solving provides a foundation for this work.

In Chapter 5, we examine how hives use democratic problem-solving systems and routines to improve and innovate, pollinating the entire organization with the most up-to-date knowledge about how to implement strategies equitably and well. In these systems, knowledge management is no longer solely conceived of as a technical venture focused on processing and storing data and information, but as the outcome of deliberate and collaborative strategic choices. Working backward from the system's ambitious goals, leaders set, enact, and maintain a vision for how all community members—including staff, students, parents, and partners—will give input but also meaningfully contribute to the generation, consolidation, capture, sharing, and application of knowledge. A collaborative improvement infrastructure supports actors at all layers of the system in sharing, making sense of, and using data to bridge daily learning into strategic progress. Democratic participation strengthens knowledge generation and builds buy-in and capacity for knowledge application, yielding better and more efficient outcomes.

In Chapter 6, we examine how learning hives harvest data to monitor and improve system design, strategy, and practice. We zoom in on the measurement and monitoring of strategy implementation at the local and collective levels. In hives measurement is no longer linked exclusively to end-stage accountability. Instead, it functions as an early alert system, prompting and enabling actors to spot and explicitly name problems and opportunities for improvement whenever and wherever they occur—and quickly swing into action to learn from and address them. Hives engage in ongoing experimentation that yields opportunities for fundamental change and improvement, not just small tweaks to head off surfaced problems. Done right, measurement communicates core values, focuses stakeholders on the strategy, and supports localized and system-wide learning. Hives home in on select measures that allow them to gauge the most important parts of strategy. They focus on elements that are essential to advancing equity, are most tightly aligned to the ultimate aim, and are able to serve as early alerts when things fall off track. Through this work, measurement allows the hive to deliberately and continually advance.

In Chapter 7, we introduce the leading through learning approach that hive leaders employ. We explore how leaders in successful organizations reject the role of know-all, tell-all director, instead building leadership capacity at each layer of the organization. In these systems, leaders are cultivators of a democratic, learning-driven culture that encourages the distribution of power, development of a collective mentality, and constant reflexivity. They are capacity builders, who develop in hive members the collaborative skills and learning behaviors that enable ongoing improvement. They are coordinators, ensuring that participatory processes are in place when and where they are needed and that learning across the organization is streamlined to accelerate improvement. And they are system architects, building and constantly refining the structures that enable collaborative decision-making and ongoing innovation. Each of these tasks requires a learning leader who both facilitates and participates in learning, examining and improving their own leadership strategy and the system's design with the same attention that they apply to the activities of other stakeholders in their system.

Chapter 8 concludes the book with steps readers can take to shift their own practice, team, or organization to a learning hive, helping readers right-size their transformation goals and start working with others to put the exercises and ideas of this book into action.

Each chapter includes theoretical foundations, vignettes of hives in action, reflection activities, tips on putting theory into practice, and cases of system and leadership redesign.

Let's get started, together!

For more resources, check out our website:
https://www.leadingthroughlearning.org.

CHAPTER 2

The Challenge

Systems differ from each other in two primary ways. First is how they identify, choose among, implement, and improve strategies. We call this the system's method of *governance*. Second is how systems enable people who are not part of their formal leadership, especially ground-level staff (teachers, for example) and people the system serves (families and students, for example) to inform and help make those choices. We call this the system's method of *democracy*. To succeed, a system's governance and democracy must be well matched to its context and goals. Many of our public school systems' designs are not so matched, keeping them from achieving what we call *educational equity*.

In this chapter, we consider three models of governance and democracy: bureaucracy, managerialism, and craft/professionalism. Although many school systems use one or a combination of these models, no one nor any combination of them has advanced educational equity at scale. To clarify the models and how they differ, the rest of this chapter strips each model down to its essential elements and identifies the model's basic assumptions (including its sources of knowledge and information), identifies when and where each model fails to achieve its stated goals, and provides vignettes of how each model has worked in public schooling. In each case, we assume that school systems' overarching goal is to meet the needs of each student, enabling all to thrive, so producing educational equity.

We start our investigation of governance and democracy with *bureaucracy*, historically the model that has dominated the nation's public school systems.

BUREAUCRACY: TOP-DOWN, RULE-DRIVEN, INDUSTRIAL-STYLE MANAGEMENT

Bureaucracy is grounded in principles of equality, defined as treating all "likes" alike. It assumes that most people are similar and that the most effective and fairest way to serve all well is to identify and apply to all the best set of resources and procedures that work in typical cases. In this way, bureaucracy strives for objectivity, seeking uniformly beneficial outcomes through uniform inputs and activities (Kocka, 1981).

In the public schooling context, bureaucracy aims to achieve both optimal student learning and equality through the implementation and enforcement of centrally developed rules that specify the resources and procedures that school districts and schools should provide children (Sizer, 2004). To do so equally, bureaucratic schooling in the United States segments students into 13 (K–12) age-based grade bands, determines what is needed for the typical student of that band, and bases the system design on providing those resources and procedures for all students within that grade.

Bureaucracy first emerged in the private sector in the 18th century as a way to facilitate industrialization in Europe and the United States. As new technologies enabled a shift from small-scale, craft-oriented systems of local production to large-scale, technically-complex mass production, factory managers faced a governance challenge: how to organize, coordinate, control, and discipline large and heterogeneous groups of workers unaccustomed to this new form of manufacturing. Many of these workers came from family farms and had moved to urban centers for the first time. Thus, owners and managers needed a way to ensure workers (1) knew what to do and did it and (2) worked for the good of the organization rather than their individual interests (Kocka, 1981). Accordingly, owners and managers formalized and regulated workflow through strict, centrally developed rules, procedures, divisions of labor, and disciplinary procedures that limited the discretion of frontline workers as they executed a narrow set of tasks (Kocka, 1981). This hierarchical model created more predictable, easily managed, and financially efficient factories that produced uniform, high-quality goods at scale.

Later, in the early 20th-century Progressive era, bureaucracy overtook public school system design. By developing what historian David Tyack (1974) has famously described as the "One Best System," public-sector reformers sought to obtain the same efficiencies in publicly educating a rapidly growing, increasingly diverse student population as industrial factories achieved through rigidly organized production lines.

Bureaucracy = Uniformity via Top-Down Rules

Bureaucracies are structured as top-down pyramids with well-developed divisions of labor (see Figure 2.1). At each level of the pyramid, supervisors oversee a "complete" set of related processes and tasks, exercising authority over those responsible for each component part.

Figure 2.1. Bureaucratic System Design (Adapted From Aghina et al., 2018)

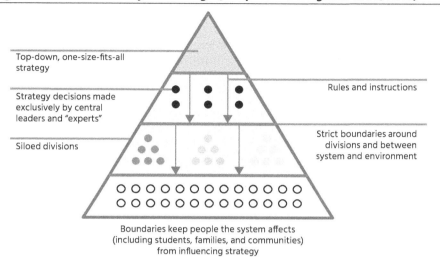

Top-down, one-size-fits-all strategy

Rules and instructions

Strategy decisions made exclusively by central leaders and "experts"

Strict boundaries around divisions and between system and environment

Siloed divisions

Boundaries keep people the system affects (including students, families, and communities) from influencing strategy

Positional leaders at the top are assumed to hold most of the knowledge and expertise needed to organize and guide the organization's core functions, while those at the bottom are assumed to have little of either (Kocka, 1981). Because those at the top are experts, bureaucracies rely on them to design the entire system's operations to meet the organization's goals and achieve its mission (Liebman et al., 2017). Decision-making is centralized and communicated via prescriptive rules that specify how lower-level employees are to perform. These rules and procedures aim to cover every important component of every employee's work process and to specify the rewards and consequences for complying with or violating the rules. Just as lower-level employees cannot be trusted to have knowledge about how to best do their work, they also cannot be trusted to follow elaborate rules. Accordingly, accountability focuses on compliance: Supervisors assess and judge employees' success based on adherence to specified protocols and procedures. This combination of one-way top-down decision-making, clearly communicated directives, and transparent and enforced compliance is key to bureaucracies' success (Volti, 2011).

If you encounter a system trying to implement a "silver bullet" solution uniformly across a broad swath of people who are required to follow an elaborate set of rules, you're likely looking at a bureaucracy.

Bureaucracy Works in Systems With Known and Stable Conditions. Bureaucracy works well when conditions and actors are similar across contexts and over time. In those circumstances, actors at the top can set and maintain organization-wide agreement on goals, structure work using well-orchestrated divisions of labor, and prescribe strategies and mandate and monitor compliance with implementation steps.

Not surprisingly, therefore, bureaucracy has proven successful in many contexts beyond the factories where it initially arose. One example is New York City's 1976 window safety legislation. To prevent child fall–related injuries and deaths, NYC Health Department experts developed and implemented a set of rules for the design, installation, and enforcement of window guards in apartment buildings on or above the second floor where children live. Enforced through legal mandates paired with inspections and criminal liability for noncompliance, the mandate has steeply diminished window falls from over 100 annually prior to 1976 to just nine in 2023 (NYC Department of Health, 2024), and inspired implementation of similar programs nationally (Toprani et al., 2018). The problem lent itself to a centrally-developed, one-size-fits-all solution, given (1) a clear and widely accepted goal (zero child-fall deaths and injuries); (2) the uniformity of actors, actions, and conditions that matter (contractors' installation of standard, relatively inexpensive, metal window guards in windows that open in residential buildings above the first floor); and (3) the small number of necessary exceptions (windows leading to fire escapes).

Bureaucracy Does Not Work in Complex Systems. Bureaucracy works well in stable and predictable systems, but not in those that are diverse and in flux. In other words, it is ill-suited for complex systems, because they are

- constantly changing, often unpredictably, in response to changes in their environment (Preskill et al., 2014);
- highly relational, defined as much by the relationships between entities (e.g., actors, teams, departments, institutions, groups) as they are by those entities themselves (McQuillan, 2008; Preskill et al., 2014), with changes in one part of the system affecting others (Preskill et al., 2014); and
- nonlinear, with multifaceted, multidirectional, and difficult to isolate causation (Clarke et al., 2017; Snowden, 2024).

In complex systems, rules cannot assure bureaucracy's principle of fair service: treating "likes" alike—and, as a corollary, treating "unlikes" differently. When faced with diversity and unpredictability, "unlikes" rather than "likes" are the norm. Work is, by definition, context-dependent. In these situations, bureaucracies often proliferate rules to cover the various permutations that might need to be accounted for or addressed. With a multitude of rules for application in different situations encountered day to day, ground-level actors find that they cannot follow all of these rules, as they inevitably contradict one another, resulting in decreased fidelity to the prescribed rules and processes (Braithwaite & Braithwaite, 1995; Churcher & Talbot, 2020). Even if all rules could be followed perfectly, they would not match actual circumstances in all cases and over time. (Those bureaucracies that instead take the approach of striving to adhere to a smaller set of rules also fail on their goal of equal treatment: Particularities will certainly be missed, resulting in "unlikes" being treated the same (Lipsky, 2010).

Beyond the number and contradictory nature of highly specific rules, bureaucracies face another challenge: Their top-down, unidirectional flow of expertise deprives them of the information needed to see and respond to diversity and unpredictability in complex systems (Clarke et al., 2017). Bureaucracies assume they don't need ideas from the base and solicit only minimal input from ground-level employees and other affected actors, depriving them of any good *direct* mechanism for influencing goals, strategies, rules, and the like despite their funds of knowledge about effective approaches (Liebman et al., 2017; Park, 2021).

Of course, from the beginning, public systems have had mechanisms for participation. In a representative democracy, elected officials are to carry out the interest of constituents and to appoint people who understand and implement what the public wants (Henig et al., 2011). These *indirect* methods also cannot assure equal treatment through the design and application of policy and rules that are right in each context. As the administrative state became more complex and more and more activity was conducted by appointed administrators, it became harder for individual voters to exercise preferences and influence action through elections alone, given the multiple issues at play and the level of generality at which they are addressed (Henig et al., 2011).

When representative democracy turned out to provide too little accountability over the policies and actions of large-scale bureaucratic administrations, interest groups developed to fill the gaps. Like representative democracy, interest groups are designed on the theory that most people want to devote their energies to their private lives, not to debate public policy (Henig et al., 2011). Interest groups (supported by members' or adherents' payment of dues or contributions and occasional signing of a petition or appearance at a rally) keep track of things for their members, tell their members how to vote, lobby elected officials to adopt legislation providing what their members want, and oversee administration of the legislation by public agencies. Bureaucracies, then, often decide what policies to implement in backroom negotiation with these groups.

But like elected representatives, interest groups can succeed only if they treat unlikes alike. Their success requires that they organize and rally members around a single or small number of interests while minimizing members' other goals or interests (Henig et al., 2011). Some interests are well represented this way (e.g., unions focused on members' salary and job security over a lifetime) but other interests are not well represented (e.g., those of low-income parents whose children spend a few years in a progression of different schools and have a broad and ever-changing set of needs and priorities). Furthermore, the time and financial resources required to organize successfully often mean that a minority of relatively privileged stakeholders retain outsized influence, reinforcing historical patterns of inequity (Yackee & Yackee, 2006). As a result, although interest groups have, by some measures, increased participation in bureaucratically governed public systems through their lobbying, litigation, union and political organizing, public information campaigns, and consumer action, they also have entrenched existing inequities and undermined key democratic principles (Liebman et al., 2017).

Bureaucracy Does Not Work for Today's Complex System of Public Schooling. Public schooling is among the complex systems ill-matched to bureaucracy. Its widespread application took hold at the beginning of the 20th century, when urban and other school systems organized around the bureaucratic principles of the One Best System (Tyack, 1974). Up to that point, public schooling had been highly localized and lacked a formal, ordered structure (Tyack, 1974). In response to compulsory schooling laws, growing labor needs, and rapid industrialization and urbanization, administrative reformers sought to rationalize public schooling and make it efficient, putting in place bureaucratic structures that would enable schools to produce a workforce-ready populace. Consolidating expertise and authority in centralized and top-down administrative agencies, students—divided along class, race, gender, and even religious lines—would proceed through a series of age-based grade bands, in each learning standardized curriculum delivered with fidelity by teachers adhering to rules imposed by their supervisors.

This pursuit of order and uniformity increasingly proved futile in public schooling, especially as access to education has become more equal and desegregated, and as the populace demanded increased customization to its needs and preferences (Liebman et al., 2017). Schools now serve a student body that is vastly diverse in terms of race, national origin, gender identity, socioeconomic status, religion, and ability, and a proliferation of goals that goes well beyond those of social efficiency (Labaree, 1997). And, unlike Ford's factory line, which produced one kind of car in one color, the widespread expectation is that individual demands for learning deserve to be met (Liebman et al., 2017). In short, public school systems' conditions, actors, goals and strategies are anything but stable, homogeneous, and well established. Yet many of today's school systems are still governed according to One Best System principles.

As in other contexts, bureaucracy in public school systems is top-down. It assumes that expertise lives at the upper levels of the hierarchy (i.e., federal, state, and local agency leaders) and not in teachers and other school staff working directly with students and families. Presumed to have little knowledge about how best to serve students and families, these ground-level actors are not trusted to exercise independent judgment in understanding the individual capacities and serving the different needs of diverse students in the broad array of classrooms, schools, and districts.

Accordingly, the system constrains ground-level actors' exercise of judgment. Central experts design system strategy, policies, and tools that are communicated to ground-level staff via countless one-size-fits-all rules. Teachers and other school staff are expected to implement directives with fidelity, even if they do not correspond well to particular student needs or contextual factors (Lipsky, 2010). Either teachers and school staff conform to the rules, demonstrating the compliance by which bureaucracies measure success, or they stray from the rules, forgoing compliance in order to meet the unique needs of their students (Liebman et al., 2017). Ted Sizer dubbed the conflict arising when teachers try at least to appear to comply with the rules, while behind closed doors subverting them in order to meet students' actual needs, "Horace's Compromise" (Sizer, 2004; Lipsky, 2010).

Bureaucratic schooling systems try to keep those outside the formal organization (families, community members) at an arm's length. Weak democratic processes, fueled by bureaucratic distrust for "non-expert" voices, have, over time, produced detached (at best) and adversarial (at worst) politics. As with other administratively complex public systems, interest group or special interest politics dominate, with groups such as teachers and other labor unions, family advocacy organizations, issue-specific advocacy organizations, and student unions increasingly providing constituencies with opportunities to advocate and gain power and representation within the system. Because bureaucracy positions these groups as agitated outsiders, rather than codesigners, these relationships are inherently adversarial in nature, with diverse and competing interests jockeying for limited attention, resources, and power—hardly fertile ground for productive partnership, collaboration, problem-solving, and innovation (Liebman et al., 2017; Yackee & Yackee, 2006). Increasing polarization at the national level is fueled by and contributes to these dynamics across state education systems and local school districts (Kleinfeld, 2023).

Consider school boards, historically seen as an exception to the partisan nature of mainstream politics—buffered via mechanisms such as off-cycle elections—now increasingly battlegrounds for debates ranging from instructional policy to cultural considerations often far removed from the core educational challenges facing public school systems (Henig et al., 2011). The system of accountability falls apart in three cases: (1) when special-interest aggregation does not proportionally represent all interests across school systems, (2) when special-interest organizations threaten and infringe on another group's constitutionally recognized values, and (3) when special-interest groups dominate other groups with weak or no representation (Liebman et al., 2017). This is particularly true when the more heavily represented interests are misaligned with the interests of the actual groups that the bureaucracy is meant to serve.

Bureaucracy's top-down system of knowledge fails to capture potentially important context and information from those closest to teaching and learning, and its weak democracy means the system is unable to capture and represent the interests of all of its actors. Lacking processes for authentic engagement and feedback, and burdened with ineffective systems for monitoring progress and impact and sharing and applying knowledge, the system cannot learn from and refine strategy in response to variation in implementation and results. When outcomes are disappointing, leaders blame teachers and school leaders for the system's failure, adopt new reforms, and double down on the same bureaucratic accountability mechanisms—increased uniformity and centralized control—that contributed to failures in the first place.

Table 2.1 (see page 37) summarizes the underlying logic of bureaucracy, highlighting its top-down, compliance- and control-oriented approach to fair and high-quality service at scale.

Bureaucracy in Action

To see how bureaucracy works, let's look at the implementation of special education in the United States.

The federal Individuals with Disabilities Act (IDEA), first passed in 1975, establishes the nation's legal framework for providing special education services and legal protections to students with disabilities (Kramarczuk Voulgarides et al., 2021). Most importantly, IDEA gives special education students a legal right to—and requires schools, districts, and states to provide them with—"a free and appropriate public education" (FAPE) in the "least restrictive environment" possible (Individuals with Disabilities Education Act, 2004). IDEA also provides federal funding for special education and related services costs.

In concept, the special education system is not bureaucratic. It is plan-based and designed to ensure access to education services tailored to each student's unique needs (Garda & O'Neill, 2020). To access these services, parents or guardians must request—and the school district must conduct—an evaluation of their child (New York City Public Schools, "The IEP Process," n.d.). If the evaluation suggests that special services are warranted, the local district must convene a team that includes the student's parents/guardians and teacher to interpret the results and develop a written Individualized Education Plan (IEP) for the child's education. This plan is a legally binding articulation of each student's unique educational needs and the goals, services, and accommodations appropriate for meeting them. Plans are supposed to place students in an education setting in which the needed services can be provided in the least restrictive way, meaning in a manner that is as close as reasonably possible to the way abled students of the same age and grade receive instruction. As an IEP is implemented, the team monitors the plan on a yearly, biannual, or more frequent basis and may make adjustments as needed.

In practice, bureaucratic implementation and enforcement undermine the flexibility that IDEA's focus on *individual* education plans otherwise would seem to promise (Garda & O'Neill, 2020; Grissom et al. 2015; Miesner, 2022; Kramarczuk Voulgarides et al., 2021). Indeed, IDEA's focus on treating all likes alike through procedural compliance prevents the substantive policy enactment required to meet each student's individualized need. In practice, "the tragic irony is that the letter of the law has become the principal barrier to achieving the spirit of the law" (Skrtic, 1991, p. 149).

Parental rights that focus on procedural safeguards, such as the right to participate in the IEP process and the right to dispute resolution, work against a focus on the quality of service provision. These safeguards, together with federal and state oversight to ensure procedural compliance and reliance for enforcement on litigation (itself far better at curing procedural problems than fixing poor-quality services), prevent nimble and responsive adjustment to the student's goals, preferences, progress, and needs. A 2016 study found that inflexibly facilitated meetings in which participants spend most of their shared time reading from a mandated script prevented authentic participation and information-sharing by students and their families, leaving problems, as well as student and parent concerns, unaddressed and solutions unexplored (Bray & Russell, 2016). The jargon-laden legal, technical, and abstract language used in IEP meetings adds barriers to authentic communication, especially when a family's first language is not English, when they are not used to presenting in formal proceedings, and when they do not understand the extent to which they can direct the agenda, as more privileged families often do. In rare instances when families redirect the script and engage authentically, the educators facilitating the meeting lack guidance on how to pivot from the policy-mandated script and proceed productively (Bray & Russell, 2016).

Procedural safeguards are also insufficient to assure plans are tailored to students' needs. Financial and budgetary constraints, alongside the rising costs of special education and increased identification rates, lead to "mounting pressure to generalize, label, routinize, and categorize children into pre-existing programs" (Hyatt, 1989, p. 724; Turnage, 2020). Indeed, many studies have found identical IEPs for students with varying needs (Catone & Brady, 2005). Students are given few assessments when IEPs are created, and these assessments are often not revisited or updated as the student progresses since many school systems are not required to do so to maintain compliance.

Teams typically are not required to update the IEP even in response to significant anticipated changes in schooling context, such as a move from middle to high school (Catone & Brady, 2005). Although teams may develop Individual Transition Plans (ITPs) to guide the student through key transition points, research indicates that ITPs often lack adequate descriptions of assessment results, age-appropriate transition planning, and insight into the student's future goals; one study of ITPs found that while approximately 80% were in procedural compliance, around 50% lacked any meaningful information or substantive services required for successful student transitions (Greene, 2018).

Enforcement of the IEP and ITP system, too, fails largely because of the limitations of bureaucracy. The focus on process over substance obscures problems with the quality of service, suggesting that things are "in order," when they are anything but. To be in compliance, districts need only follow the procedural steps outlined in the law, which are, in practice, poor proxies for quality of service (Raj, 2021). Because schools are often technically compliant—in letter, if not in spirit—the onus falls on families to advocate for their children when enacted procedures do not yield the instructional services required to help their children learn. Advocacy demands that families engage in a legalized system of procedural rights, a context in which they are nearly always on uneven footing with schools and districts. While well-resourced families may engage a specialized attorney, for the most part, parents navigate the system with little support (Ong-Dean, 2009). With or without an advocate, families are inevitably at a disadvantage given the court's assumption that procedural compliance is an adequate measure for substantive quality (Raj, 2021).

As a result of the focus on procedure over substance, there is a daunting risk that students' needs are not accurately captured and addressed, leading to poorer outcomes for students with disabilities (Kramarczuk Voulgarides et al., 2021). Procedural compliance fails to assure equitable access to high-quality services, resulting in persistent learning and achievement gaps, disproportionate discipline rates, and unequal post-school outcomes (National Center for Learning Disabilities [NCLD], 2023). Studies have found that students in special education programs score lower on achievement tests than peers with disabilities placed in general education classrooms (Cole et al., 2021). Exclusionary discipline is more common for students with disabilities, who are twice as likely as general education students to be suspended and represent 58% of students placed in seclusion or involuntary confinement despite constituting only 12% of public school students (Office for Civil Rights, 2015). This disparity is further starkly divided by race, as about 25% of Black students with disabilities were suspended in the 2009–2010 academic school year, whereas White students with disabilities had a suspension rate of 12% (Gowdey, 2015).

Finally, bureaucratic structures and rules, while apparently neutral, are highly interpretable and thus prone to bias (Kramarczuk Voulgarides et al., 2021). Take, for example, racially disproportionate rates of disability identification: Black and Latino students are two (or more) times more likely to be labeled than their White peers and also more likely to be placed in self-contained classrooms rather than "mainstreamed" in general education classrooms (Grindal et al., 2019). Both identification and tracking of these students are choices, made within the boundaries of "benign" bureaucratic structures (Kramarczuk Voulgarides et al., 2021, p. 221) that nonetheless reinforce historical patterns of inequity. The supposed neutrality of the bureaucratic process makes this bias all the more difficult to identify and challenge. Making matters worse, bureaucracy's relentless focus on compliance discourages interrogation of the systemic dimensions of racialized or otherwise biased patterns in the interpretation of rules.

MANAGERIALISM: TARGET-BASED ACCOUNTABILITY

An alternative to bureaucracy is *managerialism*. Like bureaucracy, managerialism identifies goals top-down, but unlike bureaucracy, managerialism

- shifts attention away from inputs and toward outcomes,
- assigns the determination of the means used to achieve prescribed ends to local managers, and
- rewards or penalizes employees based on their success meeting the desired ends—not by their compliance with directives specifying prescribed means (Coglianese & Lazer, 2003).

In theory, managerialism pursues equality of ends (all actors pursuing the same, centrally-set, usually quantifiable, goals) through means more conducive to equity than those of bureaucracy (equal outcomes as a result of differentiated inputs). Goal attainment drives and rationalizes strategy. Those who succeed are rewarded, and those who don't face the consequences.

This governance approach grew in popularity in the public sector, including in education, in the early 2000s, in many cases working hand-in-hand with outcomes-oriented accountability reforms at the federal and state levels, and as implemented in a number of the United States's largest school systems.

Managerialism = Strategy of Motivating People Through Targets

Recognizing the complexity of the work and the diversity of contexts and actors (those working and those standing to benefit), managerialism rejects the bureaucratic idea that uniform strategy can achieve desired outcomes across contexts. Even if there were such a strategy, managerialism lacks bureaucracy's confidence that experts at the top of the organization (1) are best placed to identify it and (2) can effectively prescribe and divide up its implementation into fixed pieces neatly assigned to workers operating according to a fixed division of labor. Managerialism assumes that the success of all such tasks depends on particular individuals' tacit instincts and intuitions as to the conditions they face. Better, therefore, to motivate managers closest to the task at hand to do their intuitive best to guide the similarly motivated and intuitive members of their workforce in pursuing the organization's well-defined goals—retaining and rewarding those who achieve the goals and letting others go. Often, local managers apply the same operating logic to their employees: Those who deliver outcomes succeed; those who don't are fired. By placing authority on those closest to the work and the ground-level conditions, managerialism seeks to fix a key issue arising from bureaucracy: the inability of those at the top to spot problems as they arise (Coglianese & Lazer, 2003).

For managerialism, therefore, much depends on four things: (1) the quality of goals set; (2) the capacity of a small set of usually quantifiable targets to demonstrate the full range of managers' success; (3) the effectiveness of the rewards and consequences attached to meeting targets; and (4) the supply of managers and employees whose motivations, instincts, and intuitions enable success.

Managerialism Works When Goals Are Easy to Define and Measure and Talent Abounds. Managerialism works when goals are somewhat limited, uniform, and easy to define and measure across contexts and at scale, and where strategy need not be defined, studied, improved, and spread. It requires clear measures of success attached to rewards and consequences, along with lots of people qualified and willing to work in the system, providing a constant source of potential employees to step up when those who are unsuccessful are let go. Targets and incentives are key to success: The model assumes that with the proper extrinsic motivation, capable managers will, through their own action and the selection of others, achieve goals. Making and applying explicit hiring criteria in selection is unnecessary, both because success criteria (e.g., charisma, diligence) may be hard to measure and because they reveal themselves quickly in practice, more cheaply than they are developed through intensive before-the-fact training or after-the-fact learning.

For example, managerialism has worked when organizations and their managers are both incentivized and constrained by profit objectives. United by the goal of maximizing profits, managers are given a great deal of discretion as to how to motivate workers, increase efficiency, and generate the largest return.

Consider a luxury handbag store. Managers who run the store are motivated by increasing profits via sales. Performance against profit targets determines success, and, in turn, determines their personal commission and job security. Companies select managers based on their proven knowledge of how to maximize profits and increase sales, as well as on their ability to manage their employees to the same goal. Managers decide how much inventory to order, how to display goods, how to motivate their employees to meet quotas, and the like. Central regional offices monitor whether managers meet their sales and profit targets, culling those who fail to do so and replacing them with those who are more effective. Managers, too, use target attainment to improve their human capital and therefore the performance of their stores, retaining and promoting salespeople with track records of success and firing those who do not meet expectations. This approach works because goals are easy to define and measure, are limited in scope, and align to rewards/consequences; there is a ready supply of managers and employees; and hiring/firing proves an efficient way to boost the quality of human capital.

Managerialism Has Not Worked in Complex Systems. While effective in sales, this approach has not worked well in complex systems with many goals, some or all of which are difficult to define and hold sufficiently stable across contexts and time. Success is hard to capture in a small number of fixed, quantifiable outcomes, making it difficult to determine fully or quickly enough who or what is working and to assign rewards and consequences accordingly. Using flawed targets for accountability leads to bad behavior, for example cheating, hiding one's knowledge, and using strategies that enable success against targets but failure on broader or more central goals (e.g., teaching to the test).

Managerialism tries to solve two of bureaucracy's problems: (1) the focus on equality of service at a cost to equity of service, and (2) the distortive influence of interest group politics. To do so, managerialism limits public participation to elections and limits the top's authority to determining ends, not means. Just as consequences apply within the system should targets not be met, this model assumes consequences will be applied to those officials who mismanage the system as a whole. But it, too, suffers from the unidirectional flow of information. Although central decision-making is solely focused on outcomes, without feedback loops and engagement with those closest to the work, the central level cannot get these decisions right. Targets become blunt. They are insensitive to local context and too narrowly focused to motivate quality service across the range of ground-level workers' activities.

Radically decentralizing strategy decisions to many different sites makes comprehensive capture by interest groups more difficult—but these groups still have an impact. Interest groups retain influence over goal-, target-, and consequence-setting at the central level, and at the local levels they retain one of the few mechanisms of influence. Managerialism's assumptions about knowledge interfere with local managers' efforts to discover what works and why with their close-at-hand workers and clients. The model trusts managers' intuitions about their workers and clients, obviating the need for explicit and direct exchange, much less joint decision-making. Without widespread knowledge generation and sharing, managerialism's success depends on the capacity to identify and hire people who have required knowledge and fire people who don't. In practice, few complex systems rarely have the talent supply needed, especially when pay is relatively low.

Managerialism Does Not Work for Today's Complex System of Public Schooling. Public schooling is among the complex systems ill-matched to managerialism. Managerialism overtook bureaucracy in a number of state and local systems following the passage of the No Child Left Behind Act (NCLB) of 2001, which required states to adopt target-centered accountability systems as a prerequisite for federal funding. Each state system was to set a timeline for schools and districts to make Adequate Yearly Progress (AYP) in the average proportion of students who reached a state-defined level of proficiency in reading and math, with a goal of universal proficiency by 2014. To set and measure AYP, the act required states to employ standards-aligned assessments in math and ELA in grades 3, 5 and 8 to evaluate each school's progress, with failing schools subject to state-defined consequences aligned to federal requirements (typically public designation as a failing school, with relatively onerous oversight, planning, and improvement goals). The law thus aimed to eliminate student, school, and district achievement gaps not (as under bureaucracy) by prescribing a particular approach to school improvement but instead by motivating schools and districts to reach prescribed levels of student learning while leaving the means of doing so to the discretion of each district and school.

As exemplified in a particularly stark way by the Atlanta district described below, no state and very few districts ever came close to meeting NCLB's overall target of universal student proficiency in reading and math by 2014. Universal targets are insensitive to local context and focused on too small a set of measurable objectives to focus and facilitate high-quality services across the full set of activities central to public schools. In the quest for success as defined by these quantifiable results, too many systems focus on achieving limited outcomes regardless of unintended consequences (e.g., the narrowing of the curriculum), exacerbating inequities already baked into the system via its bureaucratic past. Worse yet, because implementation remains unexamined, the system fails to learn and spread effective practice beyond the purview of each "gifted" manager, and there remain too few of these managers to serve schools across the country. Although the definition of ends is top-down, the definition and implementation of means originates at and never spreads beyond the bottom level. Moreover, one of the core mechanisms for accountability within managerialism, that managers and lower-level employees who underperform can be replaced, does not work within the educational context. To wit, there is not an endless supply of aspiring and effective principals and teachers.

Accountability and direction-setting through representative democracy remains limited, too. Multi-issue elections mean that constituents' education interests are not necessarily captured in their voting preferences, leaving little signal from elections alone about how to carry out those preferences when staffing administrative agencies and setting targets. To compensate for the missing information and steer the behavior of elected and administrative leaders, interest groups step in, with many of the same groups (e.g., labor unions, family advocacy organizations) employing many of the same tactics (e.g., lobbying, litigation, union and political organizing) that are used in bureaucracies.

Table 2.1 (see page 37) summarizes the underlying logic of managerialism, highlighting its target-based accountability approach to fair and high-quality service at scale.

Managerialism in Action

The cheating scandals in Atlanta in the 2000s reveal the shortcomings of managerialism when managers are pushed to achieve a narrow set of outcomes regardless of consequences (Aviv, 2014). Like many districts in the early 2000s, the public school system in Atlanta, Georgia, adopted a targets-based management approach following Congress' adoption of NCLB.

Atlanta governed its schools in accordance with the NCLB framework but set school-based targets for average proficiency that aimed to achieve universal proficiency more quickly than Georgia itself required. These targets formed the basis for rewards and consequences. Staff in schools that met targets received bonuses up to $2000, whereas in schools and classrooms that failed to meet targets, administrators and teachers faced negative performance evaluations, public "humiliation" and "ridicule," and even termination (Wilson et al., 2011, p. 355). Indeed, nearly 90% of principals were replaced during this period (Wilson et al., 2011). Atlanta's leaders set the targets based on levels they *hoped* their schools and educators could achieve but without any evidence that the levels set were realistically achievable and without accounting for differences among schools' student bodies. Schools' targets were the same irrespective of, for example, socioeconomic and academic differences between school populations. Although the targets thus ignored differences in students' academic starting points, those starting points greatly influenced whether students met targets, which focused on the average percentage of students at "proficiency" at the end of each year, not on how much progress students had made toward proficiency from the beginning to the end of the year. The system thus left the strategy for reaching uniform targets to the principal of each school, with no consideration of the nonuniformity of the learning conditions each faced.

Initially, it appeared that the approach worked astonishingly well, with schools throughout the city making impressive gains on state tests. At Parks Middle School, for example, in 2006 the percentage of 8th-graders who demonstrated proficiency in reading rose 31 points and in math the percentage who passed rose 62 points (Aviv, 2014). Parks was a struggling school by many metrics; this result was astounding. Then, in 2009, the *Atlanta Journal-Constitution* reported statistically unlikely anomalies in Atlanta testing data (Perry, 2009), and, by 2011, the Georgia Bureau of Investigation had published a report implicating at least 44 schools and 138 practitioners across the city in one of the largest K–12 cheating scandals in history (Aviv, 2014; Wilson et al., 2011). Under enormous pressure to meet performance targets, teachers and administrators had, for years, doctored student exams, erasing and replacing incorrect answers. Dozens of educators were indicted, nine were convicted, and two served time in prison (Proctor & Lupiani, 2024). Judgment was swift, and Atlanta's improvement was largely considered a mirage.

But it wasn't a mirage, at least not completely, complicating the Atlanta story and revealing managerialism's fatal flaw when applied to public schooling. NAEP performance, a more rigorous and difficult-to-game assessment than the state exams of this period, suggests that improvement *did* occur in Atlanta over the accountability period. For example, according to NAEP, between 2002 and 2013, the percentage of Black students in Atlanta at or above grade level increased 10 percentage points, compared to a three-percentage-point increase in Black student proficiency rates nationally and in Georgia (Cooper, 2016).

Impossibly high targets imposed without regard for the different challenges faced at different schools and enforced with exceptionally high stakes destroyed—and ended—what *was* working. The tragedy here is multilayered, and one that stems from governance and system design, rather than discrete decisions made by individual teachers. The managerialist approach masked real learning and improvement happening in many schools and classrooms, inhibited its systemwide spread, deprived students of the student learning experience they deserved, and exited passionate and experienced teachers prematurely from the profession. The egregiously bad definition of targets created incentives for bad behavior, despite the fact that, with the shift from a focus on inputs to one on outcomes, educators were indeed using the data and new motivations to improve learning outcomes (as demonstrated by rising NAEP scores). The governance model ignored these improvements, myopically focused on whether targets were reached. It assumed the only knowledge that mattered was *whether* principals met targets, not *how* they did so. In so doing, it stifled collective improvement, preventing the public schools from generating and spreading knowledge that could have enabled and sustained systematic improvement.

PROFESSIONALISM AND CRAFT: SELF-REGULATION BY EXPERTS

A third set of governance approaches takes a different tack. Unlike bureaucracy, which distrusts teachers and other ground-level actors, and unlike managerialism, which focuses only on principals but not on their teachers and other staff, *professionalism* and *craft* recognize that teachers, counselors, librarians, and others are experts in their own right who can be trusted to exercise discretion effectively within each of their diverse contexts.

This decentralization goes beyond that of managerialism: Professionalism and craft assume that both means and ends are locally determined. Ever popular with teachers, but difficult to implement, professionalism and craft seek to raise teachers' status, respect, and authority (Mehta, 2013).

A variety of teacher-led schools, many of them part of the Essential Schools movement, have adopted this approach. Ted Sizer launched the Coalition of Essential Schools from Brown University in 1984. The coalition comprises a network of autonomous schools committed to reforming the industrial-style model of high school that took hold with bureaucratic school governance (Sizer, 1986). Each member school commits to nine shared principles (e.g., an intellectual focus, personalization) and teachers and school leaders work to build consensus about how to operationalize those principles at their site, defining end goals (often in the form of performance standards) and means fitting to their own context and population (La Prad, 2016; McQuillan & Muncey, 1994).

Professionalism and Craft = Master Practitioners Defining and Meeting Goals Using Hard-to-Acquire Knowledge and Skills

Unlike bureaucracy and like managerialism, professionalism and craft recognize the diversity of contexts in which service provision occurs, and therefore reject one-size-fits-all rules for determining how to achieve objectives. Unlike managerialism, however, this context-specific approach includes ends (what they aim to achieve) as well as means (how they aim to succeed) (Lagemann, 2000; Mehta, 2013; Sennett, 2008). Both professionalism and craft entrust ground-level actors to determine these contextually appropriate means. This trust stems from the consummate professional's rigorous training or the master practitioner's vast experience, each demonstrated through rigorous training pathways and gating mechanisms and criteria that limit expert status and responsibility to those who are capable of providing high-quality services and sustaining the public esteem associated with their role.

Although consistent in the ways just noted, professionalism and craft differ in important principles. Professionalism assumes that determinative knowledge and skills can be made explicit, taught, and assessed. Craft, on the other hand, assumes that determinative knowledge and skills are "more art than science," which cannot be made explicit or standardized and taught in traditional classroom settings. Instead, aspiring craftspeople learn through apprenticeship—observation, practice, and rehearsal of gradually maturing elements of the craft under the direction of a master. Importantly, both approaches depend upon self-regulation. In each case, the professionals (often acting through collective structures) and craftspeople (more usually acting at local guild and company levels) govern themselves, establishing the desired direction of their work and maintaining service excellence and status through collective, more and less explicit standard-setting, observation, and review.

Professionalism and Craft Work When Self-Governances Ensure High-Quality Service. Professionalism and craft work when service excellence is dependent upon a body of knowledge and skill that is widely agreed upon and that can be obtained and assessed through rigorous training and evaluation, separating those who have achieved mastery from those who have not. Those who achieve the status of the profession or guild, then, are responsible for maintaining its status and efficacy. Relevant publics, too, play a role, acting as consumers whose behavior influences the evolution of the profession or guild.

Take, for example, the profession of law. Lawyers attend law schools accredited by the American Bar Association based on the content of their curricula, where students learn a well-codified body of legal knowledge and skills on which they are tested through end-of-course assessments and an end-of-training bar examination, and which are periodically refreshed through mandated continuing education programs. The American Bar Association governs the profession, reviewing the knowledge and evidence base of what works, refreshing and setting new standards, and making necessary changes to the training and evaluation of aspiring and veteran professionals. To see the approach in a craft setting, consider ballet. Novice ballet dancers hone their craft through hours of practice and feedback, guided by the ballet company's principals who lead them to ever higher levels of mastery. Elevation to principal is eventually declared, or not, upon review by masters who already have established themselves within the guild.

In both cases, the public has access to information needed to steer the direction of the profession through their consumption (or lack thereof) of services. The quality of service is transparent to the public in each case. It is clear whether one's client is convicted or prevails in court, and what the ballet looks like and whether it is pleasing to the viewer. Consumer behavior in combination with masters' own expert judgments shape improvements that assure the profession's or guild's success and status.

Professionalism and Craft Have Not Worked in Vast, Complex Systems. Professionalism and craft allow ground-level actors to exercise discretion in order to customize action to each context. To do so, they move away from bureaucratic inflexibility around means and immediate ends to allow experimentation with the application of specialized knowledge or know-how to myriad situations. Although this approach may work in some complex systems, it doesn't when the system is vast and provides a public good delivered through direct service across a diversity of contexts.

Professionalism and craft employ self-regulation that concentrates knowledge in a relative few rather than providing it to all actors who need it, making learning, knowledge, and expertise opaque and hard to scale. Professionals and craftspeople have our trust because they are elite; they have mastered a hard-to-acquire set of knowledge and skill through lengthy processes through which relatively few persevere. Once acquired, knowledge and expertise are often hoarded. For the artist, the rarity of the insight is what makes it art—that's what critics praise and patrons pay for; its uniqueness is crucial. For the professional, too, amassing expertise increases status and raises value, in turn reinforcing lengthy and expensive training and induction pathways that bless few as experts and turn many, many more away.

In this model, trust is unidirectional: The public trusts professionals and master practitioners, not the other way around. Professionalism and craft glorify expertise itself (even more, perhaps, than other governance models) leading their members to distrust others—students, families, community members—who lack their knowledge, experience, and carefully honed skills (Mehta, 2013; Sennett, 2008). While master practitioners and professionals collaborate extensively with each other to develop, test, adapt, and scale improvements or to solve problems, there is little to no role for authentic and ongoing collaboration with those outside of their guild. There is also limited transparency into whether, why, and how practitioners actually succeed or struggle. Only those who also have acquired the specialized knowledge over time (professional critics, collectors, large private corporations with their own legal expertise) influence service through direct engagement. Others can indirectly influence the trajectory of the profession or guild with their consumer behavior, but only with readily accessible information about what constitutes quality, which is more challenging in contexts where the criteria for what constitutes a "good" outcome are not as self-evident as they might be in a ballet performance or the outcome of a court case. Too often, that information is only available to consumers with the capacity (time, money) to achieve their own expertise. By shutting out the remaining non-experts, the system cuts itself off from knowledge about how to best meet each consumer's need.

Most action is private or internal to the guild. Lacking public transparency, there are few guards against systematic bias and fewer opportunities to customize service to constituent needs, leading to system failure in diverse, complex systems, particularly when those in the profession or guild are meaningfully different from those outside of it. The definition of service excellence is left to the judgment of those already in the guild, with few checks to ensure if the approach truly serves all well. Disconnected from their publics, they lack feedback about the quality of service from those served. Failure to attend to outcomes further enables biased practice, as is the case with craft, which resists specification and measurement of important outcomes and formal structures for achieving them. What matters most is the blessing of those who have been blessed by previous masters, not whether outcomes are achieved, perpetuating approaches that are conventional among members of the guild, regardless of their ability to serve all well.

Professionalism and Craft Do Not Work for Today's Complex System of Public Schooling. The framings of professionalism and craft appeal to many in the public education field, as they afford educators the respect that master practitioners deserve. But in their pure forms they are a mismatch for the United States' vast and diverse system of public schools. These models have been applied in small contexts since the Progressive Era, most notably in a number of the Essential Schools, which typically employ a craft model, relying on mentorship as a way of developing expertise. In these schools, educators are the decision-makers. As new educators enter the school, they learn by observation of and training by master practitioners in the same school or network of schools. Under the experts' guidance, novice educators develop pedagogical techniques aligned with the acceptable model, honing their intuition and their ability to evolve the craft based on their observation of how and what students learn. Peer educators are the most trusted source of feedback and expertise, and student work is captured through portfolios and projects that allow educators to assess learning without insisting on a level of formality or standardization that kills individuality and creativity. Because excellence is subjective and intuited by those in the guild, families are largely relegated to passive recipients of the school's services. Few have a means of providing feedback or information to improve the quality of teaching and learning; those who do are typically those who had the resources to develop their own expertise, in some cases by observing at their own child's school.

In schooling, this model has not succeeded beyond small, relatively homogeneous settings where the culture of those in the guild or profession match the culture of the children and families served. At scale, the trade-off of earning trust through elitism is a nonstarter for public schooling. Consider size alone. The size of the active teaching workforce is roughly three times that of acting physicians and roughly 2.5 times that of acting lawyers (American Bar Association, 2024; Association of American Medical Colleges, 2020; Riser-Kositsky, 2019). With a workforce that large, which must take on challenges without known solutions for each child in each context, knowledge needs to be generated, substantiated, and spread. Furthermore, the increasing diversity of our student population—with roughly 44% White students and 55% students of color—in contrast with that of our educator workforce—where 81% of public school teachers are White (National Center for Education Statistics, 2023, 2024)—introduces variability in opportunities and outcomes given the range of mindsets, skills, knowledge, and expectations that practitioners bring to bear and unexplored mismatches between those traits and students' diverse strengths and needs.

Table 2.1 summarizes the underlying logic of professionalism and craft (along with the logics of bureaucracy and managerialism), highlighting its use of self-governance to assure service excellence.

Professionalism and Craft in Action

As mentioned, a classic example of professionalism and craft as a model in education is teacher-led schools. One such effort was the Central Park East Schools of District 4 in New York City in the 1970s–1980s, led by Deborah Meier (Liebman & Sabel, 2003). Meier used the system's growing tolerance of alternative schools to establish "teacher-led" elementary, middle, and later high schools that focused on applying the "core principle of collegial attention to individual student needs" (Liebman & Sabel, 2003, p. 216).

The Central Park East Schools flipped bureaucracy's hierarchical pyramid and gave the majority of decision-making power to educators. Together, these practitioners hired and evaluated colleagues; created, implemented, and improved their curricula; and assessed student progress via expert teachers' qualitative evaluation of each student's portfolio of work. As Meier stated: "Our experience suggested that a strong school culture requires that most decisions be struggled over and made by those directly responsible for implementing them, not by representative bodies handing down dictates for others to follow. We felt the same way whether the representative bodies were composed of kids, parents, or fellow teachers" (Liebman & Sabel, 2003, p. 216).

When Anthony Alvarado assumed the superintendency in 1987 of nearby District 2, he set out to replicate the success of Meier's school-based model at scale in his district. He saw the system design—its bureaucracy—as an impediment to widespread improvement, and therefore sought to make not just changes in policy, but also changes in governance (Roberts, 2024). To start, he launched a "learning community" of principals who

Table 2.1. Summary of Governance in Bureaucracy, Managerialism, and Professionalism/Craft

	Bureaucracy	Managerialism	Professionalism/Craft
Works well when . . .	Conditions, strategy, and goals are stable, homogeneous, and well established	Goals are somewhat limited, uniform, and easy to define and measure across contexts and at scale	Conditions vary, practitioners reflect the populations they serve, and strategy and goals are best determined by those practitioners who exercise their judgment on behalf of their constituents
		Strategy need not or cannot be defined, studied, improved, and spread	There are robust pipelines of professionals and craftspeople aspiring to serve and sustain careers in the sector
Direction is set by . . .	Leaders and central experts at the top of the hierarchy	Leaders and central experts who set outcomes-based performance targets	Local practitioners who consult other master professionals/practitioners as challenges arise
Knowledge . . .	Of the leaders and central experts is made explicit through detailed rules that actors at lower levels of the system must carry out	Is tacit and its responsible discovery and use can be incentivized via performance targets and accountability	Is explicit in professionalism and acquired and refined through study, application, and assessment, including by esteemed professionals
			Is tacit in craft and developed under the guidance of master practitioners
Success is determined by and respect comes from . . .	Compliance with prescriptive and highly elaborated rules	Achievement of performance targets	Peers who have mastered the craft or have been deemed expert professionals

Table 2.1. (*continued*)

	Bureaucracy	Managerialism	Professionalism/Craft
Systematic improvement occurs when . . .	Leaders and central experts upgrade, communicate, and enforce compliance with rules that reflect new knowledge	Managers hire employees who meet performance targets and let go of those who do not	The profession or craft grows and is able to meet the demand of those seeking services
People outside but affected by the organization or agency at the center of the system influence it through . . .	Arms-length and often adversarial, episodic and interest-based engagement	Elections and selection and appointment processes that identify system leaders who determine uniform performance targets	Participation in the profession or craft; those outside are expected to comply with expert practition-ers' judgment

would work together to devise strategies for improving instruction particular to each of their schools (Alvarado, 1998). They used "study groups, seminars, and professional development around the teaching of literacy . . . to search for exemplary models of instructional practice" (Elmore & Burney, 1998, p. 7). The principal collegium organized its work around Balanced Literacy and brought in external professional developers to train staff. Principals retained much latitude over how these practices would be used at each of their schools, making improvement largely site-based and individualized, with principals and teachers focused on supporting students in realizing and improving their own learning strategies (Liebman & Sabel, 2003). Mentor teachers developed novice teachers, and classroom observations and visits helped teachers hone their craft. Management was focused on the accumulation and use of professional expertise, albeit absent explicit study of the relationships between those practices and student learning (Elmore & Burney, 1998). Standards were left implicit and resided in the individuals who already mastered their content: They were "embedded in the professional development that teachers and principals received, in the school and classroom visits that the district administrators made to schools, and in the growing professional community of teachers and principals across schools within the district" (Elmore & Burney, 1998, p. 8). Service excellence was identified by those already in the guild: "good teaching was what teachers recognized as good said it was" (Liebman & Sabel, 2003, p. 221).

Nearly a decade into his leadership, Alvarado questioned whether, absent more explicit standards of practice, expectations for students, and assessments of what they learned, the district was improving outcomes for *all* students, particularly those who were "hardest-to-teach" (Elmore & Burney, 1998, p. 9). He stated: "The only way you can answer that question is by getting agreement on what kids should know and be able to do and starting to assess their learning in some systematic way" (Liebman & Sabel, 2003, p. 221). And in fact, while the district was highly successful in the aggregate, a closer look at disaggregated data suggested significant racial and socioeconomic achievement gaps. Although the district had done better than its peers at teaching its lowest-performing students, Alvarado and his team were alarmed by *within*-district variation between their lowest- and highest-performing students, which had persisted during his tenure despite improvement in the district overall (Elmore & Burney, 1997). Alvarado and his team saw this disparity as a moral imperative for improvement: If the district was not serving those students effectively, it was not doing its job (Elmore & Burney, 1998).

In response, Alvarado's district, like other districts, states, and organizations, found new ways to design, lead, and manage their operations and engage internal and external stakeholders. The district became a learning hive, employing a combination of transparency, experimentation, and broad participation and knowledge sharing that reveals effective ways to serve individuals and groups of students, severing deeply entrenched links between student background, access to opportunity, and learning outcomes. We'll turn to a fuller discussion of this model in Chapter 3.

SUMMARY

This chapter surveys three popular approaches to governance and democracy, each with its own strengths, but each profoundly mismatched to the complex system of public education.

Bureaucracy, the foundation for the last 150 years of American public education, places trust in central leaders and experts to unilaterally set goals and map strategies to guide actors across the system to achieve them. This approach functions well when conditions are stable and aims clear, yet, in complex contexts like public education, fails to draw in the expertise of stakeholders across the system—frontline staff, students, teachers, community members—who have insight critical to meeting the demands of dynamic environments and diverse conditions.

Outcome-focused managerialism trusts local managers to create contextually specific strategies to meet high standards, which, at times, can motivate strong results and innovation. But this model rarely generates scalable knowledge about how to yield similar outcomes outside of each local leadership context, and in practice, encourages bad behavior, like cheating, that can derail progress.

And in professionalism and craft, teachers and other frontline experts are trusted to draw from a font of experience-based expertise and wisdom to design and adapt frontline strategy as needed. While appealing for its deep faith in teachers—who have historically, in traditions built around bureaucracy and managerialism, been sidelined—trust in the front line alone is insufficient to the task of solving the complex problems of public education. Because these problems are expansive and multidimensional, the perspectives of those outside the profession—distrusted in both models—are critical. And at scale, the professional silos and the closed classroom doors inherent to professionalism and craft undermine coordinated learning efforts that can spot and solve thorny problems and spur durable improvements in system practice.

We've established three approaches to governance and democracy that *don't* work. You may be asking: What *does* a governance approach well-matched to public schools look like?

It would be driven by a broad goal: Constantly adapt to meet the needs of each and every child, family, community, and moment to deliver equitable service at scale. To do so, it would draw together the best elements of each of the governance approaches discussed above to build a new model driven by constant improvement and learning. And it would do so using a democratic model of improvement that trusts and enables all community members to identify problems in their local context as they occur and quickly adapt practice in response.

Read on and meet Evolutionary Learning in Chapter 3.

Introduction to Evolutionary Learning

We ended the last chapter with discussion of what was, initially, a craft-based system: New York City's District 2. While, by many measures, the district was successful, outperforming its peers, Superintendent Anthony Alvarado and his leadership team were disturbed by within-district variation that revealed significant racial and class-based opportunity gaps (Elmore & Burney, 1998). Recognizing that these gaps presented a moral obligation for further improvement, Alvarado and his team set about transforming district governance, in the process blurring the lines between learning and doing and finding ways to balance a strong central vision and a shared instructional framework with local autonomy. Making explicit widely held but largely implicit instructional standards and goals, district leaders supported local sites to learn how to reach those standards through implementation, while holding teachers accountable for the learning happening in their own classrooms and principals in their own schools. Despite initial fears to the contrary, increased standardization did not demand uniformity; each school was able to tailor both strategy and goals to its unique context (Elmore & Burney, 1998). Opening the classroom doors that often remain closed in craft models, centrally-supported measurement (including diagnostic testing), paired with collaborative structures like professional learning communities (PLCs), intervisitations, and peer learning and evaluation, allowed the district to surface and spread learning, over time advancing its shared strategy and collective progress toward more equitable outcomes for all students.

Evolutionary Learning (EL) systems, like Alvarado's District 2, use ongoing individual, collective, and system-level adaptation to meet the unique needs of each child, family, community, and moment and deliver equitable service at scale. To do this, EL draws together the elements of bureaucracy, managerialism, professionalism, and craft that are best suited for systemwide improvement and learning. The result: A broadly democratic approach to problem-solving that trusts each member of the system to spot and address challenges when and where they occur, so that everyday doing becomes everyday improvement.

In many ways, EL-driven systems are like beehives: democratic communities in which every bee plays a part in making decisions that ensure the colony's adaptation and survival (Seeley, 2011). In late spring or summer, as colonies seek a new home, bees participate in intricate learning rituals, through which individual bees explore their larger environment. As the group consolidates this learning, they vote on a new hive location, drawing on the brilliance of their collective, and as Seeley (2011) writes, "organizing themselves in such a way that even though each individual has limited information . . . the group as a whole makes first-rate collective decisions" (p. 7).

Evolutionary Learning systems function similarly. With a goal of fostering constant organizational improvement, EL hives restructure traditional approaches to governance. Through broad and active participation, problem-solving, and research, they pair a disciplined approach to learning with an aligned suite of concepts and tools that foster collaborative learning and democratic decision-making. These ongoing learning efforts mobilize system stakeholders every day to adapt and improve strategy as a collective.

This chapter briskly walks you through EL, outlining its general principles of organizational design (captured in brief in Figure 3.1). You will finish with a working definition of EL, but also, surely, with questions: What does EL look like in practice across various types of systems? What structures, activities, cultures, and mindsets guide EL implementation? And, practically, how can I start doing this work in my organization? We explore each of these questions in turn in the rest of the book.

EVOLUTIONARY LEARNING: ORGANIZED LEARNING FOR ONGOING ADAPTATION

Schools and districts—and their broader ecosystems—are complex systems grappling with complex problems. Complex systems have a number of special characteristics that can make governance challenging, including that they are

- constantly changing, often unpredictably, in response to changes in their environment (Preskill et al., 2014);
- highly relational, defined as much by the relationships between entities (e.g., actors, teams, departments, institutions, groups) as they are by those entities themselves (McQuillan, 2008; Preskill

Figure 3.1. The Learning Hive (adapted from Aghina et al., 2018)

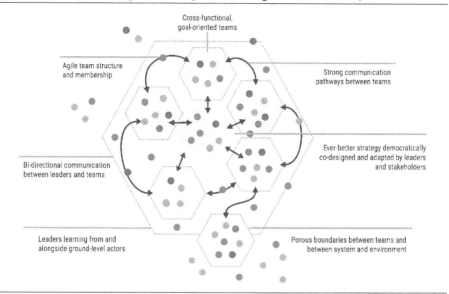

et al., 2014), with changes in one part of the system affecting others (Preskill et al., 2014); and

- nonlinear, with causation that is multifaceted, multidirectional, and difficult to isolate (Clarke et al., 2017; Snowden, 2024).

Unlike bureaucracy and most other governance models, Evolutionary Learning is designed for these conditions. Rather than assuming relative uniformity and trying to succeed mainly by treating likes alike, EL acknowledges diversity and pursues equal outcomes by treating different people and situations differently. In school systems, this essential pursuit of equity means meeting the differing needs of each student to enable all to thrive.

Complex systems in which conditions constantly change cannot rely on existing know-how and must constantly develop new knowledge (Ansell, 2011). Under those conditions, achieving equity requires delivering services so highly dependent on context that any static, one-size-fits-all strategy will fail to meet that goal. School systems, for example, demand different substantive strategies for different communities, schools, classrooms, families, and students. EL responds to these conditions by inducing and guiding people at all layers of a system to engage in ongoing inquiry to adapt, test, and improve a shared, dynamic strategy that can evolve, over time, to meet the needs of different individuals and constituencies in a quickly changing world.

Undergirded by a set of cultural and structural supports, Evolutionary Learning seeks to improve strategy and implementation through practical experimentation. It reorients operations to enable experimentation *for* children by treating every action members take as an opportunity to learn. It replaces public school systems' traditional approach to learning from experience: repeated implementation of the same strategies, practices, and processes even when they fail to enable student learning, without systematic ways to learn how to better support students in the future.

In EL hives, everyday work becomes an experiment in how to get better. Actors address complex conditions and uncertainty by working together to be more deliberate and observant about their work and its results. This requires actors closest to each element of the daily activity— leaders, ground-level staff, faculty, students, families, and/or community members—to be clear about what they believe to be true and what they expect their actions to accomplish. With that hypothesis in hand, they are then prepared to learn how and why their predictions differ from their expectations. Those insights enable the hive to more effectively address problems when and where they occur.

Using a shared learning cycle, hives innovate and address problems— deviations between what's expected and what occurs—in the regular course of daily activity. To do this systematically, actors

1. Choose an area of focus;
2. Articulate the problems to be solved;
3. Research and hypothesize potential solutions;
4. Study and refine hypotheses using experimentation; and
5. Capture learning from experiments and feedback and test and adapt solutions at wider scales and in new contexts.

You may be familiar with "continuous improvement" methodologies and tools like The Model for Improvement, improvement science, Six Sigma, or PDSAs—and wonder if by using them you've turned your organization or team into an Evolutionary Learning hive. Maybe you have! Still, although structured inquiry processes are an important component of EL, they are not the whole package. Successfully applying EL requires the full integration of individual and system-level improvement efforts into the system's daily practice—radically remaking the way work across every layer of the organization is enacted. Counterintuitive though it may seem, it is possible to use improvement tools in a bureaucratic way, if, for example, leaders mandate and assess compliance with prescribed inquiry steps, templates, and tools, prioritizing procedure over substance. In such instances, the focus becomes fidelity to the prescribed process, stifling the flexibility, substantive rigor, learning, and modification needed to ensure the process surfaces and spreads meaningful improvement. In other instances, bureaucracies may employ these improvement methods and tools not to shift governance, but rather to solve a preidentified problem, generating a solution through testing that can be mandated systemwide. In these instances, though inquiry was used to surface the solution, its use has limited effect on the system design as a whole, which ultimately treats what arises from discovery as a "silver bullet" that can be prescribed. Often, when these constrained improvement efforts fail to shift student outcomes at scale—not surprisingly, because the governance approach impedes progress on many fronts—leaders move on or deemphasize disciplined improvement as a lever for change.

In contrast, EL hives make constant, rigorous experimentation and learning the *modus operandi* for daily practice at all layers of the system, enabled by a shared vision, an embedded suite of structures and routines, and aligned cultural norms, all of which themselves are subject to investigation and refinement. In short, improvement succeeds because it is experienced by each community member as an explicit, foundational, and integral part of their everyday work, rather than as a supplement or layer atop the "real" or "core" work of the organization. In hives, actors are accountable not only for leading, teaching, coaching, or bus driving, but also for contributing to *constant improvement* of individual and collective leadership, instructional, or coaching practice across the system every day, even when they are already personally performing at a high level.

For this process to succeed, hive leaders must be able to trust actors at all levels of the system to exercise discretion to adapt, test, and refine strategy so that it addresses needs and challenges as they emerge and where they are most visible (Ladd, 2010). A culture of transparency prompts actors at each site to make adaptations explicit and share them and their results with leaders and actors at other sites in support of system-level improvement. Testing innovations by one site at others—customizing them as different conditions warrant—enables innovations over time to be applied at scale. Because these inquiries continue over the lifetime of a system, the hive's and each actor's knowledge about strategies and expected outcomes is always treated as provisional and subject to revision (Ansell, 2011). Ongoing experimentation allows hives to build sustainable strategies that improve over time while remaining dynamic enough to meet the diverse and changing conditions and needs of a complex system.

Four core activities are essential to the successful implementation of EL:

1. *Building a hive:* Cultivate systems that draw in all actors in the system—those the system employs and those it serves—to engage in robust collaborative vision-setting, strategy development, and learning.
2. *Swarming problems, innovating, and pollinating learning:* Democratize and streamline the generation, consolidation, capture, sharing, and application of knowledge to solve problems and innovate.
3. *Harvesting data to monitor and improve:* Measure process and outcomes across the system to identify what works, for whom, under what conditions.
4. *Leading the Learning Hive:* Propel innovation, enable participatory decision-making and collaboration, and serve as learners in chief.

Approaches to integrating those activities into a system's everyday work are the subject of the next five chapters.

EVOLUTIONARY LEARNING: STRENGTH FROM DEMOCRATIC STAKEHOLDER PARTICIPATION

Central to Evolutionary Learning is a theory and practice of democracy that puts consequential participation by the frontline staff and communities implementing and affected by organizational practice at the heart of each strategy's design and improvement. EL assumes that the knowledge held by central leaders is necessarily incomplete given the complexity and diversity of the systems they lead and their distance from the sites where much of the work gets done. So EL replaces the rigid top-down bureaucratic structure of strategy development and decision-making familiar in education ecosystems with flexible and interconnected problem-solving hives.

In these hives, consequential participation characterizes all stages of the work—participatory visioning, goal definition, strategy design, implementation, and improvement (Ansell & Gash, 2008; Bianchi, 2021). EL hives identify and strategically tap the diverse cohort of people they will need to set ambitious aims and implement effective practice at scale, moving beyond inherited relational structures that have produced current inequities. In school systems, this means softening the entrenched boundaries that have divided various groups—central offices and schools, administrators and teachers, expert educators and families, schools and communities—boundaries wrought, at least in part, by governance systems like bureaucracy, managerialism, professionalism, and craft that purposefully resist democratic processes needed to inform and forge strong, shared visions for the future (Liebman et al., 2017). Leaders in EL systems build trust with all; highlight participants' interdependence; set the conditions for meaningful and productive conflict and deliberative democracy (Dewey, 1927/2012); and find areas of commonality that can catalyze progress (Ansell, 2011; powell, 2019).

Schools and districts are a particularly important site for this work because they are many people's primary points of contact with public institutions and government itself. Democratic processes in schools function as a meaningful, sustained, and experiential civic curriculum for students, families, and their communities (Giroux & Penna, 1979; Henderson et al., 2016; Lenzi et al., 2014; Liebman & Sabel, 2003; powell, 2019). A system's approach to engagement and participation communicates which voices are valued both in the system and in the larger democratic context (Giroux & Penna, 1979; Justice & Meares, 2014). Inclusive approaches to participation can empower communities and build democratic dispositions with effects far beyond the schoolhouse door, including by fostering increased trust in the legitimacy of schools and other public institutions (Anyon, 1980).

In practice, coordinated participation helps the system diagnose, respond to, and learn from persistent and enduring challenges, get early warning of environmental changes, and identify and quickly act on opportunities to improve system practice. This approach activates the powerful knowledge and wisdom that remains latent in bureaucratic, managerialist, professional, and craft systems—each of which has its reasons for not attending to what teachers, students, families, and/or communities know. This is not participation for participation's sake; it is *the only way* to ensure that organizational strategy and practice is responsive to the needs of students and communities and to what those constituencies know about how to meet their needs. It is ultimately the only way to accelerate progress toward equity at scale (Allison, 1984; Anyon, 1980; Giroux & Penna, 1979). Over time, this work cultivates communities in which all stakeholders continuously develop stronger understandings of, learn from, and influence the systems they are part of as a matter of course.

EVOLUTIONARY LEARNING: BORROWED FEATURES WELL-MATCHED TO COMPLEXITY

EL builds on the effective features of other governance models while eliminating elements mismatched to the complexity of public education (see Table 3.1). From bureaucracy, EL retains structured operations, a belief that knowledge can be made explicit and transferred, and a commitment to public, rather than private interests, while shedding bureaucracy's stifling rules and hierarchies, top-down perspective on knowledge transfer, mistrust of line employees' exercise of discretion, susceptibility to pressure from interest groups not representative of the system's main clients and constituents, and struggles to reach collective consensus before taking action. From managerialism, EL retains a sharp focus on outcomes and the flexibility granted to local actors exercising discretion in pursuit of success, but drops narrow high-stakes targets and dubious assumptions about the opaqueness of knowledge held only by a small number of intuitive leaders and implementers. And from professionalism and craft, EL retains a faith in line actors' preparation, access to knowledge, exercises of discretion, and commitment to a profession or craft's shared quality standards, internally driven motivation, and bottom-up learning, while rejecting assumptions that knowledge is exceptionally difficult to acquire and spread and thus is limited to experts who are susceptible to narrow conventional or elitist norms.

This fusion of elements drawn from each governance approach produces a model well-equipped to support the pursuit of equity across diverse educational contexts.

For easy comparison of the Evolutionary Learning model to those we discussed in Chapter 2, see Table 3.1, which adds EL to the summary table of governance models shown at Table 2.1.

EVOLUTIONARY LEARNING: NEW APPROACHES TO LEADERSHIP

In EL systems, leaders abound. By rejecting the top-down, rigid definition of leadership and expertise so common in education systems, EL empowers stakeholders across the system to take responsibility for and lead learning and strategy refinement efforts in their domain of influence.

Orchestrating this expanded network of empowered frontline leaders are a handful of actors whom we call *positional leaders*. Positional leaders play an important role in steering, coordinating, and advancing continuous learning aligned with the system's aims, strategy, and practice. While effective positional leaders often, though not always, hold traditional leadership roles—think superintendents and principals, executive and deputy directors, and team leaders—learning hives define their role not as a hero or general at the top of a hierarchy, charged with directing the behavior of others, but rather as a "learner in chief," charged primarily with facilitating learning and, in that way, getting the best out of everyone they lead, while learning alongside their collaborators and giving their best (Spear, 2009).

Table 3.1. Summary of Governance Models Including Evolutionary Learning

	Bureaucracy	Managerialism	Professionalism/Craft	Evolutionary Learning
Works well when . . .	Conditions, strategy, and goals are stable, homogeneous, and well established	Goals are somewhat limited, uniform, and easy to define and measure across contexts and at scale Strategy need not or cannot be defined, studied, improved, and spread	Conditions vary, practitioners reflect the populations they serve, and strategy and goals are best determined by those practitioners who exercise their judgment on behalf of their constituents There are robust pipelines of professionals and craftspeople aspiring to serve and sustain careers in the sector	Conditions are diverse, complex and unstable, and identifying goals and effective strategy requires new knowledge that is best derived from the ongoing experience of people active in and served by the system
Direction is set by . . .	Leaders and central experts at the top of the hierarchy	Leaders and central experts who set outcomes-based performance targets	Local practitioners who consult other master practitioners/ professionals as challenges arise	Central actors in collaboration with local actors employed or served by the organization
Knowledge . . .	Of the leaders and central experts is made explicit through detailed rules that actors at lower levels of the system must carry out	Is tacit and its responsible discovery and use can be incentivized via performance targets and accountability	Is tacit in craft and developed under the guidance of master practitioners	Is developed through problem-solving enacted by all system actors, made explicit, and shared through disciplined knowledge management processes

(continued)

49

Table 3.1. (continued)

	Bureaucracy	Managerialism	Professionalism/Craft	Evolutionary Learning
Knowledge . . .			Is explicit in professionalism and acquired and refined through study, application, and assessment, including by esteemed professionals	
Success is determined by and respect comes from . . .	Compliance with prescriptive and highly-elaborated rules	Achievement of performance targets	Peers who have mastered the craft or have been deemed expert professionals	Improved processes and outcomes using collaboratively developed measures of success and capacity to help others achieve such improvements
Systematic improvement occurs when . . .	Leaders and central experts upgrade, communicate, and enforce compliance with rules that reflect new knowledge	Managers hire employees who meet performance targets and let go of those who do not	The craft or profession grows and is able to meet the demand of those seeking services	Actors at all levels of the system, including those who do and are affected by the work, are transparent about success and failure and collaborate in continuously surfacing, testing, refining, and incorporating insight into strategy and practice
People outside but affected by the organization or agency at the center of the system influence it through . . .	Arms-length and often adversarial, episodic and interest-based engagement	Elections and selection and appointment processes that identify system leaders who determine uniform performance targets	Participation in the craft or profession; those outside are expected to comply with expert practitioners' judgment	Active participation in and the resulting transparency of ongoing activities and efforts to improve them

This approach to leadership draws on the strengths of both top-down and bottom-up models. Centralized positional leaders help track learning across the system, keeping it anchored to a common vision and goals and, over time, accelerating improvement. At the same time, positional leaders work to amplify the unique expertise of ground-level stakeholders who participate actively in direction-setting through local discretion and meaningful influence on decision-making (Liebman et al., 2017).

Leading the learning work of a hive is no mean feat. Successfully orchestrating improvement requires an ability to hone rich understandings of and constantly attend to nuanced processes of knowledge development across the organization, so the system itself can evolve and get better at identifying and addressing problems (Ansell, 2011). In particular, positional leaders must support the development and refinement of the system's vision, strategy, standards, and operational learning structures. In EL systems, system design and leadership decisions guide actors doing and affected by the work to operate as a coordinated learning community, adapting quickly to challenges and changes in conditions, learning from one another's successes and failures, and advancing toward shared goals more quickly. Unhampered by internal and external organizational boundaries, these leaders build bridges across—and ultimately break down—the structural and interpersonal silos that can obscure innovations and stall progress.

EVOLUTIONARY LEARNING IN ACTION

You may be thinking: this all sounds great, but what does it look like in practice? Look no further than the High Tech High CARPE College Access Collaborative convening. Walking into the room, there's something different in the air. Excited chatter fills a bright, breezy room flanked by a kindergarten playground sparkling with laughter. High school students, teachers, college advisors, principals, and district staff eagerly reconnect with peers from neighboring schools and districts, providing updates on progress made since their last meeting, three months earlier. In describing his vision for progressive education, John Dewey (1899, p. 22) wrote that "there is a certain disorder present in any busy workshop," an observation resonant with the scene today. Drifting in and out of conversations, however, it's easy to pick up on a clear vision and ethos: an optimism that improvement is not only possible but already in motion.

High Tech High is a school-development organization, home to a network of charter schools and the High Tech High Graduate School of Education (GSE), and is known for its pioneering approach to project-based learning and continuous improvement. In 2018, it launched the CARPE College Access Collaborative (CARPE), a learning community designed to accelerate progress on college access and success outcomes in comprehensive public and charter high schools throughout Southern California. Spearheaded by High Tech High GSE's Center for Research on Equity and Innovation, the network has supported over 30 school-based improvement teams—each a collective of school and district leaders, teachers, counselors, school staff, and students—in using High Tech High's unique approach to experimentation and improvement. As a community, the network has collaboratively identified challenges and built shared strategies to address college access and success pain points, in the process fundamentally shifting how participating schools conceptualize and approach learning, decision-making, and change.

In short, in CARPE, network leaders have built a hive: a dynamic and agile community composed of an integrated web of members motivated by a shared vision of rigorous measurement; a commitment to constant, collaborative learning across traditional boundaries; and a drive to share that learning with others to meaningfully and sustainably shift outcomes for all students.

How does a hive, like CARPE's, function—and how can you start building your own?

CHAPTER 4

Build a Hive

VIGNETTE: HIGH TECH HIGH CARPE COLLEGE
ACCESS COLLABORATIVE

In the sunny California meeting room described in Chapter 3, High Tech High's CARPE College Access Collaborative (CARPE) hive feels joyful, organic, and effortless. But this unstudied atmosphere belies a system carefully designed and facilitated by a team of experienced positional leaders. Since the network's inception—when we started studying CARPE's work—these leaders have rejected governance approaches mismatched to the network's complex, evolving goals and contexts. Instead, CARPE's leaders have built a system driven by Evolutionary Learning.

CARPE's governance model extends to network members the same experiential learning strategy High Tech High employs in K–12 classrooms. Riordan and Caillier (2019) write that the community "enact[s] a powerful symmetry of practice; the adults learn as we hope the students will" (p. 142). In CARPE, this means that network leaders and participants alike learn through *doing* and *experimentation*. As a hive leader explained to us, "The 40,000 foot view is, get [network participants] doing the work—don't talk to them about it. Do it with them. And then push for inquiry."

For CARPE members, all work leads toward the network's shared vision: improving the college access, matriculation, and success rates for Black, Latino, and/or low-income students. A collectively developed theory of action articulates an evolving hypothesis for progress toward that outcome, naming FAFSA completion, the college application process, collegiate belongingness, and summer melt as key levers for change. This theory, paired with High Tech High's user-friendly approach to continuous improvement, brings structure and coherence to the learning work happening across schools while leaving plenty of room for local customization and innovation.

To accelerate improvement and wider-scale impact, CARPE leaders enable broad participation from a diverse pool of members. Member schools range from large, comprehensive public schools to college-prep charters to High Tech High's own project-based charters. In each of these contexts, school-based improvement teams include a cross section of actors, including district and school leaders, administrators, frontline educators, after-school staff, community members, and high school students.

A network structure designed to encourage peer collaboration and knowledge exchange across the expansive, evolving community spurs collective progress. As one hive leader explained, "We really wanted to work on connecting schools to each other, building that sense of CARPE identity, like, 'I'm learning not just from the [network] leadership team but I'm learning from the other people in the network.'" CARPE's leaders pair schools facing similar challenges for facilitated, biweekly working meetings. Cross-school affinity groups convene to tackle shared problems of practice. Coaching relationships allow network leaders to regularly get "into the weeds" with teams—not just to impart wisdom and guide practice, but also to learn from participants how network strategy is being adapted to meet local needs. These various touchpoints and relationships help foster a strong in-group identity, grounded in shared values and norms, including a commitment to problem-solving, reflexivity, belief in the power of collaboration, and, above all, a sense of optimism, joy, and fun.

Building a functional hive has been anything but straightforward. CARPE's network structure has changed over time because hive leaders apply the same rigorous improvement lens to network design, practice, and leadership as they do to the network's college access challenges. Since launch, the structure and composition of teams; criteria for inclusion in the network; approaches to connecting members; and ways of consolidating, capturing, and scaling knowledge have shifted. A constant, however, has been the pursuit of ever better, grounded in a fierce commitment to improving outcomes for young people.

This investment has paid off. In just 5 years, from 2018 to 2023, network schools demonstrated remarkable gains in student college access and enrollment outcomes. Financial aid application completion in the network rose between 11 and 18 percentage points, suggesting that nearly 1,100 additional students completed financial aid forms as a result of CARPE's work. And college enrollment rates in network schools rose by 3.8 percentage points, even as the COVID-19 pandemic disrupted schools and drove declining enrollment rates nationally. Across High Tech High member schools, in particular, college enrollment rates for 2022 graduates climbed to 82%—the highest rate in San Diego

County—as a result of changes in programming spurred by network learning (Taketa, 2023).

There is power in a hive. What does it take to build one?

THE EVOLUTIONARY LEARNING HIVE

A learning hive is the dynamic, coordinated community of people, relationships, systems, routines, and practices that drive creative exchange, learning, and innovation in EL organizations. In hives, change is the constant, as members pursue better and better approaches to organizing people, relationships, and practice to advance meaningful improvement. This pursuit requires hives to blur the line between doing and deciding so that the organization can nimbly adapt to challenges and changes in conditions, learn from successes and failures, and progress toward shared aims more quickly.

Hives orient all activity around a central vision and approach to learning. A shared strategy and three core questions guide work at each layer of the organization (Langley et al., 2009):

1. What are we trying to do, and what will success look like?
2. Is what we are doing working as expected?
3. How might we improve what we are doing?

To answer these questions, hives equip all members to act as directors *and* doers, implementers *and* problem-solvers, and facilitators *and* participants. A learning culture supports these learning structures; in particular, a community orientation and mindsets and membership responsibilities that enable constant improvement, reflexivity, and collaborative democracy.

STRUCTURES AND ACTIVITIES

Hives seek a "symmetry of practice" (Riordan & Caillier, 2019), p. 142 in which structure enacts stated values—including problem orientation, critical and action-oriented reflection, and member participation. A shared strategy and approach to learning guide activities at each layer of the hive. Flexible teaming structures provide positional leaders and frontline staff with opportunities to learn in tandem to constantly improve system-level strategy. By thinking more expansively about who has a stake in system work—and how they might participate in improving it—hives democratize improvement.

Orient All Activity Around a Shared, Evolving Strategy and Approach to Learning

Like bureaucracy, EL hives organize their work using a strategy that outlines the causal logic between a system's inputs, actions, outcomes, and results. But a huge distance separates how, why, and by whom strategy is developed and improved in EL and in bureaucracy. Rather than functioning as a *de facto* contract, designed by central leaders to mandate practice and constrain discretion in relatively stable contexts, in learning hives strategy serves as an evolving compact: a provisional hypothesis, developed as a collective, about how actors across the system might effectively coordinate practice in uncertain conditions (Edmondson & Verdin, 2017).

A good strategy articulates a hypothesis about the relationships among the following elements:

- *Inputs*: Resources, actors, and conditions that need to be in place to start implementing actions.
- *Actions*: Steps various actors within the system, including leaders, need to take to make progress toward outcomes and impacts.
- *Outcomes*: Shorter-term changes expected to result from actions that will lead to the desired impact. Typically, these are changes in attitudes, behaviors, and early results.
- *Impacts*: Longer-term changes the organization wants to achieve, including in student outcomes (Austin et al., 2021).

In a nested system, local strategies, nested with the broader system theory, support aligned learning at each layer of the organization.

The value of a strategy lies in the degree to which it makes the logic of work explicit. Strategies challenge collaborators to detail the unstated norms, vague understandings, and linguistic symbols that haphazardly guide work in many organizations and that, when tacit, confuse and derail collaborative efforts (Follett, 2013/1940). By articulating assumptions and hypotheses about how activities at each layer of the system contribute to a shared vision of success, members clarify areas of misunderstanding, work through sites of disagreement, identify shared interests, surface creative approaches to collaboration, and reach "thin consensus" (Sabel & Victor, 2022, p. 7) on how to move forward and evaluate progress.

Critically, in EL systems, strategy is merely a starting point for learning and improvement. It answers the hive's first learning question—*What are we trying to do, and what will success look like?* With that answer, actors at each nested layer of the organization use a shared learning methodology to interrogate the second and third questions. As a matter of course, during strategy implementation, hive members use data to understand whether *what they're doing is working as expected*. Whenever the answer is "no," they seek to understand *how they might improve*, typically using some variation of the following steps (which will be discussed in detail in Chapter 5):

1. *Select areas of focus*: Hive members identify high-leverage areas for improvement.
2. *Conduct root cause analysis*: Hive members collaboratively explore the underlying causes of gaps between expected outcomes and results.
3. *Develop a theory of improvement*: Hive members generate a hypothesis about how they predict proposed interventions will improve outcomes, drawing from both field knowledge (i.e., empirical research) and personal and organizational experience. These ideas are captured in a shared theory.
4. *Conduct short-cycle testing*: Hive members experiment with proposed interventions, sometimes using rapid-cycle testing processes like the Plan, Do, Study, Act (PDSA) cycle (Langley et al., 2009).
5. *Scale up and spread improvements*: Leaders integrate successful adaptations into system-level strategy and the daily practice of the organization, adjusting application as needed across contexts.

Because strategy is provisional and subject to investigation using this learning methodology, EL systems do not belabor the development process. They move quickly to implementation, seeing on-the-ground practice and experimentation as the primary lever for refining their hypotheses. Working within the boundaries established by a shared vision and strategy, norms, and practice standards, implementers exercise discretion, adapting elements of strategy to meet local needs. With this discretion, however, comes responsibility: the system relies on all hive members to use the system's learning methodology to name problems, test adaptations, and communicate new learnings so that system-level strategy and implementation can be improved.

This method is particularly suited to complex contexts, like public schools, where a high degree of uncertainty requires constant innovation. Hives bring together top-down and bottom-up approaches to governance and problem-solving to destabilize the status quo, in part through the constant interrogation of concrete problems. From the top, a provisional central strategy helps organize diverse actors with varying functional roles, motivations, and goals around shared objectives and approaches to the work. Much responsibility for the testing of strategy, problem identification, and innovation, however, is diffused across the front line, where challenges are most acutely felt and expertise regarding local implementation is highest. Positional leaders' role becomes incentivizing and scaffolding learning, mining and supporting assessment of local innovation, "piecing together" local improvements, supporting sensemaking and application of learning at the organizational level, and responsively adjusting strategy—including its targets and aims—throughout this learning process (Sabel & Victor, 2022, p. 3). This feedback loop, alongside increasingly blurred boundaries between system leaders and the front line, allows systems to stop questioning "*whether* change is possible," and begin asking *how* to motivate it across various contexts (Sabel & Victor, 2022, p. 9).

The High Tech High CARPE College Access Collaborative is guided by a shared strategy and a learning methodology that bring purpose and direction to ground-level learning across a diverse collective of districts, schools, and actors. The network's theory of improvement, represented in a driver diagram, articulates the connections between the network's aim and the constellation of actions members theorize will facilitate progress toward that goal. Initially outlined by leaders before the network's launch, the first version of the theory (see Figure 4.1) was presented to members at CARPE's first convening as a hypothesis that was "possibly incorrect, definitely incomplete" and ripe for revision. This framing positioned participants as cocreators, who immediately began proposing revisions, identifying secondary drivers, and revising the diagram.

Those suggestions were integrated into the working theory, elements of which school improvement teams began testing immediately as they pursued improvements in financial aid application completion rates. As teams tested research-backed interventions (e.g., initiating individualized student support, encouraging early completion of forms) promising local innovations emerged (e.g., in-school application support through class pull-outs). Over time, hive leaders helped members spread successful interventions across the network, capturing them in CARPE's strategy as broad standards, including practices like: "Share the 'why' & push for early completion" or "Proactively support students & families to complete." By 2024, the driver diagram had been formally revised many times as a direct result of numerous rounds of frontline implementation and testing.

Cultivate Organizational Structures That Make Doing and Learning Inseparable

Learning hives are structured to blur what Follett calls the "sharp line" between strategy and execution (as cited in Ansell, 2011, p. 72). Understanding that local challenges are the grist for system-level improvement, hives

Figure 4.1. CARPE College Access Collaborative's First Driver Diagram

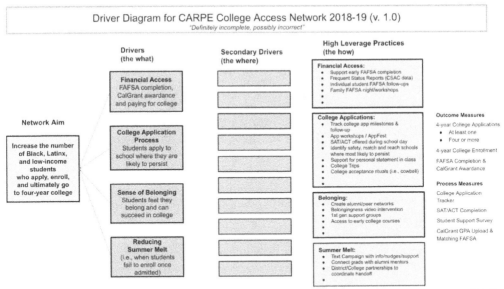

Driver Diagram for CARPE College Access Network 2018-19 (v. 1.0)
"Definitely incomplete, possibly incorrect"

If we want to improve our AIM, then we need to focus on PRIMARY drivers, through SECONDARY drivers, and one way to do that is through a CHANGE IDEA.

build organizational structure to enable habitual feedback loops between strategy and implementation. In practice, this dynamic disrupts traditional ideas about where expertise lies—in the many doers rather than the few directors—and enables the system to adapt system-level strategy more quickly and democratically. Over time, such an architecture supports self-sustaining problem-solving efforts; the generation, spread, and application of knowledge; and system improvement.

To this end, positional leaders foster an evolving "network of communities" (Snowden, 2012), strengthening communication pathways between members with differing functional roles, sites of work, and domains of expertise (Milgram, 1967). No single organizational chart captures what an EL organization looks like because they are highly contextual and constantly in motion, responding to new learning and shifts in context (Satell, 2015). A positional leader's ongoing role is monitoring, informing, and shaping the system's network of relationships, attending to evidence of emerging organic connections and, when necessary, formalizing them via new structures. Throughout this process, hive leaders position themselves as gardeners rather than engineers, understanding that they can influence, but not control, the development of human relationships (Snowden, 2002b).

Teaming structures that promote a sense of stability for organizational actors, while remaining flexible, are essential. Individuals are assigned to their home team(s) based on their core functional responsibilities. In a district, a home team for an ELA teacher might be their school-based content team; for a principal coach, the central office's leadership development team. Given members' focused work on similar day-to-day tasks, positional leaders ensure that home teams have time, space, and routines that encourage frequent contact and co-learning. Over time, these practices help teams develop trust, share knowledge, and solve problems together (Russell et al., 2019). What makes these home teams especially important in EL systems is their proximity to various aspects of strategy implementation. They are well positioned—and, critically, empowered by positional leaders—to spot, sound the alarm about, and address issues when and where they occur, communicating adaptation of strategy to central leaders who coordinate further testing and, as warranted, central strategy change. In this way, *every* team in a hive is a strategy team.

Positional leaders build ties between various home teams via clusters developed around shared context, practice, and learning goals. In districts, a cluster of grade level teams may be arranged between schools serving similar student populations, while principal coaches might be clustered with other central office teams that provide professional development. Clusters pursue learning goals aligned to system strategy, meeting somewhat frequently (e.g., in monthly meetings) and using the system's shared problem-solving methodology. Relational ties between cluster members may be somewhat weaker than those of home teams, but because members bring a greater diversity of experience to bear, clusters can help disrupt inertia and spark innovation (McCormick et al., 2011). Clusters thrive when their members find value in their relationships with peers and go out of their way to nurture these connections, for example, by connecting between formal meetings (Kinlaw et al., 2020). Effective positional leaders initially curate these groupings and then monitor where natural relationships emerge, over time adapting membership to find a balance of commonality and difference—in context, capacity, and learning interests—that will increase buy-in and motivate disruptive thinking and innovation.

As local- and system-level problems come to the fore, often signaled during the learning efforts undertaken by home teams and clusters, positional leaders initiate a third type of grouping: cross-functional, goal-oriented teams, tasked with end-to-end responsibility for a particular challenge. Powered by a diverse set of representatives—including hive members like students, families, community members, and outside experts—with varying expertise and access to local sites of implementation, the team addresses challenges that span traditional organizational boundaries, moving beyond siloed tinkering and toward systems-level solutions. The lifespan of these teams varies depending on the needs of the organization. Some dissolve once a challenge is addressed, others evolve to address new facets of a problem, and still others persist, becoming integrated into the stable architecture of the organization.

For example, to investigate a marked increase in chronic absenteeism, a district hive might initiate a cross-functional team composed of school principals, attendance clerks, counselors, nurses, family outreach coordinators, families, and students. As the context-specific root causes of absenteeism become clear—perhaps including scheduling—positional leaders might elect to refocus team membership, for example, releasing nurses and bringing in teachers and additional administrators. If shifts in scheduling ameliorate the chronic absenteeism issue, the team might disband; if they raise other challenges or possibilities, team membership and tasks might again evolve.

Finally, positional leaders cultivate time and space for hive members across their system to come together as a full organizational team for learning, celebration, and socialization. The informal, light-touch connections forged in these spaces develop the organization as a highly-connected, "small world" network, wherein members belong to tight-knit groups (via home teams, clusters, and cross-functional teams) yet also maintain more casual relationships with a broader swath of the organization (Milgram, 1967; Uzzi et al., 2007). Such an organizational structure expedites knowledge sharing and makes the organization more resilient in the face of disruption and change.

This hive model relies on competent teams. To build team capacity, positional leaders collaborate with members to develop clear expectations, roles, and working norms. Measurable standards for team excellence, shared directly with members and those supporting capacity development (e.g., coaches, team leads) define success and allow positional leaders to monitor their own leadership practice. If teams fall short, positional leaders and teams interrogate where organizational structure, team design, and their own approach to support could be improved.

Make Permeable Boundaries Between Leaders, Implementers, and Those Served

Positional leaders lead from the ground. They embed themselves in frontline work and team-learning processes as often as possible so they can better understand implementation, experience challenges directly, and learn at pace with hive members. Positional leaders are in frequent contact with ground-level staff and actors, including through regular check-ins;

frequent site visits; and, in some cases, formal roles on various implementation and cross-functional teams (The Learning Accelerator, n.d.).

In the CARPE Collaborative, hive leaders coach school-based improvement teams in addition to their strategic planning responsibilities—departing from the practice of many school improvement networks, where coaches sit on teams that report to, but do not include, network leadership (Kinlaw et al., 2020). CARPE's hybrid structure allows leaders to anticipate and understand emerging challenges and quickly adapt their leadership approach and network strategy in response.

This practice has had a tangible impact on network practice and student outcomes. For example, to improve completion rates for the Free Application for Federal Student Aid (FAFSA), CARPE's network leadership team recommended that all teams test a promising network-generated innovation: targeted class pull-outs to support completion during the school day. While coaching a school at a convening, Stacey Caillier, a network leader, learned that the school team had not implemented the intervention for a seemingly minor reason: There was no one to run hall passes to classrooms after a new state policy had reduced the number of aides at the school. In other organizations, where system leaders and frontline staff are in contact only infrequently, leadership might never have realized that this small, but real, logistical challenge was standing in the way of successful implementation. Instead, the strong feedback loop enabled by the proximity of network leaders to school teams allowed CARPE members to flag the issue immediately. Caillier worked with the school's teachers and administrators that same day to adapt the intervention to their local context via shifts in scheduling.

As positional leaders learn from implementation, they also ensure that ground-level hive members have formal roles at various points throughout the strategy development process. In these touchpoints, frontline hive members work alongside positional leaders to articulate, refine, and adapt system-level strategy. Leaders design these collaboration spaces so that all actors can engage fully, not merely as token observers or "voices in the room." They recruit and convene a consistent group so that rapport and trust can be established, develop and facilitate the implementation of community agreements, use protocols to support voice equity, listen closely for what is *not* being said, and most importantly, give all hive members a full vote when decisions are made (Feicke, 2007).

In this work, hives consistently adapt to ensure they include those closest to and most impacted by various aspects of strategy in decision-making. For example, CARPE launched in 2018 with adult-only improvement teams, drawing in student perspectives primarily through empathy interviews and surveys. But network leaders and participants soon realized that these limited touchpoints were falling short of meaningful inclusion—and that, as a result, the network was missing an opportunity to produce stronger solutions to the network's most acute college access challenges. So CARPE leaders swung into action, piloting a student fellowship wherein students from several schools worked on a parallel track to the adult network, aligning to the same core strategy to surface, test, and refine their own ideas about how to improve college access outcomes, including hosting a highly-successful, youth-led workshop on the college application process for younger students.

The pilot allowed the network to learn how to best support and engage students in improvement efforts, and in the year following, network leaders began asking adult school-improvement teams to include two students in their core membership, in particular pushing teams to invite to participate students further from college success. Through their direct integration on teams, students were able to participate in real time, supporting stronger problem understanding, flagging instances where adult interventions were off the mark, and surfacing and testing their own ideas. For example, as adults on one team discussed emailing an application checklist to seniors, a student member immediately flagged a potentially fatal flaw in the plan: her peers rarely checked email. The student suggested that seniors would be more likely to see such a communication on the school's virtual gradebook system, and the team immediately altered their plan. Of the effort, network leader Sofía Tannenhaus said: "We have well-intentioned adults trying to do meaningful work to improve student outcomes. And an essential piece of that process is hearing from students directly. That can take many forms, but students need to have a seat at the table in order for us to really move the needle. And it's equally important to have adults really willing to learn from students and lean in with curiosity."

Expand Participation

To surface, get to the root of, and address complex problems, hives look beyond the network of existing relationships that have contributed to the status quo and bring together a broader cross section of actors from within and beyond the formal boundaries of the organization. This requires partnering with those who have been marginalized, reinvesting in challenging relationships, and finding new allies.

Beyond engaging proximate hive members like students and families, hives attend to the "inconvenient" relationships (Innes & Booher, 2016) that most systems are designed to avoid. Key to this work is a belief that conflict is not a problem to be solved but instead one of the most important drivers of improvement (Ansell, 2011). Excluding members who ask tough questions and challenge existing practices ultimately leads to weaker strategy and unresolved tension that will emerge again and again (Follett, 1919). Positional leaders seek out and harness conflict, facing up to difficult relationships and, often with the help of trusted intermediaries, inviting hive members into thoughtfully facilitated learning spaces organized around shared challenges. This problem orientation is essential: it asks participants to move away from critiques of other member's values and beliefs—and toward a practical assessment of a particular problem at hand. This approach allows for creative integration (Follett, 2013/1940), in which alternate paths forward are identified.

Creative integration can work even in instances where relationships begin as entrenched and bitter standoffs. Ansell (2011) describes one such situation: in the 1980s, Las Vegas, then one of the fastest-growing cities in the United States, began encroaching on the habitat of the endangered desert tortoise, violating the Endangered Species Act. Leveraging an exception in the Act that allowed development if a habitat protection plan was proposed to mitigate harm, Clark County initiated a collaborative deliberation process that convened all affected stakeholders, including local governments, developers, and environmentalists. Interested parties were "beating down the door" to participate in the process (Raymond, 2006, p. 49), seeing it as the only way to defend their own interests. But while they wanted a seat at the table, at first, participants engaged in collaboration begrudgingly—or as one participant described, "hating each others' guts and ready to slit each others' throats"—bringing fundamentally oppositional values, concerns, and proposed solutions to bear (Ansell, 2011, p. 178). Ansell notes that early meetings were "violent" (p. 169), even requiring a weapons check throughout the first two years of the process.

Ultimately, however, the initiative was successful: the group emerged with a shared, mutually agreeable plan that allowed land development outside of the turtle's prime habitat. This success was enabled by facilitators who led a face-to-face deliberative process that asked participants to find new common ground, rather than sacrifice their core values or interests. Early work centered on forging a shared problem definition, a process that helped each side reframe the boundaries of the challenge. Years of extended meetings, meals, and exploratory trips together seeded personal relationships and helped participants see each other as legitimate collaborators, in turn, enabling more productive conflict. Through this work, hive members imagined creative solutions that honored each party's values and did not require compromise on any members' core concerns. This example underscores that collaborative governance can, even in the context of caustic social conflict, lead to strategies that accommodate mutual gains (Ansell, 2011).

Beyond attending to challenging relationships, hives identify *missing* relationships, looking beyond the immediate system to identify actors—policymakers, innovators, experts, and advocates inside and outside education—with whom they might build forward-looking partnerships. Rejecting the dichotomy of "in here" and "out there," hives understand that the borders erected around system elements, including the organization's formal boundaries, are artificial and porous and that, in practice, what happens "out there" is intertwined with what happens "in here." To identify relational gaps that, if filled, could advance improvement, hives return to their strategy and hypothesize the highest-leverage points of improvement. They engage in problem analysis that encourages blue sky thinking about what might be possible if they targeted levers beyond the organization's immediate locus of control. And then they go big, initating and cultivating relationships today that will contribute to transformative change tomorrow. The Mississippi marathon is an example of this principle in action. Rather than constraining decision-making to the state department of education, the initiative's leaders brought together a coalition of funders, researchers, policymakers, higher ed faculty and administrators, frontline practitioners, teachers, aides, and families—all working to address the deepest roots of the state's literacy crisis.

To tap into this broader range of member expertise, hives move beyond the informal, *pro forma* touch points long used in education, creating instead formal and integrated structures through which all members meaningfully and democratically influence strategy and decision-making as part of their daily work. Cultivating a dynamic, holistic view of their immediate system and environment, hives "get the right participation" and "get the participation right" (Glicken, 2000, p. 306), acknowledging that, in education systems, time and capacity is precious. Fully cross-functional member participation in every decision is unrealistic and, indeed, unnecessary, as each hive member holds different areas of capacity and expertise and will not be a necessary contributor to each shift in strategy. Positional leaders account for these realities, strategically prioritizing the participation of different members when and where it's most important.

In practice, this means that positional leaders toggle between participation modalities tailored to both hive member and system needs and capacity, moving up and down a participation ladder (Arnstein, 1969; Bens, 2017; González, 2019), below, ordered from more to less intensive participation, while ensuring that all hive members have opportunities to participate at each rung.

1. *Defer:* Positional leaders task a cross-functional group of hive members with developing, testing, and refining strategic initiatives at the local or system level. Leaders may support facilitation, but ultimately, they defer to the decisions made by the group.

   » For example, in an initiative to refresh their school support model, positional leaders at school support organization Partners in School Innovation shied away from top-down shifts in strategy, instead tasking a temporary, cross-functional working group with the redesign process. In line with Partners' core value of centering proximate voices, the frontline coach who had initially raised concerns about the strategy led the group through the redesign process. After months of collaborative work to refine the provisional model, Partners' leaders reshuffled team membership, tapping another functionally diverse group of staff—this time with expertise in data systems, evaluation, implementation, and program design—to monitor the implementation of the new model across partnership contexts.

2. *Collaborate:* Positional leaders work closely with hive members to co-lead and cofacilitate strategy development, implementation, or improvement. In practice, collaborative approaches may function as a capacity-building step necessary to transitioning toward "defer to" strategies.

   » In CARPE, as new school-based improvement teams set up norms, routines, and ways of working, hive leaders know success will depend on strong team function. To build a strong foundation for that work, leaders work closely with teams, offering vetted guidelines on roles, structures, and norms and then working with local participants to adapt those structures to meet local needs. In early team meetings, coaches cofacilitate meetings with participants, over time handing off responsibility to the local team lead. This early capacity-building exercise builds skills that allow hive leaders to increasingly defer to the discretion of those local teams as they mature.

3. *Consult:* Positional leaders gather input on strategy from hive members using tools like surveys and empathy interviews. Unlike the use of consultation in many traditional bureaucracies, learning leaders seek out feedback from hive members *before* decisions have been made, bringing provisional strategies to members throughout the development, implementation, and improvement process. Making early drafts of strategy public before they are finalized and

polished can be uncomfortable for positional leaders accustomed to bureaucratic and managerialist approaches. But in hives, expediting the learning processes requires that relevant parties have the opportunity to provide input early and often.

> » Consider again the network strategy hive leaders presented to CARPE participants at their first convening. When network members came together, positional leaders used a consultative approach—presenting a provisional theory, seeking feedback from participants, and then integrating comments into the network's strategy. At this juncture, consultation was appropriate, given that network members were new to the work and continuous improvement processes. Over time, the refinement of the network's theory became more and more collaborative, with ground-level experimentation directly moderating changes to strategy.

4. *Inform:* Positional leaders provide hive members with relevant information about strategy without seeking feedback. Implementation of this approach in learning hives differs from its execution in bureaucracies because culture supports transparency and system architecture facilitates bidirectional communication, in which hive members have the freedom to adapt strategy in their local context, offer feedback, or opt into a more actively participatory role.

CULTURE AND MINDSETS

Hives share a powerful vision and understand their interdependence in achieving it. As positional leaders facilitate boundary-crossing learning activities across the system, they make the connections between that work explicit and visible to hive members. Through this process, the community builds a sense of collective momentum by, as john a. powell (2019) writes, "co-constructing a larger *we*."

While the particularities of culture differ across hives, effective learning communities share a number of baseline orientations to their work. Evolutionary Learning occurs at the intersections of problem-solving, reflexivity, and deliberation (Ansell, 2011). In hives, these are not just activities, but also mindsets and foundations for a culture that is, in many ways, at odds with those of bureaucracy, managerialism, and craft. To unsettle and replace entrenched ways of thinking, positional leaders are as intentional about building culture as they are about building structures, understanding that "community is a process" (Follett, 1919, p. 576) and must be cultivated. First, positional leaders make culture and mindset explicit, helping hive members see and unpack their existing worldview and inbuilt assumptions (Pourdehnad et al., 2006). At the same time, leaders name learning dispositions, model them in their own practice, and weave them through the organization's vision, norms, structures, and routines.

Problem-Solving Orientation

In hives, community members embrace problems as concrete opportunities for improvement. While this practice is scaffolded by the problem-solving cycle (discussed in greater detail in Chapter 5), sustainable improvement requires more than rote progression through a formal set of procedures constrained to discrete initiatives and moments in time. Members must build patterns of thinking organized around the three questions outlined earlier in this chapter—and lived out as a default orientation to daily action: What are we trying to do, and what will success look like? Is what we are doing working as expected? And how might we improve what we're doing?

An effective learner's disposition is grounded as much in "solving" as it is in "problem;" in a practical optimism based on the belief that better is always possible. Positional leaders help cultivate this mindset by developing in hive members a sense of individual and collective self-efficacy, or a belief in one's own capacity to enact behaviors that support the achievement of goals (Bandura, 1977). Self-efficacy is critical in learning systems because it affects whether people set ambitious goals and feel motivated to pursue their aspirations.

An expedient route to self-efficacy is evidence of success, a condition that neatly aligns with EL's predilection toward action. Moving quickly from theory to execution—rather than getting stuck in perfecting an untested hypothesis—leads to quicker learning and, ultimately, quicker wins (Weick, 1995). Positional leaders motivate action and leverage strong measurement practices to celebrate early successes, naming explicitly how those milestones contribute to progress toward the system's strategic aims. And leaders showcase breakthroughs across the system, motivating self-efficacy by demonstrating the attainability of success (Bandura, 1977). Over time, drawing connections between victories garnered across local contexts can contribute to the development of *collective* efficacy (Bandura, 2000), wherein hive members attribute success to the collaborative work of the collective.

Deliberation and Fruitful Conflict

A key attribute of hives is the structures that help members work across the boundaries often reinforced in other governance models. With increased collaboration comes increasing interchange of perspectives and, inevitably, increased conflict. Hives do not avoid or smooth over disagreement but instead harness it for learning, pursuing "fruitful conflict" (Ansell, 2011) through which community members bring out and examine differences, investigate and reformulate problems, and, at best, produce creative new solutions that do not require compromise from any party (Follett, 1940). As Follett writes, "As conflict—difference—is here in the world, as we cannot avoid it, we should, I think, use it. . . . We talk of the friction of mind on mind as a good thing" (p. 30).

In mature hives, this type of deliberation happens both formally, in carefully facilitated spaces, and informally, as part of daily practice. Over time, as participants see the value in the process and better understand their peers, the nature of conflicts changes. Deliberation begins closer to the root of challenges, is navigated more gracefully, and surfaces integrative innovations that meet the needs of more hive members more often.

To cultivate this type of productive deliberation, positional leaders foster three key dispositions in the hive (Ansell, 2011). First, community members enter deliberative spaces with an openness to having their minds changed. Second, hive members see themselves as members of a collective, and in this belief, agree to sacrifice some degree of individualism and autonomy. And, third, hive members see themselves as co-owners of collaborative processes: deliberation, though at times facilitated by positional leaders, is shaped by all who participate. In combination, these three mindsets advance fruitful conflict.

At the root of each of these three mindsets is earned trust: trust that others in the collective share a vision for the work, that they bring to the table expertise and informed analysis, that they will follow through on commitments, and that they will be transparent about successes and failures. Positional leaders support the development of trust first by modeling it, placing confidence in the community and deliberative processes. Positional leaders may participate in and express disagreement, but once provisional decisions are reached, they commit to helping test, measure, and track outcomes. In this way, leaders share power with the collective (Berwick, 2009) and inspire trust.

Leaders begin this process by cultivating, surfacing, and making explicit shared values and ways of being that are unique to the hive. Those values are coconstructed through relationship-building with and between actors, both professionally and personally. Ultimately, members of the community must develop "joint appreciation," acknowledging each other's legitimate place within deliberative processes (Ansell, 2011). Positional leaders create time and space for face-to-face interaction as often as possible and include activities that help hive members build personal connections and get to know each other

Forming a collective also means recognizing differences and the strengths and perspectives that each hive member brings to the work. Heterogeneity in perspective and experience is what allows communities to build nuanced understandings of inequities and make progress toward addressing them. The collective "we" does not require that members assimilate, but asks instead that the boundaries of the system become more expansive, flexible, and inclusive (powell, 2019). To this end, and especially in long established communities, positional leaders push the group to interrogate regularly norms and ways of being ("This is how we do things here") to accommodate new perspectives and solutions. Almost paradoxically, leaders celebrate individuality to cultivate belongingness, making clear the tangible value each member's perspective contributes to successful pursuit of equitable outcomes. In turn, trust and belongingness help motivate greater ownership of process, growing the social connections and confidence needed for productive deliberation.

CARPE's positional leaders are intentional about building each of these mindsets—and as a result, have built a functional deliberative collective. When members joined the collaborative, they became part of the larger High Tech High community, whose formal bedrock design principles of equity, personalization, authentic work, and collaborative design, alongside unique ways of being like joy, humor, positivity, curiosity, and care, shape the structure and strategy of improvement. Leaders go out of their way to make community values visible, capturing them in meeting norms, sprinkling them liberally across the network's tools and protocols, and articulating them verbally during coaching and at full-network convenings. But CARPE leaders know that naming values isn't enough—they model them in their own practice and help participants do the same. There is, for example, a playfulness in the way CARPE leaders facilitate convenings that models the joy High Tech High has found so critical to sustaining improvement work. They demonstrate the power of a key community value—as participants find convening activities engaging, learning concepts "stickier," and the work enjoyable enough to persist—and present a model for how participants might bring that value to life in their own work.

CARPE's success also relies on network leaders who cultivate and maintain a sense of community identity. As a multidistrict collective with a leadership team that cannot mandate participation, network leaders have to incentivize participation by making CARPE a community to which participants truly want to belong. This depends, first, on drawing clear lines around the network, defining and differentiating it from other groups members belong to. Leaders began by giving the network a unique name and welcoming participants to the network with cohesively branded tools, resources, and personalized notebooks all stamped with the network's bold logo and punning tagline, "Seize the challenge to improve college access." The collective identity proposed by the network's name has helped cultivate a sense of belonging, kinship, and collegiality. Because most network participants do not work in the same schools, traditions like raucous post-convening events, complete with DJs and dancing, have been essential to expediting the development of community bonds. Equally essential are the efforts leaders made to build deep, personal relationships with each team, getting to know members on both a personal and professional level. A testament to such efforts was a coach recognizing how appreciated personalized "FAFSA Nagging Queens" t-shirts would be by a team that had proudly embraced the label. Such seemingly small expressions of care are of critical importance to the network's improvement goals; when adults, like children, feel seen and feel a sense of belonging in a community, they're more prepared to be vulnerable, collaborate, share and learn from failures, and invest time in the success not just of their team, but of the entire collective.

SUMMARY

In this chapter, we explored what it means to build a learning hive. Using Evolutionary Learning, hives blur the sharp line between strategy and execution, drawing on the expertise of hive members across the system to support ongoing adaptation and improvement of strategy to meet the needs of each community and moment. Constant learning becomes business as usual as hives align to a shared vision and use the organization's learning methodology to integrate doing and improving, continuously assessing whether strategy is supporting progress toward goals. When it is not, hive members take action, rigorously experimenting with new approaches and sharing new insight with others. The system is organized as a web of learning relationships that strengthen community and accelerate improvement. This network is not exclusive; hives broaden the scope of participation and include a wider cohort of hive members in decision-making, lowering barriers between system leaders, ground-level staff, and students, families, and communities. Positional leaders orchestrate this work, tapping the expertise of various actors when and where it is most relevant to system challenges. Emerging from and contributing to this work is a strong culture that values a shared problem-solving orientation and commitment to collaboration and fruitful conflict.

This approach to participation positions hives to implement the democratic problem-solving and knowledge management approach we discuss in Chapter 5, one that draws on the wealth of expertise at each layer of the system to enable problem-solving and continuous innovation.

STARTING THE SHIFT: REFLECT AND ACT

In this section, three activities will help you reflect on the degree to which your system exemplifies the hive qualities and get started on mapping an actionable strategy.

1. Self-Assessment: Reflect on your current practice, taking stock of where your system and approach to leadership is closer to and further from exemplifying the qualities of a learning hive.
2. Map Your Hive: Visualize your current system, identifying relational strengths and missed opportunities for stronger collaborative pathways and feedback loops.
3. Articulate a Strategy: Develop or refine an existing strategy to support learning in your system.

You can complete these activities alone, in 1:1 settings, or in larger groups.

Self-Assessment

Has your organization set conditions for, invited, and facilitated systematic and meaningful participation from hive members in learning, improvement, and decision-making across your system?

- To what extent does your system design engage hive members in the development, implementation, and refinement of your agendas, goals, and problem-solving?
- Think about a hive member participation experience you've observed that exemplifies what you would like yours to look

like. What made that experience successful? How might you
incorporate similar practices into your system?

- Think ahead to a decade from now. Visualize two contrasting
scenarios: (1) Your system achieves equitable practice at scale,
and (2) Your system does not achieve equitable practice at
scale. What role did hive member participation play in each
scenario?

- When and how have you shifted your understanding of challenges,
decisions, and system design based on hive member insight?

- Have you productively engaged hive members within and beyond
your system?

- When and how have you involved the hive members closest to
various problems you're trying to solve? When and how have you
excluded those individuals?

- Alternatively, are there places where your reliance on positional
leaders creates bottlenecks in your learning and improvement processes? Where and when do you need positional leaders to come
in and out of problem-solving processes?

- What relationships among members and groups in the hive stymie
productive learning and improvement? As a leader, how might
you help foster more productive connections?

- What high-impact partnerships have you *not* developed because
they seem out of reach? What adversarial relationships do
you avoid that, if nurtured, might open up new inroads to
improvement?

- Which innovative organizations or actors working outside your
immediate field could you partner with or learn from to accelerate
change?

- Which of the following approaches have you used most often with
hive members? When and with which hive members have you
used different approaches? Why?
  » Inform: Provide hive members with relevant information
  » Consult: Gather input from hive members
  » Collaborate: Ensure hive members' capacity to play a
    leadership role in the development and implementation of
    decisions
  » Defer: Foster democratic participation and equity by bridging
    the divide between hive members and governance through
    community-driven decision-making

- In what ways, if any, have you facilitated collaborative spaces to
draw out fruitful conflict? How have you used protocols to scaffold
equitable collaboration?

Mapping Your Hive

To build an effective hive, it is helpful to create and maintain an evolving *system map*: a shared list or diagram that outlines the core elements of your immediate system and environment and the relationships between those elements. Completing this exercise visually—ideally in person, with pen and paper—can make collaborative development easier, surface new relationships between system elements, and cultivate the type of holistic view that can be challenging to see in writing. Use the template in Figure 4.2 along with these instructions to work through this exercise.

1. Name the teams and hive member groups you lead, directly influence, or serve.

Figure 4.2. System Mapping Template

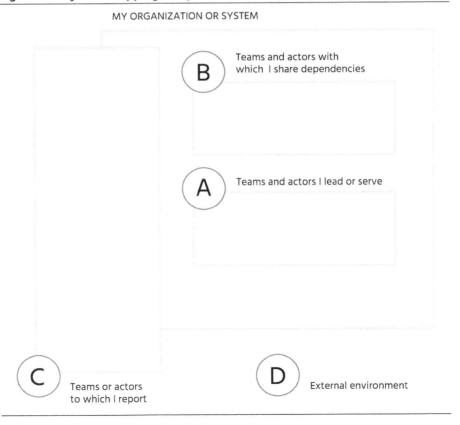

    a. Write the name of those teams and any relevant hive members on pink sticky notes, and place them in Section A of the activity template.

    b. Draw out the connections each group or hive member has to the others, naming both formal (e.g., meetings) and informal (e.g., relationships between members) pathways that connect them. Use lines and arrows to illustrate and label those connections.

2. Consider the lateral teams and hive members within your system that you do not directly lead but with which you share tasks, responsibilities, and work.

    a. Write the names of those related subsystems, teams, and hive members on blue sticky notes, and place them in Section B of the activity template.

    b. As you did in Step 1, draw out the connections each of these groups or hive members have to each other, using lines and arrows to illustrate and label connections. Do the same for hive members and groups in Section A.

3. Name the institutions, groups, and hive members that you formally report to.

    a. Write the names of those organizations, groups, and hive members (e.g., departments or leaders within your organization, state agencies) on green sticky notes, and place them in Box C on the activity template.

    b. Draw out the connections each of these groups or hive members have to each other. using lines and arrows to illustrate and label connections. Do the same for hive members and groups in Sections A and B.

4. Name any external systems and hive members that directly or indirectly impact the outcomes of your work

    a. Write the names of those external systems and hive members (e.g., peer organizations, interest groups) on yellow sticky notes, and place them in Section D on the activity template.

    b. Draw out the connections each of these groups or hive members have to each other, using lines and arrows to illustrate and label connections. Do the same for hive members and groups in Sections A, B, and C.

5. Step back and assess your diagram, adding missing hive members, groups, institutions, and connections.

6. Once you are confident that your map represents your system as it currently is, reflect on how you might make your organization more hive-like. Consider:

   a. Which hive members and groups from the larger environment
      are missing or sit on the edges of your map? How might you
      include them?
   b. What structural changes could you make to:
      i. Facilitate stronger learning connections between
         positional leaders, frontline staff, and those you serve?
      ii. Reduce the space between doing and learning?
      iii. Facilitate cross-functional problem-solving?

Articulate a Strategy

In hives, an explicit, collectively-developed strategy helps anchor all activities to a common vision and aims for the work. Strategies may take
many forms but always draw out how inputs and actions support progress
toward short-term aims and long-term impacts. Effective EL systems often feature nested strategies, where system teams and initiatives develop
activity-specific logic models mapped to parts of the organization's broad,
system-level strategy.

   Throughout the rest of this book, each Reflect and Act section will
build on an explicit articulation of your system, team, or initiative-level
strategy. If your organization or team already has one, excellent; assess
your existing strategy using the criteria below, adapting it as needed. If your
organization does not have an existing, explicit strategy, use the activity
below to develop a working draft.

Step 1: Articulate a High-Level Theory of Action

A theory of action is a high-level summary of how your system's actions will
lead to its intended impacts and outcomes. An effective theory of action (a)
illustrates your theory about the causal chain between actions, outcomes,
and impacts, (b) can be measured, and (c) remains relatively consistent but
adaptive to learning as you implement your strategy (Austin et al., 2021).

   Often, a theory of action is organized in the following format (see
Figure 4.3): "If we do X (actions), then Y (outcomes) will occur. As a result, we will achieve Z (impacts)" (Austin et al., 2021).

   To build a Theory of Action, use the following steps (Austin et al.,
2021)

   1. Start, seemingly in reverse, with Impacts, articulating no more than
      three long-term goals in the "As a result" box. As you craft these
      statements, think about what your organization hopes to achieve 3
      to 5 years from now, including shifts in student outcomes.

Figure 4.3. Theory of Action Template

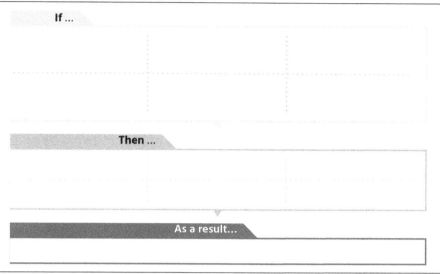

Source: Austin et al. (2021).

2. Working backward, develop three to four outcome statements in the Then box. These should be the shorter-term results of the everyday work occurring in your organization—think changes in behavior, mindset, and early results that will lead, over time, to your impacts.

3. Draft up to six If statements that articulate the high-level actions you and those you work with will take to achieve your outlined outcomes and impacts. Note that your actions do not need to line up 1:1 with your outcomes or impacts.

4. Assess your Theory of Action as a whole, using the following questions to guide refinements in language and content.
   a. Is your language clear, precise, and accessible?
   b. Will the theory, as written, easily communicate your vision with various hive members?
   c. Is there a clear logic connecting your actions, outcomes, and impacts?
   d. Is the theory responsive to your problem statement?
   e. Is the theory feasible to achieve in the timeframe you have outlined?
   f. Is the theory inspirational? Will it motivate action?

5. Before moving on to Step 2, test your theory with hive members and advisors, refining as needed.

Step 2: Articulate a Detailed Strategy

Next you will develop a more detailed logic model that outlines what your Theory will look like in action.

One tool you can use for the purpose is the Operationalized Theory of Action, or OPTA (Figure 4.4). An OPTA typically consists of more detailed descriptions of the three elements you outlined in your Theory of Action:

- Impacts: longer-term changes you aim to achieve.
- Outcomes: shorter-term changes you expect will lead to the desired impact (changes in attitudes, behaviors, results).
- Actions: steps you need to take to implement your strategy.
  . . . and one additional element:
- Inputs: resources, actors, and conditions that need to be in place for you to start implementing your strategy (Austin et al., 2021).

Use the following steps to outline your OPTA. Keep in mind that each organization's OPTA may look different; customize the format provided in Figure 4.4 to fit your needs (Austin et al., 2021).

1. **Articulate your short-, medium-, and long-term goals.**
   a. Use the "As a result" impacts from your Theory of Action to generate a list of measurable impacts. List those impacts in the Impacts column, sorting them chronologically with the nearest-term impact at the top, the longest-term impact at the bottom.
   b. Translate the shorter-term outcomes ("Thens") from your Theory of Action into the Outcomes column as a list of concrete, observable outcomes. Order these outcomes from short to long term. Note that your nearest-term outcomes will often be changes in mindsets, followed by changes in behaviors, followed by any changes in short-term results that arise from different behaviors.
2. **Articulate the inputs and actions needed to achieve your goals.**
   a. Translate the actions ("Ifs") from your Theory of Action into a series of measurable, ongoing actions. Ensure that each action has a subject that makes evident which hive members are

Figure 4.4. Operationalized Theory of Action

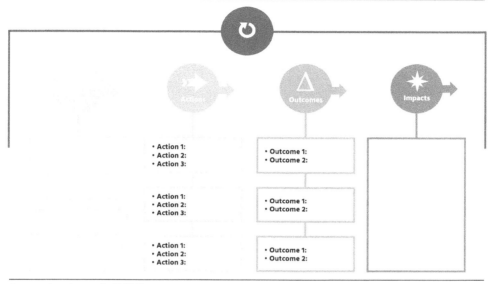

Source: Austin et al. (2021).

responsible for implementing the action. Order these actions
chronologically in the Actions column.

b. Reflect on which inputs will enable your organization to
enact the actions you have outlined. Include resources,
actors, and conditions that will need to be in place to advance
your organization's strategy. Write these in the "Inputs"
column.

3. Group actions and outcomes into workstreams, if useful.

a. As needed, reorganize your Actions column, clustering
aligned actions into workstreams to foster clarity and
coherence.

b. Turning to the Outcomes column, assess whether
there are sets of outcomes that more directly align
with your new actions workstreams. If so, group those
outcomes and indicate links between associated actions and
outcomes.

4. Review, revise, and refine the OPTA.

a. Review the OPTA, in particular checking both overarching
and intermediate causal pathways for missing elements. Add
components as needed so that hive members will understand
the logic of the strategy and how this logic will bring about the
desired changes.

b. Compare the OPTA and your theory of action to ensure tight alignment between the two, iterating as needed between the two diagrams.

c. Review the OPTA language to be sure that it is clear, accessible, and illustrates how the strategy will produce its intended outcomes.

CHAPTER 5

Swarm Problems, Innovate, and Pollinate Learning

VIGNETTE: PARTNERS IN SCHOOL INNOVATION

Partners in School Innovation is a school support organization that seeks to "transform teaching and learning . . . so that every student thrives." Since 1993, Partners has worked with dozens of schools and districts nationally, reaching over 1 million students. The organization seeks out and supports some of the most complex public school systems in the country, adapting its model to local school and district contexts with the goal of building adult capacity to lead, teach, and learn in service of educational equity. Over the last three decades, Partners has seen great success, with a consistent quality of work that has allowed most partner schools to outperform their peers by substantial margins—particularly among Black, Latino, and multilingual students. For example, over a multiyear effort with Dr. Tanner G. Duckrey Public School in Philadelphia, Partners supported a robust school transformation effort which produced growth in both predictive indicators (e.g., adult uptake of improvement mindsets and behaviors) and student outcomes. Results from the annual Pennsylvania System for School Assessment (PSSA) indicates that the partnership had a strong positive effect on student learning: In the school years 2016–2019 the percentage of students scoring at the highest proficiency levels on both the English Language Arts and mathematics assessments doubled, while the percentage scoring in the lowest performance bands decreased by 17% and 14%, respectively. The results at Dr. Tanner G. Duckrey are emblematic of the impact Partners has had in other schools and districts nationally.

So what is Partners' secret? In short, the organization is a learning hive that has implemented a participatory learning system that allows the organization to generate, capture, and spread knowledge and apply it to innovate and solve challenges. Using a shared vision and learning methodology to guide discovery, the organization moves beyond technical changes that address the superficial manifestations of problems to fundamental shifts in practice that systemically address the roots of recurrent issues.

Partners' learning approach succeeds because its culture is grounded in a deep belief in the capacity of *all* people—children and adults alike—to learn, improve, and spur transformative change. As Jae Fusco, a team leader at Partners, notes, "The culture at Partners is that we believe in people, and our systems are then built to try and center this belief." Flexible teaming structures, strong relationships, and a democratic approach to learning and change are the manifestation of that belief. As people generate knowledge about how to address challenges, a robust knowledge management infrastructure supports knowledge capture and sharing processes that help actors across the system adapt, scale, and apply what is learned to meet the needs of each context they work within.

Throughout this chapter, we'll explore this democratic knowledge management model and investigate how Partners and other organizations have used it to coordinate learning and make progress toward equitable service at scale.

KNOWLEDGE MANAGEMENT IN PREDOMINANT GOVERNANCE MODELS

Knowledge is information in action—the know-how and context used to make decisions, solve challenges, and innovate to reach organizational goals (Drucker, 1993; Nonaka & Takeuchi, 1995; O'Dell & Grayson, 1998; Snowden, 2002a). Knowledge management is an organization's approach to generating, capturing, sharing, and using that knowledge (Snowden, 2002a). All organizations manage knowledge, whether or not their approaches are explicit or effective. In public systems, providing equitable service relies on applying knowledge to spot and address two types of problems: issues that emerge through the daily implementation of strategy and emergent and enduring complex challenges.

An organization's approach to governance is, in large part, founded on its perspective on knowledge. The difference among governance models is rooted in their respective answers to several questions:

- Who has knowledge? Who generates knowledge?
- How do we communicate and integrate knowledge into practice?

Each governance model answers these questions differently, with implications for how work is organized, decisions made, and strategy executed.

In Bureaucracy, Knowledge Comes From the Top Through Rules

Seeing conditions, people, and contexts as being relatively uniform—that is, with a simple cause-and-effect relationship between actions and results, problems and solutions (Snowden & Boone, 2007)—bureaucracies assume that a great deal of knowledge about execution of the organization's core tasks already exists and can be made explicit. In short, bureaucracies see knowledge as an object that can be easily shared (Alavi & Leidner, 2001) and believe that there is a known and communicable best practice for most tasks (Snowden & Boone, 2007).

Bureaucratic leaders are selected because they are presumed to possess this knowledge. Ground-level staff, on the other hand, are assumed to lack the knowledge and expertise necessary to successfully carry out their core functions. A leader's responsibility, then, is to find ways to transmit their knowledge to implementers, controlling frontline practice to guarantee uniformly high-quality service at scale.

To do this, leaders organize knowledge transmission much like a factory-based assembly line, wherein knowledge is delivered, unidirectionally, from expert central leaders to frontline staff as detailed procedure and rules. This industrial approach and orientation to knowledge management has provided a blueprint for American schooling since the late 19th century (Bowles & Gintis, 1976; Dewey, 1899; Tyack, 1974). Today, while the landscape of school governance is a great deal more heterogeneous than it has been historically, bureaucratic perspectives on knowledge still dominate.

Of course, in practice, bureaucratic approaches to knowledge sharing and application play out much more messily. The complexities of instruction in diverse classrooms across diverse schools require frontline staff to use their own knowledge and discretion every day to adapt instructional strategy and curriculum (Lipsky, 2010). Bureaucracies tend to either (a) punish or ignore these adaptations, incentivizing inaction and missing the opportunity for learning, or (b) create new rules to constrain them, a Sisyphean task given the raft of novel situations and decision points encountered by frontline staff each day. In the latter condition, rules proliferate at such a rate as to make their use impractical (Braithwaite & Braithwaite, 1995). Ironically, while the proliferation of bureaucratic rules is intended to make knowledge transfer more efficient and practice more standardized and transparent, in practice, these rules breed inefficiency and give managers less control and less insight into what is actually happening in the field, as workers "go underground," hiding their real practice to paint a picture of compliance (Snowden et al., 2011, p. 124).

In Managerialism, Knowledge Is Tacit and Lives With Talented Managers

Managerialism acknowledges that providing service and solving problems across differing contexts is complicated—and that there is likely more than one right way to achieve strong results (Snowden & Boone, 2007). As in bureaucracy, a small number of gifted leaders are believed to have the tacit knowledge necessary to achieve strong outcomes; here, these gifted leaders are not central experts, but instead local managers appointed and given the discretion to direct activity as needed to meet centrally-established, high-stakes performance targets (Coglianese & Lazer, 2003). With minimal central regulation bounding action, managerialism encourages innovation by incentivizing managers to leverage their mostly tacit knowledge to build contextually-tailored strategies that produce stronger and stronger outcomes (Coglianese & Lazer, 2003). But this freedom comes with high-stakes strings attached: When managers and frontline workers do not meet targets, they are swiftly removed and replaced.

Unlike in bureaucracy, knowledge in managerialist systems is understood to be innate, difficult to codify, and challenging to transfer. This means that insight on process, or the precise path talented leaders take from action to results, often remains a black box: Managerialist organizations know when systems are working but are often unable to identify the precise ingredients of success (or are uninterested in doing so), be they a manager's superior knowledge, their ability to access others' know-how, luck, or even cheating (Aviv, 2014; Coglianese & Lazer, 2003). This makes it difficult to isolate and pressure-test effective practice and scale it from one part of the system to others. The competitive nature of these systems, wherein managers receive rewards for outperforming peers, further disincentivizes knowledge sharing.

In Professionalism and Craft, Knowledge Is Held by Professionals and Frontline Staff

Professionalism and craft share the assumption that local conditions and needs are so particular that knowledge must be dynamic (Mehta, 2013; Sennett, 2008). In both, those with experience on the frontlines of service—rather than leaders and managers—possess the expertise and context necessary to adapt practice to context (Lagemann, 2000; Mehta, 2013; Sennett, 2008).

Craft and professionalism diverge on whether and how frontline knowledge can be made explicit. In professionalism, knowledge about how to execute the core functions of a profession like teaching can be codified and acquired through study, application, and assessment, including by esteemed professionals (Mehta, 2013). Competitive professional schools that control entry into the profession and ongoing self-regulation through licensure and collective discipline ensure that accepted bodies of knowledge and ethical standards are consistently embedded in practice (Mehta, 2013).

In craft, knowledge is tacit and difficult to transfer because it is grounded in experience and, to some degree, innate talent (Sennett, 2008). Expertise is cultivated slowly and experientially over time through apprenticeship with master practitioners. This model of knowledge transfer—tacit-to-tacit socialization (Nonaka, 1994)—is evident in a number of the arts, in which aspiring artists train under the watchful eye of those already deemed masters.

Both models can work in smaller, more homogeneous contexts, where needs are relatively uniform. But in a large, complex, and highly diverse context like the U.S. public education system, an elitist approach to knowledge—one that sees expertise as valid only when proffered by members of a small circle of elites—misses key opportunities to draw insight from those with alternative perspectives, including those served by the profession (customers, patrons, clients, or students) and those outside of the profession. Further, incentive systems in both models encourage knowledge hoarding rather than sharing, preventing widespread application of insight. Even if incentives were otherwise, in craft, knowledge transfer is particularly difficult, given that it is innate and tacit, offering limited ability to identify, extract, and share practice across contexts at scale, even within the guild.

All Three Are a Mismatch for Education

Each of these approaches to knowledge is ill-suited to solving the challenges that arise in the context of American public education, where systems are complex, conditions dynamic, and needs of communities multifaceted. The pursuit of equity—providing service tailored to the needs of each community, context, and moment in service of universally strong outcomes—requires understanding knowledge as inherently dynamic. In short, there will always be something to learn in order to provide equitable learning experiences at scale.

KNOWLEDGE MANAGEMENT IN EVOLUTIONARY LEARNING

Evolutionary Learning assumes the need for ongoing discovery, given that conditions are uncertain and solutions to our most pressing problems have yet to be discovered. Its approach to knowledge is well matched to complex systems that are constantly changing, interconnected, and relational. In this context, adaptive challenges—problems that require new learning and changes in organizational practice and behavior (Heifetz et al., 2009)—are common. Solving them to provide effective service across diverse contexts requires evolving and highly localized know-how that no leader, manager, or practitioner alone possesses. Hives build knowledge management systems that harness collective learning and expertise to close the gap between these challenges and the knowledge needed to solve them.

Evolutionary Learning hives employ elements of each model's perspective on knowledge (captured in Table 5.1)—for example, bureaucracy's attention to making knowledge explicit, managerialism's commitment to shared success standards, and craft and professionalism's respect for the expertise of the frontline—and add in something new: a disciplined approach to experimentation that draws in the know-how and capacity of each person in the system.

Table 5.1. Knowledge Across Governance Models

	Bureaucracy	Managerialism	Professionalism/ Craft	Evolutionary Learning
Who has knowledge—or will be valuable in helping us generate it?	Leaders and central experts	Talented managers	Professionals and practitioners	Actors throughout the system, especially those most proximate to implementation or closest to various problems of practice
Once we have knowledge, how do we share and apply it into practice?	Knowledge is made explicit through detailed rules that actors at lower levels of the system must carry out	Knowledge is tacit and its responsible discovery and use can be incentivized via performance targets and accountability	In professionalism, knowledge is explicit and acquired through study, application, and assessment In craft, knowledge is tacit and developed under the guidance of master practitioners	Knowledge is made explicit and shared through disciplined knowledge management processes

Hives generate knowledge in response to two types of problems: (a) issues emerging out of everyday practice and implementation of strategy and (b) emergent and entrenched "wicked" challenges that are complex, layered, and challenging to define (Bellamy et al., 2005; Cannon & Edmondson, 2005). Interrelated problem-solving on both fronts powers a broader goal: continuous improvement of system strategy and practice at large.

In all arenas, hives recognize the dynamic nature of knowledge and design participatory knowledge management practices as a cycle that uses the daily implementation of strategy as a driver of learning. Understanding that "knowledge cannot be treated as an organizational asset without the active and voluntary participation of the communities that are its true owners" (Snowden, 2012), positional leaders ensure that *everyone* in the system—students, families, custodial staff, teachers, counselors, bus drivers, administrators—plays a part in generating, capturing, sharing, and supporting the application of knowledge that allows the system to make better decisions and solve problems. The networked structure of the hive discussed in Chapter 4 establishes the formal and informal learning relationships that enable the participatory nature of the knowledge management cycle.

Hives conceptualize their knowledge management efforts as a cycle of four overlapping activities (Figure 5.1).

- *Knowledge Generation:* Hives employ a shared learning methodology to articulate problems and opportunities and scaffold the development and discovery of knowledge to address them.
- *Knowledge Consolidation & Capture:* Hives make sense of, make explicit, and organize knowledge, so it can be shared more widely to enable action across the system.
- *Knowledge Sharing:* Hives use active and passive communication strategies to communicate knowledge with those who need it.
- *Knowledge Application:* Hives support the adaptation and use of knowledge in problem-solving and ongoing improvement.

While the knowledge management cycle rarely plays out as a neat or linear process, this broad framework helps hives ensure that they translate local learning to transformative innovation and improved practice at scale. This approach to knowledge management is grounded in the Dewyian conception of *learning as doing* through experimentation and action, rather than through a static "knowing" and transfer of expertise. In this chapter, we will explore how you can enact a participatory

Figure 5.1. The Knowledge Management Cycle

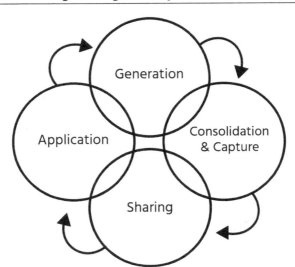

knowledge management model in your hive, starting with the culture that enables innovation and then exploring the structures and processes that drive learning forward.

CULTURE AND MINDSETS

In hives, knowledge management is grounded in an organizational culture that establishes learning as the core function of the organization and each of its members (Fullan, 2020). Hives succeed because they quickly address the daily issues that get in the way of strong performance and think big, challenging "the way things are done" in service of improved practice. In schools, this means using learning and knowledge management structures to experiment with changes that challenge the orthodoxy of public education's established grammar (Tyack & Cuban, 1997).

This requires a different approach to problem-solving. Rather than patching up emergent challenges within the boundaries of the dominant paradigm, hives must build a membership that proactively engages in constant, critical questioning of the norms, mindsets, values, and beliefs that underlie problems (Argyris, 1977). This requires each hive member to act as a steward of improvement who looks out for, raises, and responds to issues in the system, even when those issues fall outside their immediate work or domain of influence. Positional leaders set the conditions for this type of collaborative action by ensuring that hive members feel safe to fail as they problem-solve and innovate.

Make It Safe to Fail While Refusing to Accept Failure

Hives are, in some ways, "preoccupied" (Weick & Sutcliffe, 2015, p. 45) with failure. Persistent system deficiencies are not tolerated: errors, mistakes, and breakdowns are identified and addressed when and where they occur—when memory is fresh and evidence available—even if issues seem insignificant or do not result in immediate harm.

Yet, almost paradoxically, building an organization that can identify and address problems in this way requires a certain tolerance for error and acceptance of productive failure (Kapur, 2008; Kapur & Bielaczyc, 2012). Hives understand the impossibility of a perfectly designed system or strategy in uncertain and changing contexts: There are simply too many complexities and variables to predict (Spear, 2009). It is only through *doing*—the implementation of strategy—that these problems become visible and solvable. If people are incentivized to hide errors and leave concerns unreported, improvement and innovation are stymied, and the system puts itself at risk for stagnation and catastrophic failure. A culture where people feel safe to flag problems and make mistakes as they experiment to solve them is particularly important in fields like healthcare, nuclear energy, aviation, and education in which the human consequences of persistent errors can be grave. NASA's Challenger and Columbia disasters, for example, were both attributable, in part, to an organizational culture that normalized system failures and deviance from standard practice and inhibited candid communication about safety concerns, eventually resulting in the death of 14 astronauts (Vaughan, 2016).

Building a culture that enables productive failure requires hives to reconceptualize problems as the grist for improvement, rather than negative outcomes to be avoided. Dr. Alan Cheng—the superintendent of New York City's Consortium, Internationals and Outward Bound High School District—notes of his district's approach: "To make it safe to fail, we celebrate risks, normalize setbacks as learning opportunities, and focus on progress over perfection." Leaders refuse to tolerate persistent system dysfunction while challenging the link between error and punishment, treating failure as neither "good" nor "bad," but as a natural condition of uncertainty. To incentivize the immediate identification of challenges, leaders recognize and celebrate individuals and teams who sound the alarm on problems—even when addressing those issues makes the organization's immediate work more complex (Cannon & Edmondson, 2005). People are reprimanded not for failures, but for failing to report and learn from them.

Consider a classic example of a hive from outside of education: Alcoa, the aluminum production company. Aluminum production can be a dangerous business, and in 1987, the chances of being injured on the job at Alcoa were around 2% annually, meaning that over a typical 25-year career, employees had a nearly 40% risk of injury. Seeing the situation as untenable from both a human and fiscal perspective, Alcoa's incoming CEO, Paul O'Neill, set reducing employee injuries to zero as the company's focus. In service of this objective, all safety incidents were to be reported to O'Neill directly within 24 hours.

In one well-documented case, a business unit president at Alcoa was fired after failing to properly investigate and learn from an apparently minor safety issue at an assembly plant he supervised (Spear, 2009). His employee reported a bout of nausea and was sent home; the worker recovered, returned to work, and the illness went unexplained—and unreported. Weeks later, when several additional workers reported similar symptoms, an investigation determined the cause to be indoor air pollution, a serious safety issue with an evident solution. The unit president was let go—not because the unit had underperformed with regard to revenue or customer satisfaction, but because he had created a culture where staff felt comfortable allowing small safety issues to fester and become significant problems.

The goal of this approach is not a divestment from personal responsibility, but a redefinition of what actors are responsible for: not the initial failure itself, but any failure to learn from it. This culture allows the organization to leverage experimentation to accelerate organizational learning (Cannon & Edmondson, 2005). When hive members feel that it is safe to experiment—and when they work within scaffolds that enable *productive* failure—they free up mental capacity to contribute to collective improvement efforts, rather than focusing on self-protection (Schein, 1993). They are also more likely to learn quickly, be creative, and innovate (Heifetz & Linsky, 2002). The hive's knowledge management and measurement processes enable this approach by mitigating risk through smaller scale experimentation and the use of ongoing formative measurement that surfaces failures promptly.

When Everyone Contributes, Everyone Improves

Strong knowledge management starts and ends with people. Ultimately, a hive's greatest knowledge management assets are not technical tools, but its members' passion for the work—and their sense of personal and collective efficacy (Bandura, 2000), or belief that they can effect positive change in the organization.

For the hive to succeed, hive members must see themselves and their peers as agents of change with valuable knowledge and a role to play in shaping the organization's improvement (Ansell, 2011; Fullan, 2020). Mehta and Fine (2019) call this "an ethic of contribution," a belief that makes it more likely that members will be intrinsically motivated to work toward ambitious goals (Bandura, 2000), collaboratively engage in creative problem-solving and innovation (Kim & Shin, 2015; Liu et al., 2015), and, through these efforts, produce positive outcomes (Bandura, 1993; Goddard et al., 2000; Gully et al., 2002; Hattie, 2012). As researcher John Hattie (The Learning Pit, 2018) explains, collective efficacy is not "just growth mindset. It's not just 'rah-rah' thinking. It's not just 'Oh, we can make a difference!' . . . It is that combined belief that it is 'us' that causes learning."

To foster this ethic of contribution, positional leaders use participatory principles in their approach to problem-solving and knowledge management and reinforce a sense of collective agency and competence (Ansell, 2011). In their daily practice, all members of the community—leaders and frontline workers, veteran and novice staff, adults and young people—have decisional capital in shaping the learning agenda of the organization through their participation in identifying, prioritizing, and solving problems. Through this shoulder-to-shoulder learning and doing in service of shared goals—where system actors observe their contributions influencing improvements in personal, local, and system practice—collective efficacy and ownership of organizational improvement bloom.

In reflecting on the importance of agency, New York City superintendent Alan Cheng notes that, without a sense of ownership of learning and change:

We turn people into compliance robots, like 'My job is only what's in my inbox. When it's clear, I'm done.' . . . For educators to do their best work, they have to feel a sense of belonging . . . they need to feel like people deeply understand and know them, and they need to feel a sense of efficacy about their work. They need to be able to have a level of optimism about the future, and that happens when they feel like what they do makes a difference. You do that by asking people to set goals they can make a difference in.

STRUCTURES AND ACTIVITIES

With a culture conducive to innovation and learning, hives mobilize continuous problem-solving across the system, orienting all knowledge management efforts toward the application of knowledge to support ever better practice. From this perspective, individuals and groups use a shared learning methodology to flag challenges and sequence daily and longer-term improvement. As learning emerges, the collective engages in sense-making via consolidation efforts that surface the knowledge most relevant to organizational priorities and challenges. Hives make that know-how explicit through capture processes that enable communication with key audiences. As the hive shares knowledge and supports its application in new contexts, the cycle begins again as actors across the system contextualize, test, and adapt knowledge to address local needs.

Orient All Activity Toward the Application of Knowledge

The singular aim of knowledge management in any hive is to use knowledge to improve practice, a perspective embedded in our definition of knowledge: information *in action*. EL systems are focused on organizing activity so that each hive member is able to apply the most timely and relevant know-how to their work at any given moment. To do this well, organizational practice must be structured to articulate a clear, if sometimes winding, path between the generation of knowledge and its use.

By making the application of knowledge the explicit goal of learning, hives reject the common conception of knowledge management as a technical exercise concerned primarily with the storage and organization of information. Instead, it becomes a people-driven change project, concerned chiefly with behaviors, beliefs, needs, motivations, and relationships (Snowden, 2002a). Enabling application is no simple task. Sharing knowledge with people is one thing; getting them to use it—internalize it, integrate it into their own practice, continue testing, refining, reshaping, and reinventing it—is entirely another. Among the most effective strategies for ensuring uptake of new learning is including those who have a stake in projected changes as active participants in knowledge generation efforts. As discussed throughout Chapters 3 and 4, hives seek to empower and enable joint experimentation by people who (a) understand or experience problems, (b) will be responsible for implementing solutions, and (c) can lower or raise barriers to change. This method is *practical*, in that it allows hives to draw out the critical expertise of each of these actors, and *strategic*, in that it ensures that those who will need to change understand and feel ownership of new knowledge. The use of this approach diminishes the importance of the persuasive and coercive change management tactics often used in other governance contexts.

As they plan and enact learning activities, positional leaders and knowledge generators reflect on the shifts in behaviors and mindsets implicated by new knowledge and iterate on their knowledge management approach. In particular, they seek clarity on *who* might need to change and at each stage of the learning process adjust who is involved in knowledge generation, consolidation, capture, and sharing. They ask and answer:

- What is our learning goal? What shifts in behavior and mindsets may be implicated by the knowledge we generate?
- Based on that goal, who may be key audiences for the knowledge we generate? What might motivate these audiences to act on new learning? In what ways could we involve these key audiences in the generation process so that they are cocreators, rather than mere recipients of, knowledge?
- What relationships and influence do we already have with these key audiences? What relationships and influence do we need to invest in building?
- Whom should we engage early in the generation process because we anticipate they will either (a) be champions of change, or (b) stand in the way of implementation?
- What obstacles might audiences face in applying new knowledge? How might we begin to mitigate those obstacles?

The answers to each of these questions are hypotheses, subject to continuous iteration as learning progresses. And, of course, application will not be the end of learning processes—as generated knowledge is applied in new contexts, the cycle begins anew, inciting a new cycle of generation, sensemaking, capture, and sharing of learning.

Use Experiential Problem-Solving to Generate and Surface Knowledge

In hives, the entire system, each of its components and strategies, and all forms of daily practice are experiments in how to best apply knowledge to accomplish the system's goals. To this end, hives embed into daily operations a shared learning methodology that prompts continuous identification, development, and testing of solutions for two overlapping types of problems raised earlier in this chapter: (a) daily issues arising from implementation and (b) novel and enduring wicked challenges (Bellamy et al., 2005; Cannon & Edmondson, 2005). The learning outputs of these problem-solving efforts enable an overarching goal: ever better improvement of the system as a whole.

In the first instance, as actors across the system implement and examine data about their daily work, they identify areas where system and local strategy are not performing as predicted. As these "everyday organizational failures" emerge (Cannon & Edmondson, 2005, p. 301), hives treat them as early warning signs and empower local actors to sound the alarm and surface, generate, and test interventions to address them (Bellamy et al., 2005). Immediate attention allows hives to quickly learn from and correct system issues, preventing them from snowballing into larger problems (Cannon & Edmondson, 2005). In this way, EL encourages continuous, small-scale, parallel testing of new ideas across the system. This practice is exemplified by the daily problem-solving process at Toyota, where line workers are encouraged to halt the production line by pulling a physical *andon* cord and initiate problem-solving when and where they observe product or process deficiencies (for more details on the *andon* system, see Chapter 6; Rother, 2009).

In some cases, these everyday issues are *technical*, meaning that they can be addressed by applying existing expertise or experimenting with self-evident shifts in practice. Solving such challenges does not require major changes in organizational practice, values, and beliefs (Heifetz et al., 2009), but their resolution is essential to enabling effective practice and can drive organizational improvement. At other times, daily challenges are more *adaptive* in nature—meaning that defining the base problem is difficult and that solving it requires new learning and deeper shifts in the way the organization functions, including changes in how people think, behave, and work with each other (Heifetz et al., 2009).

As frontline staff field technical and adaptive daily challenges, the hive also tackles the second category of problems: emergent and entrenched wicked problems that stand in the way of equitable service at scale (Rittel & Webber, 1973). Wicked problems are complex, multidimensional, and difficult to define. Understanding and addressing their manifold impacts requires sustained, coordinated problem-solving across the organization; here, think of the challenge of making sure all children are provided learning experiences that enable them to achieve literacy. Many of the technical and adaptive problems that arise in daily practice are symptoms of these wicked challenges.

For both types of challenges, hives use a continuous improvement (CI) learning methodology to understand the problem and to generate, discover, contextualize, and test new ideas and existing insight on how to solve it. CI approaches abound (e.g., the Model for Improvement, Carnegie Foundation for the Advancement of Teaching's approach to improvement science, Results Oriented Cycles of Inquiry, Kaizen/Lean, Six Sigma), and while the particularities of these methodologies differ, they are all designed to support the hive in answering the three learning questions (Langley et al., 2009) introduced in Chapter 3:

1. What are we trying to do, and what will success look like?
2. Is what we are doing working as expected?
3. What changes can we make to improve what we're doing?

When the answer to the second question is "no," each of these methods helps the system generate knowledge about the third, using some variation of the steps (introduced in Chapter 4): (1) Select areas of focus, (2) conduct root cause analysis, (3) develop a theory of improvement, and (4) conduct testing cycles.

1. Select Areas of Focus. The system's shared strategy (see Chapter 3) acts as an anchor for improvement (Nonaka, 1994), ensuring that knowledge generation activities across the system can be woven together to amplify progress toward shared goals. To identify particular areas of focus within the strategy's frame, hives use the data gathered through measurement routines (see Chapter 6) to spot emerging problems and track persistent challenges. With this insight, positional leaders support individuals and groups in using a number of overlapping criteria to prioritize problems, asking (Austin et al., 2021):

- Is the problem a priority for the organization and its community members? Is solving this problem urgent?
- Is the problem strategically connected to the organization's mission and strategy?
- Does the problem result in disparities by race, ethnicity, and other identifiable categories in the service level, quality provided, or in outcomes and impact?
- Is it possible to address the problem with currently available resources? If not, what resources are needed?
- Will resolving the problem drive meaningful improvement?

In each organization and at different points in time, the criteria for identifying priority improvement areas are weighted differently. Critically, however, as problems are deprioritized, they are not forgotten; hives recognize that breaking apart complex challenges, while practically necessary, raises the risk of misdiagnosing root causes and obscuring possible solutions. Interrelated issues are kept in view, with hives sequencing subsequent problem-solving cycles to address each manifestation of the challenge in turn (Ansell, 2011).

As problems are prioritized, positional leaders work with hive members to identify members who might contribute to problem definition and knowledge generation processes. Again, deciding who should be involved in each problem-solving venture is both a practical and a strategic exercise. Leaders consider who might bolster learning efforts—typically those proximate to the problem or those with relevant specialized expertise. At the same time, thinking backwards from application, the hive strategically considers who might enable or prevent strong uptake of knowledge once developed and includes those members as early as possible. Positional leaders help craft participation strategies that engage each relevant actor, tapping them variously as leaders, codesigners, experimenters, and consultants in the learning process.

2. Conduct Root Cause Analysis. Once an area of focus is identified and problem-solvers are engaged, hives explore observed gaps between expected outcomes and results, thoroughly unpacking problems before proposing solutions. Proceeding from W. Edward Demming's perspective, popularized in the continuous improvement community as the idea that every system is perfectly designed to get the results it gets, positional leaders support causal analysis that moves past symptoms and toward the underlying foundations of problems. Root cause analysis is no simple task, as cause and effect is rarely straightforward in complex contexts like the U.S. education system (Clarke et al., 2017; Preskill et al., 2014). Hives account for these conditions through their mobilization of a broad cross section of actors with different expertise and experience with the problem, including those closest to and most affected by it. This collaboration helps make visible a fuller scope of the issue.

Shared tools like process maps, the 5 Whys protocol, and fishbone diagrams can help scaffold this process, though in more mature hives, the lines of thinking these tools prompt may become second nature. Notably, formal and informal root cause analysis processes begin and end with data that initially define the boundaries of the problem and later draw out its nuances. Both quantitative outcome data (e.g., student outcomes) and qualitative street-level data (Safir & Dugan, 2021), derived from empathy interviews, surveys, observations, and shadowing, are critical.

Throughout this step, positional leaders help the hive orchestrate pacing. They understand that time spent developing a strong problem understanding ultimately drives the development of stronger solutions, but also that any initial root cause analysis is merely a provisional theory to be revised as the hive learns. Organizations that move too slowly through root cause analysis—a condition often teasingly called "admiring the problem"—risk inertia and lost momentum, especially when community members are unconvinced of the value of the learning methodology.

3. Develop a Theory of Improvement. Once the hive has an initial hypothesis about the roots of the problem at hand, members generate interventions and innovations predicted to improve process and lead to stronger outcomes (Bryk et al., 2015; Langley et al., 2009). As potential interventions emerge, problem-solvers predict how and why they will work in a theory of improvement, in particular attending to the question, "How would we recognize success if it happened?" (Sparrow, 2000, p. 150), or, in other words, articulating what "good" looks like. To make this standard explicit, the hive often sets a provisional benchmark (e.g., a percentage point increase in the number of students demonstrating mastery of a concept). In other cases, success may be relative (e.g., this idea works better than others for one group of students) or qualitative (e.g., a set of shifts in mindsets expected after the implementation of a collaborative learning cycle). Through this process, hive members build a deeper understanding of proposed ideas, identify areas of misalignment with peers, make sense of how interventions will interact with each other and with existing practice, anticipate implementation challenges, and articulate shared expectations and standards for success.

Interventions included in a theory of improvement may be locally developed innovations (e.g., locally specific adaptations to scheduling) or adaptations of existing knowledge (e.g., contextualizing an effective practice from the literature on literacy instruction). While there is no such thing as a perfect intervention, some are better positioned than others to motivate the transformative improvement necessary to achieve ambitious equity goals. To find the right suite of change ideas, hives draw on their current evidence base to make informed predictions of what will produce success, often selecting many interventions to try out in parallel, low-stakes trials.

Most of all, hives understand that there is no perfect theory or change idea either, and move quickly from theorizing to testing, where predictions are borne out or refuted (Langley et al., 2009). Before they make this move, however, the problem-solving group returns to the question of application, considering who might be implicated by implementation of various aspects of the theory at scale and integrating those audiences into the knowledge generation process as early as possible.

4. Enact Short-Cycle Testing. Hive members test proposed interventions, using rapid-cycle inquiry processes like the Plan, Do, Study, Act (PDSA) cycle (Langley et al., 2009). The goal of testing is to generate knowledge about whether interventions articulated in the theory of improvement function as predicted, should be integrated into local strategy, and are ready to be used in other contexts. In contrast to bureaucratic systems, where promising ideas are often implemented across the system immediately, in hives, interventions are piloted on a smaller scale to limit risk and ensure that ideas will be applied in ways that are contextually relevant.

The steps of the PDSA cycle are as follows:

1. Plan: Testers determine the scale of the test and develop an action plan, including where, for how long, and at what scale testing will occur; who will be involved; and what data will be collected to measure outcomes. At this stage, testers capture specific predictions about the impact of the intervention so they can assess the gap between anticipated and actual results.
2. Do: Testers enact the intervention, gathering data, tracking results, and making note of any deviations they make from the testing plan.
3. Study: Testers and other relevant actors come together to compare actual results with predictions. By collaboratively analyzing data—often using visualizations like frequency tables, line graphs or run charts, bar graphs, scatterplots, and pie charts—and observations and insights from the testers, the team gleans insight for the next problem-solving cycle and the overarching theory of improvement. In particular, looking across their data, the group asks itself whether, for whom, and under what conditions the change idea worked.
4. Act: Testers make sense of what they've learned and decide whether to abandon, adapt, or adopt the intervention for the next round of short-cycle testing. Ideas are abandoned when they fail to demonstrate success, even after repeated testing, or when the challenges associated with implementation outweigh the benefits of the idea. Ideas are adapted when they exhibit promising results but fail to fully meet articulated needs, for example, serving some populations of students but not others. In instances where the intervention has achieved strong outcomes across a diversity of contexts, leaders may opt to adopt and scale the intervention for further testing in new contexts, a process that in turn often spawns additional adaptations and refinements of the intervention, or new ideas entirely.

In enacting their chosen CI learning methodology many bureaucratic organizations focus on the fidelity of implementation and documentation of process by ground-level staff, like teachers. Hives move away from this approach, tailoring and applying the chosen methodology as "a compass, not a map" (Mehta et al., 2022), using as a North Star consistent uptake at every layer of the organization, rather than perfect implementation of the process. Snowden (2003) writes, "A good tool fits the hand and is largely forgotten despite its usefulness; a bad tool . . . too often requires not only the hand, but also the brain, to be bio-reengineered to enable its use" (pp. 116–117). Sustainable improvement routines become a tool that fits the hand: an intuitive rhythm for learning that all members of the community, including leaders, can reasonably apply to their daily practice.

Part of making the implementation of the methodology manageable is determining how to tailor its application to the type of challenge faced. For many of the technical problems encountered in daily practice, diagnosing a problem and finding solutions may require a less formal application of the process. Ground-level actors are empowered to implement changes to strategy and assess their efficacy in the moment, moving through the steps of the learning methodology to rapidly diagnose the problem, identify and apply a solution independently or in collaboration with system experts, and assess its efficacy. This quick problem-solving is essential to daily improvement and relies on hive members who have internalized the learning methodology to the degree that it is almost second nature (Rother, 2009). Critically, as hive members encounter and solve these technical issues, they do not stop at patching up the immediate challenge before them. The hive's learning methodology prompts double-loop learning—a reflexive questioning of the boundaries of the problem and the organizational values, norms, mindsets, and goals that allowed it to occur (Argyris, 1977). This rapid sensemaking process allows hives to quickly address daily problems to improve service delivery, while drawing insight from those problems to inform longer-term adaptive problem-solving and behavioral change.

Here, consider Partners in School Innovation's use of their learning methodology, Results Oriented Cycles of Inquiry (ROCI), a five-step cycle—(1) partner, (2) set goals, (3) plan, (4) act, and (5) assess, reflect, and adjust—that anchors all improvement efforts in shared goals and habits. The organization threads ROCI through each element of their work, but staff do not see it as a set of technical procedures so much as a problem-solving mindset. In 2018, as the organization launched several lower-dosage, network-based support models for schools, frontline implementers noticed that the organization's long-term strategy for partnerships—honed over decades and articulated in a suite of strategy documents and tools—wasn't functioning as intended; less frequent touchpoints with schools in the new networked model presented novel time and resource constraints. In the immediate term, this was a technical problem that implementers were able to solve relatively quickly in daily practice by picking and choosing which elements of strategy to enact—and which to leave behind. During this quick, daily adaptation of strategy, implementers applied ROCI relatively informally.

While this technical fix was functional and allowed daily work to proceed, implementers didn't address the problem and forget it. As each regional team opted to enact different elements of the strategy, it became clear that practice *across* regions was becoming increasingly inconsistent, making it more challenging to learn in tandem. Implementers raised a concern that there was a fundamental mismatch between the organization's long-term shared strategy for partnerships and this new way of offering support through networks. Hive leaders recognized that a sustainable fix would require major shifts in the organization's norms, goals, and mindsets about partnership—and a different approach to the problem-solving process.

Getting to the root of and sustainably addressing the type of adaptive challenge Partners implementers had surfaced depends on deeper shifts in the way an organization functions and how people think, act, behave, and interact with others (Heifetz et al., 2009), change that often requires a more formal, cross-functional, and longer-term application of the problem-solving process to disrupt the status quo (Aguilar, 2016).

With a view from the organizational "balcony" (Heifetz et al., 2009), positional leaders work closely with hive members to make sense of each type of challenge faced and prioritize when and where to invest in larger-scale problem-solving efforts. Signals that challenges are adaptive include difficulties defining the problem, failed attempts to apply previously successful solutions, a sense that new learning is in order, a need for the input of other hive members, and a general sense of disequilibrium (Heifetz et al., 2009). At Partners in School Innovation, repeated *andon* pulls— signals from the front line that the organization's long-term partnership strategy was not working as designed—suggested to organizational leaders that they had an adaptive challenge on their hands. They convened a temporary crossfunctional team, led by a frontline implementer, to address the challenge. The team collaboratively applied ROCI to make sense of the problem, understand its root causes, and develop a theory to address it by way of a new strategy for network-based partnerships. As that strategy was piloted, hive leaders helped shift the core membership of the problem-solving team to bring on staff who could support measurement and continued refinement of the strategy as learning emerged through its application.

Consolidate and Capture Knowledge

Hives consolidate and capture the knowledge generated during individual and local problem-solving processes so that it can be integrated into individual, collective, and organizational practice to support improvement and decision-making (Snowden, 2003). In practice, consolidation and capture often begin at the individual and local level during the Study and Act stages of PDSA testing. In organization-level consolidation and capture processes, the hive thinks beyond the distributed contexts in which knowledge has been generated (e.g., an individual classroom, a team, a network) to synthesize learnings to support improvement across the broader system.

In many systems, particularly bureaucracies, "capturing" is synonymous with "codifying"—writing things down and storing them in a shared repository. Knowledge is treated as an object (Alavi & Leidner, 2001) that can be removed from context, formally documented, and disseminated across the organization: Think here of the shelves in a district central office stuffed with dusty manuals. While relentless codification is perhaps the default approach to preserving knowledge, it is not a productive one in complex contexts, and, in fact, is fundamentally at odds with the needs of these systems. Comprehensive, undiscerning capture requires an unending investment of resources—time, capacity, attention, space—that, in practice, rarely help frontline staff access and make use of knowledge. Even worse, it often saps the substantive problem-solving energy and momentum from what otherwise would be productive experimentation. Endless documentation becomes the goal, pushing compliance with process rather than the genuine pursuit of knowledge to the forefront. The possibility for human exchange is lost as knowledge is codified, separating the knowledge from the knower and, in so doing, the knower from the seeker.

EL-driven systems take a new tack, understanding the capture stage most of all as a welcome opportunity for collective sensemaking about what new insight is worth capturing and how locally generated knowledge might be applied to the broader system to improve practice and solve organizational problems (Kurtz & Snowden, 2003; Weick, 1995). Weick et al. (2005) write that "Sensemaking starts with chaos" (p. 411), meaning that, in their daily work, organizational actors encounter a cacophony of new learning, events, actions, and conditions. Sensemaking is about stepping back and asking, "What's the story [here]?", and then, "What do I do next?" (Weick et al., 2005, p. 410–412).

In hives, these "stories" and action steps drive the spread and application of knowledge, taking local insight and bringing it to a broader stage.

Because knowledge generation processes are typically bound to a specific problem, local context, and moment in time, the capture stage is an important "way station" (Taylor & Van Every, 1999, p. 275) from which the hive collaboratively clarifies, externalizes, and generalizes tacit understandings of how local learning might apply to others in the organization. Knowledge generators themselves are integral to this process. Chris Thorn, a national leader at Partners in School Innovation, puts the central question, "Who gets to decide which evidence gets considered? This is democracy. Who decides at every level, from parents and kids up to the board, which learning gets collected and gets represented to levels above and below?"

Working with positional leaders, who hold special context about the larger system, knowledge generators collaboratively explore the following questions.

- What did we learn, and how do we know? What does success look like?
    - » During this stage, the hive identifies the learning emerging from local experimentation that is most relevant to progress on strategic priorities and challenges. Broadly, this step supports synthesis (i.e., drawing together and making sense of local data and insights as a collective set of learning) and reduction (i.e., culling down ideas to those most likely to support improvement). To identify the learning worth capturing and sharing, the hive returns to—and, as needed, refines—their definition of what "good" looks like, articulated in theories built during the generation stage, looking at the outcomes or evidence that demonstrate the efficacy of various interventions or the strength of new learnings.
    - » Using this shared standard of "good," the team assesses new knowledge. Sometimes, hives do this using a relatively formal process. For example, leaders in the CARPE Collaborative use a systematic routine (Figure 5.2) to support network-level consolidation (High Tech High Graduate School of Education, n.d.). Coaches track which teams have implemented, for example, various proposed financial aid interventions (e.g., early FAFSA completion, class pull-outs) and the quality of implementation on a simple scale from 1 (not implemented) to 3 (strong implementation). The team then compares implementation quality with results, identifying schools that have demonstrated significant increases in FAFSA completion and using the inevitable variation in implementation across

Figure 5.2. High Tech High Consolidation of Learning Routine

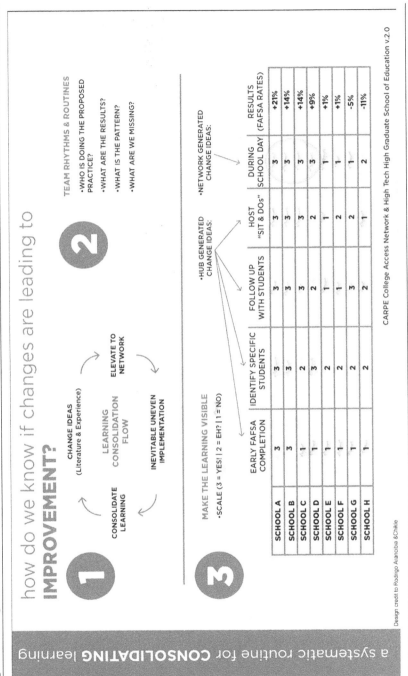

how do we know if changes are leading to
IMPROVEMENT?

1

CONSOLIDATE
LEARNING

CHANGE IDEAS
(Literature & Experience)

LEARNING
CONSOLIDATION
FLOW

ELEVATE TO
NETWORK

INEVITABLE UNEVEN
IMPLEMENTATION

2

TEAM RHYTHMS & ROUTINES
•WHO IS DOING THE PROPOSED PRACTICE?
•WHAT ARE THE RESULTS?
•WHAT IS THE PATTERN?
•WHAT ARE WE MISSING?

3

MAKE THE LEARNING VISIBLE
•SCALE (3 = YES! | 2 = EH? | 1 = NO)

•HUB GENERATED CHANGE IDEAS:

•NETWORK GENERATED CHANGE IDEAS:

	EARLY FAFSA COMPLETION	IDENTIFY SPECIFIC STUDENTS	FOLLOW UP WITH STUDENTS	HOST "SIT & DOS"	DURING SCHOOL DAY	RESULTS (FAFSA RATES)
SCHOOL A	3	3	3	3	3	+21%
SCHOOL B	3	3	3	3	3	+14%
SCHOOL C	1	2	3	3	3	+14%
SCHOOL D	1	3	2	2	3	+9%
SCHOOL E	1	2	1	1	1	+1%
SCHOOL F	1	2	1	2	1	+1%
SCHOOL G	1	2	3	2	1	-5%
SCHOOL H	1	2	2	1	2	-11%

CARPE College Access Network & High Tech High Graduate School of Education v.2.0

Design credit to Rodrigo Arancibia &Chikie

a systematic routine for CONSOLIDATING learning

103

sites to assess the strength of different ideas. When strong practices are identified, the team promotes them for further testing or, if evidence is strong enough, captures them in the network's shared theory of improvement and other knowledge artifacts.

Consolidation need not always be so formal. For example, a district instructional lead and group of principal coaches might reflect on small shifts each coach has made in weekly coaching strategy. Anchoring discussion to key focus areas (e.g., stronger self-directed learning) and a shared definition of success articulated in theories of improvement (e.g., evidence that principals are independently using the learning methodology), the team sorts through coaching interventions and surfaces those that netted stronger outcomes, adapting their shared strategy for coaching accordingly.

- Who is our knowledge most relevant to? What elements of knowledge are most relevant to them? What changes in behavior do we expect our knowledge to inspire?
  » As the hive synthesizes knowledge emerging from local contexts—and identifies new learning worth sharing with others—the hive makes sense of that knowledge in the context of the larger system. Insight emerging from local generation routines is often highly specific to the environment in which it was developed, so generators and positional leaders collaborate to identify the dimensions of new knowledge most relevant to various individuals and groups. This requires finding a balance between (a) retaining context on the conditions necessary to success, while (b) generalizing to draw out broad standards and principles, avoiding the bureaucratic tendency to prescribe particularities of practice. Consider, again, an intervention surfaced during the CARPE consolidation process: offering FAFSA completion support during the school day. Each school's implementation of this idea differed, with some schools using class pull-outs, others offering drop-in support during lunch hours, and still others making FAFSA completion an academic class assignment. The team synthesized these approaches as broad guidance to provide in-school support for completion.

As knowledge is surfaced and refined, the hive keeps application in clear view, identifying key audiences and the changes in behavior, structure, and practice they aim to inspire. The hive articulates the current practices, mindsets, and behaviors implicated by new knowledge—and what type of changes will be necessary. The answers to these questions help inform how knowledge will be captured.

Again, this type of sensemaking often begins *during* knowledge generation because, in practice, the steps of the knowledge management cycle often overlap. Hives push themselves to make explicit the sensemaking happening before and during the generation stage, *while learning is happening,* even, and especially, when the work feels novel, messy, and unclear. Human memory is reconstructive, rather than static: As we have new experiences and learn new things, our memories change (Lacy & Stark, 2013). This means that the further we get from the events that catalyze learning, the more distorted our interpretations and narratives of change become (Salmen et al., 2023). We also tend to assign retrospective logic to events, meaning that once the outcomes of a series of actions are evident, we construct coherent and linear narratives that align with and confirm personal and organizational values, beliefs, and assumptions to explain those events. While these narratives are essential tools for sensemaking and communication, they can also obstruct nuance, suggesting simple causal relationships in place of what are more likely complex ones (Snowden, 2002a).

Collaborative sensemaking can help account for and balance these realities. Opportunities to externalize are threaded throughout each step of the hive's improvement methodology: As individuals and small teams work on challenges, they make explicit how they understand problems, their theories of improvement, change ideas, predictions, data, outcomes, and findings. These early inputs support productive capture later.

Capture Knowledge to Inspire Action

As consolidation and sensemaking progress, knowledge creators and positional leaders capture knowledge in ways that motivate and enable action by key audiences. Weick et al. (2005) write, "To share understanding means to lift equivocal knowledge out of the tacit, private, complex, random, and past to make it explicit, public, simpler, ordered, and relevant to the situation at hand" (p. 413). In this way, capturing knowledge is a continuation of the sensemaking process, which allows members to translate data and insight from local learning efforts into knowledge worthy of scale to a broader audience.

Captured knowledge may take a variety of forms including

- New standards and modifications to strategy;
- Stories, bite-site narratives, and talking points;
- Trainings, lesson plans, and demonstrations;

- Videos and podcasts;
- Diagrams, illustrations, and graphics; and
- Formal writing like articles, reports, and change packages.

The variety of formats used to capture knowledge distinguishes hives from most other organizations, which tend to inflate the importance of written codification, setting an unreasonable expectation that people can comprehensively record everything they are learning. Again, in hives, capture is not about writing everything down, but about understanding what has been learned and finding ways to transmit that knowledge to potential users in ways that allow them to act and, when relevant, providing them with explicit guidance on next steps for implementation. Weick et al. (2005) write that, "Students of sensemaking understand that the order in organizational life comes just as much from the subtle, the small, the relational, the oral, the particular, and the momentary as it does from the conspicuous, the large, the substantive, the written, the general, and the sustained" (p. 410).

To that end, to reach different audiences, hives often capture knowledge in multiple formats, adapting the content, level of detail, format, and tone as needed. Regardless of intended audience, captured knowledge does not function as an unchangeable directive for implementation, but instead as a starting point for continued iteration; an added layer of context to help shape practice and enable stronger decision-making.

Baltimore City Schools' networked improvement communities present a strong example of this practice. Given their goal of influencing instructional practice across the district, the leaders of the network had, since launch, been thoughtful about capture, working with schools to develop detailed change packages about the effective strategies emerging from learning processes. But as leaders attempted to scale practices beyond the network, they quickly realized their first audience would be district leaders, who had the influence to spark changes across the system. The network leadership team began sharing change packages and detailed summary decks with district leaders to communicate the rich learning emerging from the network. Despite this effort, the team saw little impact on district decision-making and practice.

After mapping their knowledge management practices, network leaders realized that they were missing an important step: the curation of knowledge and development of communication tools appropriate for this new audience. District leaders had limited time and were overwhelmed by the complexity of the information presented in the change packages; they needed clearer descriptions of how the new knowledge coming out of the network was connected to district priorities—and the steps they could personally take to advance change. Network leaders shifted their capture strategy, preparing succinct verbal elevator pitches to take advantage of both formal and unplanned touchpoints with cabinet-level leaders, which helped ensure that ideas emerging from the network gained traction at the district level.

Critically, in hives, capturing knowledge is not the end goal. Dave Snowden (2008) writes that the process of "taking things from our heads to our mouths (speaking them) to our hands (writing them down) involves loss of content and context. It is always less than it could have been as it is increasingly codified." In the next section, we unpack how hive members help mitigate this loss of context by actively shepherding captured knowledge across the organization.

Create Space, Routines, and Roles That Enable Active Knowledge Sharing

Once captured, local knowledge is shared so it can support innovation and problem-solving across the hive. Knowledge sharing is, at base, about cultivating the trust, relationships, and communication pathways necessary to motivate application. Hives use these pathways, at times, to proactively scale new knowledge in response to immediate issues facing the broader organization; for example, implementing a tiered literacy support model in new schools. But as important is the "just-in-time" sharing that allows hive members to access institutional knowledge at their own pace as novel problems emerge in day-to-day practice; for example, insight on how to better support newcomer students in response to demographic changes in a district. Knowledge sharing is an essentially human activity, which means it is not entirely controllable. But in hives, positional leaders attend to fostering a networked organizational structure where active sharing methods, a network of communication pathways and routines, and attention to organically emerging relationships all encourage productive knowledge exchange.

Engage in Active Sharing. Most public institutions rely mostly on passive sharing. In this approach, knowledge is externalized, codified, and diffused, often through access to knowledge storage systems like databases and repositories (Crosswaite & Curtice, 1994; Gagnon, 2011). Passive approaches to knowledge sharing can be appealing because they are cost-effective and convenient, and on their face seem to support efficient spread of knowledge. But by themselves they rarely advance the effective application of new knowledge at scale, in large part because the impetus for the discovery and interpretation of knowledge falls to knowledge seekers alone. In many busy public systems, accessing codified knowledge is challenging; most knowledge artifacts are stored not in highly organized databases, but in catch-all repositories, where valuable insight gets mixed in with outdated and irrelevant content. Even when seekers are able to locate relevant knowledge, it has often been captured without the nuance and context necessary to be responsive to local needs. Lacking direct access to the knowledge generators who hold that nuance and context, seekers then struggle to effectively apply knowledge to their immediate problems.

For all these reasons, hives see passive sharing as necessary but insufficient for promoting productive knowledge application. EL systems prioritize active approaches where human connection animates and contextualizes knowledge.

First among active sharing strategies is the hive's commitment to joint experimentation, through which those closest to challenges actively participate in efforts to create, test, and refine knowledge. Starting from generation, the hive involves those who will be pivotal to the application of new knowledge in efforts to develop and test it. Consider, for example, Partners in School Innovation's inclusion of frontline implementers in their effort to reshape their partnership strategy or CARPE's inclusion of principals, teachers, and counselors on school-based improvement teams. This practice means that active sharing can be experienced not as an extra step in the improvement process but instead concurrently with generation, consolidation, and capture. In this way, hives enable *sharing through doing*.

The hive leverages the dynamism of its organizational structure to further enable active sharing. As knowledge emerges from local contexts, positional leaders flex teaming structures, creating thoughtful pairings and groupings that allow local generators to share new knowledge directly with peers through its application in new contexts. The goal of this practice is not merely transmission of knowledge, but the cultivation of reciprocal learning partnerships that support knowledge's active application and refinement. Don Berwick talks about the value of this type of active sharing (Caillier, 2021):

> That third-party document tends to end up on a shelf, you're lucky if anyone reads it, and then if people read it, it's still a long way from implementation. The beauty of the visit, of the actual peer-to-peer encounter, is that the dynamics of learning can be so robust because I can say, "Wait a minute . . . you just did that. I don't understand it. That's not what you told me. Why did you do it that way?" Or, "Could you explain a little more about this?" Or, "Wait a minute. I'm left-handed. You're right-handed. How do you think that would . . ." We actually can have a dialogue, which you can never have

in the third-party report. And so I find it a much more motivating, agile instructive way to learn. It's viscous.

At Partners, the frontline implementer who helped redesign the organization's partnership model used this approach as she brought the new strategy back to her regional colleagues and enacted it alongside them, actively sharing it with them through the act of implementation.

Hives do, of course, use more familiar approaches to active sharing to reach members not directly involved in generation: dialogue, coaching, training, and even interaction on virtual platforms—like Partners' use of Mighty Networks, an interactive networking platform that allows staff, former and current school- and district-based partners, and external collaborators to share and discuss new learning. In hives, these activities are designed to invite the type of bidirectional communication that supports further excavation of tacit context (Fullan, 2020) and continued sensemaking through which both generators and seekers contextualize, clarify, and refine knowledge. In hives, active and passive methods are often paired. In a school, for example, to encourage uptake of an instructional strategy captured passively in a lesson plan, a teacher might enact the method with coteachers in their classroom.

While the hive's teaming structures and learning spaces (see Chapter 4) naturally encourage active sharing, at times, and especially in larger organizations, additional shepherding is needed to help knowledge cross social boundaries (Aldrich & Herker, 1977). For this purpose, hives tap knowledge brokers, intermediaries, or messengers tasked with facilitating reciprocal knowledge exchange between various groups and communities (Meyer, 2010). To this end, brokers enact "processes of translation, coordination, and alignment between perspectives" (Wenger, 1998, as cited in Meyer, 2010, p. 121).

Brokerage rests on the idea that people are more likely to engage with and use new knowledge when it is communicated to them by a person they trust and when it is appropriately contextualized (Long et al., 2013). Brokers are most effective when they:

- Have expertise about the knowledge being shared, often having been involved in or familiar with the ground-level work to generate, test, and adapt it;
- Are trusted in and considered credible by the communities they work with; and
- Understand each community they are communicating with and can help bridge and translate knowledge from one context to the other.

Mature hives tailor their brokerage strategy to each situation, observing which organizational actors naturally sit at the "peripheries" (Meyer, 2010, p.122) or at the intersection of multiple learning communities, and providing guidance, time, space, and expectations to support and formalize their brokerage role. In districts and schools, coaches (e.g., principal, instructional, and improvement coaches) are often particularly agile brokers, having a foot in both the worlds of leadership and of ground-level implementation. Given their system-level view, positional leaders are similarly positioned to play a brokerage role—provided that they have, to some degree, perspective on ground-level work through their active engagement with frontline experimentation and learning efforts.

Guide, Don't Control, Knowledge Flow. Understanding that their role is to influence, rather than control, the flow of knowledge (Von Krogh et al., 2000), positional leaders cultivate pathways that facilitate reciprocal knowledge exchange. From their central vantage point, positional leaders leverage organizational structure to cultivate learning relationships by adapting teaming structures and membership and creating shared learning spaces to connect people working on similar challenges. They help set the conditions for trust and scaffold learning routines in these spaces to encourage productive knowledge sharing; for example, by establishing the cadence and guiding design principles for learning meetings, helping the hive set common standards to determine when knowledge is worth sharing, and providing protocols for dialogue.

At the same time, positional leaders avoid overly prescriptive approaches to knowledge exchange. Diverging for a moment to the world of urban planning, consider "desire paths," the off-road trails naturally created by foot traffic in parks and other public spaces. While unplanned, these paths often represent the most efficient route between popular destinations. Good landscape architects do not ignore this user feedback; they adapt design in response, often installing paved pathways along similar routes. Hive leaders follow a similar principle. If the conditions are right—if there is time, space, and trust—people will naturally seek out and share knowledge when needed (Snowden, 2012). A positional leader's role is most powerful when leveraged to ensure these conditions are in place and to look out for and encourage organically developing relationships and groupings (Fullan, 2020). Over time, leaders adapt formal structures to enable and amplify those relationships, an approach that is often more effective than investing resources into top-down collaboration and knowledge sharing structures without evidence of their value. Fullan (2020) summarizes this approach to leadership succinctly: "Control freaks need not apply: people need elbow room to uncover and sort out the best ideas. Leaders must learn to trust the processes they set up, looking for promising patterns and looking to continually refine and identify procedures for maximizing valuable sharing" (p. 100).

Support the Application of Knowledge

As sharing progresses, hives support the uptake of new knowledge to support problem-solving and decision-making across the organization. Ideally, many of the people enacting new knowledge have been directly involved in its generation. But of course, it is impossible for every hive member to be involved in every generation process, and so there is always a need for change management efforts. Seeing change as an ongoing process, rather than an event (Hall & Hord, 2006), hives understand that each person brings different interpretations of, reactions to, feelings about, and capacity to implement new learning (Hall & Hord, 2006). Part of effective application relies on recognizing these various perspectives on shared knowledge and expectations for change.

A number of common personas are often present in change efforts and help target support (Chu et al., 2024). *Rookies* and *skeptics* are members newly introduced to knowledge who are, respectively, open to or uninterested in making change. *Navigators* have begun to make changes, yet still require support to make the most of those shifts. Present, too, in any change effort, are *challengers*, who have deep expertise in new knowledge, but who remain unconvinced about its value, either broadly or in their own context. *Supporters* mirror challengers in their experience level but feel generally positive about the impact of new knowledge. Hive members inevitably move between these personas as they encounter, experiment with, and make sense of new knowledge.

Mapping individuals and audiences to these personas helps the hive appropriately tailor support and motivate action. The hive asks:

- What motivates this person or group to act?
- What resources—people, time, money, knowledge—do they need to act?
- What conditions need to be in place for them to act?
- What obstacles do they face? How can we help mitigate those obstacles?

As they answer these questions, facilitators develop a tailored blend of interventions to support—and learn from—each group, including

- Reiterating the vision behind recommended changes;
- Facilitating training and other processes to strengthen baseline understanding of new knowledge and its application;

- Providing the resources (e.g., money, tools, time, staffing) necessary to support uptake of and continued experimentation with changes;
- Regularly checking in on implementation progress and seeking out feedback and data to understand implementation challenges;
- Providing continued feedback and support on implementation; and
- Returning to and revising both knowledge artifacts and sharing strategies in response to learnings from this process (Hall & Hord, 2006).

The hive uses various combinations of these interventions to inspire uptake of a given change. For example, having been recently introduced to new knowledge, both skeptics and rookies typically require additional time and support to process and understand the reasoning behind change. The hive works closely with both groups to provide the resources and build the mindsets and skills needed to integrate new knowledge into practice, including by providing additional training and opportunities for mentorship from champions of the work. Hives spend additional time with skeptics to diagnose the roots of negative feelings so they can be appropriately addressed. Navigators, on the other hand, often require more targeted support: They are familiar with new knowledge—and willing to begin implementing changes—but are misapplying it in the process. Left uncorrected, this can lead to frustration, disappointing results, and misguided perceptions that knowledge is invalid or ineffective. Those facilitating change work closely with navigators to identify misalignments and build capacity in those areas, checking in regularly to discuss progress (Chu et al., 2024).

Given their deep experiential understanding of both shared knowledge and strategies for implementation, challengers are seen as critical learning partners. Broadly, hives see the concerns challengers raise as legitimate and learn from their resistance (Fullan & Miles, 1992), enacting responsive adaptations to the base knowledge, capture formats, sharing strategies, and implementation support to address it. Hives seek to understand critiques, provide evidence that increases confidence in the validity of knowledge, and engage challengers in collaborative problem-solving processes to address key issue areas, at times pairing them with the most experienced supporters (Chu et al., 2024).

Supporters have the potential to act as champions for the work, catalyzing stronger uptake and implementation across the system. Hives uplift and reinforce supporters' positive feelings, position them as leaders and experts in the change effort (e.g., tapping them as mentors and knowledge brokers), and identify resources that might help take their implementation to the next level (Chu et al., 2024).

As hives work toward change, they ground their efforts in a shared refrain: To meet the needs of differing people, contexts, and moments and achieve equity, knowledge must be responsive and dynamic. Knowledge management is a cycle, so application is not really the end. As Freire (1996) writes, "Knowledge emerges only through invention and reinvention, through the restless, impatient, continuing, hopeful inquiry human beings pursue in the world, with the world, and with each other." As knowledge is applied in new contexts, new implementers return to generation, using the system's learning methodology to reimagine, test, and refine that knowledge in service of ever-better practice, stronger decision-making, and innovation.

SUMMARY

In this chapter, we explored how hives synchronize the system's problem-solving efforts, aligning generation activities to shared organizational problems to amplify their impact. Positional leaders help hive members consistently apply the organization's learning methodology in their daily practice and in collective learning spaces to draw out powerful insight and solutions that might otherwise lay latent across the system. As new knowledge emerges, positional leaders support sensemaking, working with hive members to capture knowledge in ways that will enable and inspire better practice in the broader system. They foster sharing strategies that tap into and take advantage of the hive's network to both scale ideas that solve existing problems and make knowledge accessible when and where new challenges emerge. All of this work, and a keen attention to the human side of change, supports the application and ongoing refinement of novel and long-standing institutional knowledge. A principle threaded throughout each stage of a hive's knowledge management process is a commitment to setting the conditions that enable and prompt strong behaviors, rather than leaning on ineffective mandates that overly formalize organic, human processes and relationships.

STARTING THE SHIFT: REFLECT AND ACT

In this section, three activities will help you reflect on the degree to which your system enacts strong knowledge management practice and how you might improve.

1. Self-Assessment: Reflect on how your organization conceptualizes knowledge management.
2. Map and Assess Existing Knowledge Management Practices: Develop a working map of existing knowledge management structures and routines.
3. Plan Backwards from Application: Build the muscle of mapping backwards from the application of knowledge by outlining a process map for a knowledge management effort.

You can complete these activities alone, in 1:1 settings, or larger groups.

Self-Assessment

1. As a leader, how do you support the development and application of knowledge in your organization?
2. How does your organization define *knowledge* and *knowledge management*?
   a. Do you have a shared definition?
   b. Does that definition align with the four knowledge-management steps (generation, consolidation and capture, sharing, and application) outlined earlier in this section?
3. When and how (if at all) does your team or organization put in practice each of the four steps of the knowledge management process? When and why does it work? When and why does it fail or fail to happen? What do you do instead?
4. How does your team or organization learn? Does your learning process constitute a learning methodology? If so, is it simple and user-friendly? Accessible to all users? Designed and communicated as principles and processes, rather than rules? What core questions should users ask and answer during each step of the learning methodology?
5. When do members of your community feel valued in the knowledge generation, consolidation and capture, sharing, and application routines? When do they not? Why?

Map Your Existing Knowledge Management Practices

To build an effective knowledge management strategy, it can be helpful first to understand how existing activities—some that you perhaps have not explicitly tied to knowledge management—may already be contributing to your efforts.

1. Describe your network/organization's knowledge generation routines including:
    a. Regularly scheduled meetings to identify and discuss challenges
    b. Routines to test proposed solutions
    c. Routines to collect and review data from solution testing
2. Describe your network/organization's knowledge consolidation and capture routines including:
    a. Consolidation and sensemaking routines to surface the most important and relevant learning emerging across contexts
    b. Capture routines to record and prepare to communicate new knowledge
3. Describe your network/organization's sharing routines including:
    a. Active and passive approaches to sharing
    b. Identification and support of knowledge brokers
4. Describe your network/organization's application routines including:
    a. Identification of the audience for knowledge
    b. Integration of key audiences into knowledge generation, consolidation, capture, and sharing processes
    c. Development of change management strategies for various audiences
    d. Routines to revisit and revise change management strategy as knowledge is applied

With a working list of existing processes, interrogate where there are gaps and missing connections in your work.

Plan Backwards From Application

As you embark on a specific problem-solving effort, it can be helpful to anticipate your process by planning backwards from the application of knowledge at scale. A swimlane process map can help your team articulate and visualize linked activities across each knowledge management step and stage, identifying and mitigating gaps in your plan before and as you implement.

1. Identify the goal of your knowledge management efforts and plot it as a terminal in the lower right-hand corner of your swimlane template (Figure 5.3).
    a. Ask:
        i. What is our system's shared, long-term aim?
        ii. What knowledge application goal will position us to achieve that aim? To articulate this goal, think about:

  1. What type of knowledge will need to be spread and be applied?
  2. Who will need to apply this knowledge? How might we engage those audiences as cocreators throughout our effort?
  3. At what scale will knowledge need to be applied?
2. Backwards map your knowledge management system from that goal using the four knowledge management stages as a frame.
  a. Ask:
   i. If our goal is the application of new knowledge at the scale we've articulated, what preceding knowledge sharing activity must take place?
   ii. What knowledge consolidation and capture activity must precede that sharing activity?
   iii. What generation activity precedes those consolidation and capture activities?
  b. Write down those activities and plot them vertically on your map, connecting each activity to the last with an arrow.
  c. Continue to plot backwards, differentiating between processes and decision points by using the rectangular and diamond icons, respectively.
  d. Plot until you have reached a logical starting point in the generation lane. It's likely that your system generates knowledge in many different ways. For this activity, choose just one generation starting point. If the mapping activity proves useful, consider developing several maps that begin at

Figure 5.3. Swimlane Process Map

Generation	Terminal
Consolidation & Capture	Process
Sharing	Decision Point
Application	Direction

different knowledge generation starting points, making note of where your different maps converge.

   e. Reflect on your map using the following questions as a guide:

      i. What have we learned about our knowledge management process?

      ii. After mapping, have we identified any parts of our process where we are not attending to the full knowledge management cycle? Why do we think those gaps exist? Where and how can we implement new activities, supports, or tools to mitigate gaps in our process?

      iii. Are there any activities on our map that are not assigned to or owned by an actor or group? Who might take the lead on those tasks? What support can we offer to assist with that work?

CHAPTER 6

Harvest Data to Monitor and Improve

VIGNETTE: MISSISSIPPI LITERACY INITIATIVE

Let's return, for a moment, to the Mississippi marathon discussed in Chapter 1. Mississippi's journey has been full of discovery, driven by a commitment to transforming literacy instruction and guided by a learning method that revealed which strategies worked, for whom, and in what contexts. From The Barksdale Reading Institute's (BRI) launch in 2000, the Barksdale team, the Mississippi Department of Education (MDE), higher education, and school system partners tested ways to implement the science of reading and scale up those practices. Hypothesizing that one major driver of improvement would be properly training teachers before they reached classrooms, BRI first funded salaries of faculty members who would act as science of reading champions, introducing practices into the state's educator preparation programs (Butler, 2024; Mahnken, 2022). BRI studied the effect of this approach, measuring the amount of time in pre-literacy coursework devoted to phonics instruction, finding, in Butler's words, "no impact" (Mahnken, 2022). Not satisfied with a simple response to *whether* it worked, Butler investigated *why* it didn't, yielding three crucial insights, in her words: "Faculty didn't know the science. One of the findings was that they really didn't influence each other. And there was no requirement of what they had to teach" (Mahnken, 2022). This learning shaped future, more effective efforts at influencing preservice training, including training for faculty on evidence-based literacy practices and adjustments to preservice licensure requirements (Burk, 2020; Butler, 2024; Pellegrini et al., 2018).

Measurement also played a crucial role in determining effective practices in classrooms and figuring out how to spread them statewide. In demonstration sites, observations of classroom practice combined with measures of student learning revealed instructional practices and elements of the literacy block essential to student learning. These measures also revealed flaws in the theory of scaling and informed future emphases on school leader buy-in and capacity and coaching (McBride, 2021). Even after the Literacy-Based Promotion Act (LBPA) passed, MDE continued to use multiple measures and data collection methods, including classroom observations and surveys, to assess and improve strategy and implementation (Folsom et al., 2017). Former Mississippi Department of Education Literacy Director Kymyona Burk explained,

> Each month, our literacy coaches collected not only quantitative data, such as results from screeners, but also documented the areas they had to provide coaching, classroom instruction, monitoring. They documented components in each school that needed help. In trying to make an impact on student achievement, we needed to know the story behind why numbers were that way. They would submit the data to our office. They would also submit to the principal of the school, and then also the district designee.

Adjustments to strategy went beyond small tweaks, such as combining, rather than keeping separate, teacher and administrator training and making coaches available to principals as well as teachers. For example, in the years following the passage of the LBPA, the state updated state assessments and made significant increases in its early childhood investments (Mahnken, 2022).

Measurement isn't limited to the state and its R&D partners. It penetrates every level of the system. Districts use data from classrooms and schools to inform their strategies, which fit within the statewide framework but are customized to their local contexts (RMC Research Corporation, 2019). Educators use measures of learning and achievement—those on daily assessments, screeners, and state assessments, among others—to tailor instruction to students' needs, intervening as early as possible to make sure students are academically on track (RMC Research Corporation, 2019). Measurement determines promotion to 4th grade and focuses adults on "changing their behavior" to make sure children are not behind at that critical juncture (Collins, 2022). Measurement is also used to inform the content, implementation, and improvement of Individual Reading Plans (Collins, 2022). As Burk (2022) explained, "The goal is to screen students as early as kindergarten for reading deficiencies and begin interventions early. At the same time, we will keep monitoring a student's progress and communicating with their parents and families. We don't just want to say that we want children reading by the end of third grade. As a state agency, we had to be committed to helping them get there."

In this hive of activity, BRI, the state agency, districts, schools, and others harvest data needed to identify opportunities for improvement and innovation and test, adapt, and sustain what works. Measurement functions as an early alert system; an engine for ongoing, shared learning; and a source of transparency and mutual accountability.

Figure 6.1. Measurement Priorities in Bureaucracy

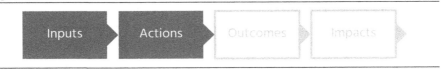

MEASUREMENT IN PREDOMINANT GOVERNANCE MODELS

Bureaucracy Measures Inputs and Compliance

Contrast the use of measurement in the Mississippi literacy case with how measurement is used in other dominant governance models, starting with bureaucracy. To measure success, bureaucracies primarily assess (1) inputs and (2) compliance with specified rules and procedures (as modeled in Figure 6.1).

Measured inputs are often quantifiable proxies, or signals, for starting conditions that likely affect the delivery and quality of services. In schools, these include things like levels of per pupil funding, class size, length of school day, and average years of teacher experience. Many inputs are proxies of key conditions that appear to be costly or challenging to measure. For example, average years of teacher experience is a proxy for teacher expertise. In this and many other cases in education, the proxy is a distant one; extant research establishes only a weak link between years of teacher experience and teacher expertise (Kini & Podolsky, 2016).

Bureaucracies also measure actions, but typically only with regard to whether those actions comply with rules and procedures (Ansell, 2011). This focus prompts ground-level actors to document the steps they take to deliver services, making clear the extent to which the enacted procedure reflects the prescribed procedure (Braithwaite & Braithwaite, 1995). Checklists abound, both to help ground-level actors follow rules and to monitor the extent to which they are followed. Because bureaucracy relies on procedural uniformity at every level, supervisors and third-party reviewers also have detailed protocols and rules for monitoring the activity of lower-level employees or other regulated actors (Braithwaite & Braithwaite, 1995).

In bureaucratic systems, gaps between what is actually measured and the intent of the measurement can lead to proliferation of measurement. Additional (and often distant) proxies or fine-grained steps are used to constrain and assess activity in the hopes of getting a better read on the intended construct.

One might think that these finer-grained indicators would increase reliability in measurement. In practice, the opposite is often the case. In the same way that finer-grained and more fully elaborated rules increase—rather than reduce—the need for discretion when working across diverse contexts (think Horace's Compromise explored in Chapter 2—superficially complying with rules while subverting them behind closed doors), finer-grained and more elaborate measures can lead to increased discretion and less reliability in measurement. In what's called the paradox of reliability, reliability in measurement is more likely to be achieved when it is not the central measurement goal (Braithwaite & Braithwaite, 1995).

Consider the 1995 comparative study on nursing home regulation in Australia and the United States that identified this paradox. In Australia, nursing home regulators employed 31 broad standards, whereas in the United States, regulators were expected to apply hundreds. Although the finer-grained American measures were intended to increase the reliability and validity of evaluations, the opposite happened; the laundry list of indicators were impossible to remember and use, not least because some measures contradicted others. The search for precision also meant increasing the extent to which the measures were proxies for target constructs. In Australia's case, adhering to a feasible number of standards meant making them broad and subjective, lessening—and in some cases, eliminating—the distance between the construct and the measure. Contrast the two approaches of assessing the quality of the nursing home environment. Whereas the Australian model simply measured "homelike environment," the U.S. indicators assessed such finer-grained items as "number of pictures on the walls" and "infection-control practice as related to bedsores," hindering a holistic and reliable assessment of the issue in question (Braithwaite & Braithewaite, 1995).

Managerialism Measures Achievement of Performance Targets

In managerialism, measures of success focus on outcomes, not inputs and processes (as modeled in Figure 6.2). Leaders of organizations and systems

Figure 6.2. Measurement Priorities in Managerialism

define performance targets for subordinate levels and actors in the system (Coglianese & Lazer, 2003). Managers measure performance against those targets, using achievement (or lack thereof) to define success. The myopic focus on outcomes inhibits learning and innovation in complex systems. Absent an explicit focus on how and why some strategies work better than others, effective practice is hidden, and is, in some cases, further obfuscated by false signals of success from bad behavior (e.g., cheating) motivated by a targets-driven management approach.

Returning to the managerialism example in Chapter 2, the focus of measurement in Atlanta Public Schools was achievement levels in ELA and Math as first set at the federal level by the No Child Left Behind Act. Georgia defined a set of achievement targets for its districts and schools using this federal framework and ensured an assessment system that would enable annual monitoring of performance (Coston, 2011). These targets were passed as performance mandates to Atlanta districts and schools. Measurement of performance relative to targets was used for motivation and accountability purposes, with individuals, schools, and districts meeting or exceeding targets receiving operating autonomies and other types of rewards, and those failing to meet targets experiencing consequences, including, in some cases, termination (Strauss, 2015; Wilson et al., 2011). In Atlanta's case, this measurement approach gave rise to cheating, which led many to conclude that achievement gains were a mirage, thereby foreclosing the opportunity to identify and spread the real, but hidden, improvements and innovations taking place in schools across the city.

Professionalism and Craft Measure Mastery of Practice

In professionalism and craft, measurement is no longer top-down. Success equals skill mastery as defined by professionals and expert practitioners and focuses on individuals' mastery and service excellence (or actions, as modeled in Figure 6.3) (Mehta, 2013).

Measurement of individuals' readiness and skill begins at training and induction (Liebman & Sabel, 2003; Mehta, 2013). In professions, this

Figure 6.3. Measurement Priorities in Professionalism and Craft

measurement is often standardized by those within the profession and is focused on proficiency in both theoretical and applied knowledge, evaluated through performance-based and written assessments (Mehta, 2013). In craft, mastery is measured through applied demonstration of skill, with satisfactory performance left to the judgment of those already in the guild (Mehta, 2013).

Once inducted, regulation of members' performance continues internally, with professionals and craftspeople monitoring and assessing the performance of their peers. In professions, this measurement continues to be reliant on explicit indicators of success, such as performance standards. Different from rules, performance standards are broadly defined and flexibly applied (Noonan et al., 2009). Rather than specifying discrete, step-by-step protocols or procedures, they create norms about high-quality service (Braithwaite & Braithwaite, 1995; Noonan et al., 2009).

In craft, post-induction measurement continues to be based more on intuition and tacit indicators of excellence than on explicit performance standards (Sennett, 2008). As with professionalism, assessment focuses on how well the individual performs their art, though the assessment of excellence remains with other masters, with little need to explicitly justify their determination.

Let's look at classic examples of each, starting with lawyers. Aspiring lawyers' readiness for the profession is first measured at the time they apply to law school, both through their performance on a standardized exam (the LSAT) and through their demonstrated track record of success (through their law school application). In many cases, performance standards and other explicit criteria are used to determine which candidates are accepted into law school. Once in school, law students' readiness for the profession is assessed through additional written exams and applied performance tasks in theoretical and experiential courses. Measurement of individual readiness occurs again at the conclusion of law school and before graduates become lawyers, this time through the bar exam. Those that pass this exam are deemed eligible for the profession. Once in the profession, lawyers are required to continue acquiring a certain number of educational credits by attending workshops, courses, or other formal lessons to retain their status as a qualified attorney, and ascend the ranks of firms and other workplaces based on appraisal by their more esteemed peers.

Turning to craft, let's look at visual artists. Aspiring visual artists' readiness for the guild is first measured, for those pursuing formal training, at their application to art school. This application often occurs via a portfolio representing their body of work to date, including their art and statements elaborating the meaning of their work and the directions they would like to pursue over the course of their study. Faculty artists review these applications to determine which candidates are accepted into art school. Once in school, art students improve their craft and demonstrate readiness for an art career via critiques of their produced work, both by their peers and by faculty artists. Students' training culminates with shows of their work. Those that are well received earn the recommendations of and introductions made by faculty and other master artists to pave their way into the guild.

Artists' success continues to be measured by fellow artists and connoisseurs of art, who assess greatness not by some objective set of performance standards, but by subjective, often difficult to define, criteria (Sennett, 2008). They know greatness when they see it, and they make these judgments known to other artists, art connoisseurs, and the public in order to elevate the work of masters.

In both professionalism and craft, the use of measurement in self-government hampers the explicit discovery and spread of improvement and innovation. Focusing measurement on selection, training, induction, and practice at the exclusion of goals or outcomes leaves professions without a means of problem solving or improving. Like distant proxies in bureaucracies, focusing on process, absent results, prevents insight into what works. Measurement of expertise by experts alone, without a user-centered or outcomes focus, makes the models vulnerable to biases and risks perpetuating practices that may work for some but not others.

All Three Are a Measurement Mismatch for Education

While these measurement approaches effectively support the pursuit of goals in some sectors and contexts, they are not well matched to the measurement needs in education writ large. Our education system is vast, diverse in context and constituency, and works to support a diversity of goals, all of which ultimately aim to ensure children lead thriving lives (D. Harris, 2020). The diversity of context, constituency, and goals gives rise to another source of diversity: strategy. Education systems have yet to discover and implement strategies that ensure consistent achievement of goals and ultimate aims at scale. In the absence of a single, winning strategy, education systems must therefore use measurement to enable ongoing learning and discovery.

The measurement approach associated with each of the three predominant models fails to enable this ongoing learning and discovery. Their limitations arise from a number of factors: a too limited view on expertise and decision-making authority over measurement, misalignment or inadequacy of what is measured, misalignment of who measures and how that measurement occurs, and misrepresentation of the role measurement plays in accountability for system performance.

MEASUREMENT IN EVOLUTIONARY LEARNING

In learning hives, measurement propels ongoing discovery of how to best customize and enact strategy to meet goals at all levels of the system, from the individual to the collective (Ansell, 2011; Spear, 2009). It is designed to support coordinated and equity-advancing progress at scale in the face of great diversity of contexts, actors, and goals, supporting the continuous evolution of strategy and implementation in light of changing circumstances (Yeager et al., 2013).

Because individual and collective learning and customization are the constants (Spear, 2009)—rather than uniform implementation of uniform strategy—evolutionary learning uses measurement as

- an early alert system, prompting and enabling actors to spot and explicitly name problems and opportunities for improvement whenever and wherever they occur—and to quickly swing into action to learn from and address them;
- an engine for ongoing, shared learning, enabling actors to study the implementation and effect of their strategies, making visible what works, why, and what improvements might be made; and
- a source of transparency and mutual accountability, making visible to all how the system is designed and performs and creating a sense of responsibility for interdependencies.

Measurement fuels the hive's problem-solving methodology, integrating measurement into system design, culture, and practice. Measurement enables the system and each component part to ask and answer: "How well does my strategy work, for whom, and under what conditions?" (Chabran & Norman, 2018). It requires every system level and each component part to

- measure process and outcome, service and effect;
- measure quality (how well) and quantity (how much);

- set before-the-fact performance expectations;
- gather information in ways that support collective improvement;
- structure operations to routinize measurement and meaning making; and
- attend to and address deficiencies and disparities.

Done right, measurement communicates core values, focuses hive members on strategy, and supports localized and system-wide learning and knowledge generation. Positional leaders prioritize measures that allow them to gauge the most important parts of strategy, those that are essential to advancing equity, most tightly aligned to the ultimate aim, and able to serve as early alerts when things fall off track.

Throughout the hive, leaders amplify common performance expectations so that everyone, no matter where in the system they operate, has a clear picture of success and therefore knows when it is and is not achieved. They also reject the inevitability of persistent failure, designing systems that detect deviations so that they may be addressed instead of designing systems that perpetually tolerate deviations or generate workarounds (Spear, 2009).

By demonstrating time and again that what happens in one area of the system affects others, measurement unifies; by demonstrating that what is uncovered, discovered, and improved in one area expands the capacity of the whole, measurement transforms, allowing the system to deliberately and continually advance. Table 6.1 captures the EL approach to measurement in contrast to that of other governance models, inspired by Chabran & Norman (2018; compare with Tables 2.1, 3.1, and 5.1).

STRUCTURES AND ACTIVITIES

Leaders coordinate the selection and monitoring of a constellation of measures for the system as a whole and all component parts, including the department, division, initiative, team, and individual levels. In school districts, this often means measuring system, school, and classroom-level strategies. Data harvested through these efforts are activated through a collaborative improvement infrastructure that supports actors at all layers of their organization in sharing, making sense of, and using data to bridge daily learning into strategic progress. That infrastructure and associated problem-solving practices are discussed in detail in Chapters 4 and 5.

Table 6.1. Measurement and Data Usage in Governance Models

	Bureaucracy	Managerialism	Professionalism/ Craft	Evolutionary Learning
Who *decides . . .*	Leaders of organizations and system	Leaders of organizations and system	Professionals and expert practitioners	Leaders of organizations and system confirm and update co-created overarching framework
				Actors throughout operationalize framework to work within context-specific conditions
. . . what is measured.	Quantifiable inputs	Performance outcomes and targets	Mastery of profession or craft during training, induction, and key milestones of career	Hypotheses at all levels of the system and its component parts
	Adherence to rules and protocols			Quality and quantity of inputs, drivers, and outcomes
Who *measures . . .*	Leaders and managers	Leaders and managers	Professionals and expert practitioners	Everyone
. . . and **why.**	To assess compliance	To hold accountable	To gain and retain status in the profession/ craft	To learn, improve, and generate transparency and mutual accountability

Figure 6.4. Measurement Priorities in Evolutionary Learning

| Inputs | Actions | Outcomes | Impacts |

Align Measures to Inputs, Activities, and Outcomes, Measuring Service and Effect

Unlike in bureaucracy, managerialism, professionalism, and craft, measurement in Evolutionary Learning focuses on the entire causal chain, from inputs to activities to outcomes to impacts (as modeled in Figure 6.4). Thus, the first step in building a measurement framework is to develop a strategy for whichever part of the system is the focus (see Chapter 4 for guidance on strategy development).

With strategy in hand, learning hives then attach *process* and *outcome* measures to their strategy, employing measures already in use where they are valid and discontinuing those that are superfluous.

- Process measures provide "leading" or early indicators of progress toward expected outcomes and impact (Bryk et al., 2015). They are often attached to inputs or activities in strategy and make visible whether these efforts are carried out as planned. Importantly, learning hives use outputs not as an end unto themselves, but rather a process measure revealing whether activities were carried out as designed. In Mississippi, one process measure for efforts to improve teaching training was the time faculty spent teaching Science of Reading in higher ed preservice classrooms.
- Outcome measures provide "lagging" or later indicators of success and are measurable after some or all parts of strategy have been implemented (Bryk et al., 2015). They are often attached to the outcomes or impacts of strategy. In Mississippi, outcome measures include student scores on the Mississippi state reading assessment and on NAEP.

When measurement resources are scarce, hives focus on measures that are attached to strategy elements most critical to improvement and success, most linked to equity (or inequity), and that provide the strongest on- (or off-) track signals.

In designing measures for each part of the strategy or causal chain, hives use measures that:

- *Tightly align to strategy.* Even though most measures are to some degree proxies, the goal is to use measures that are as close to the strategy (processes and outcomes) as possible (Austin et al., 2021).
- *Aggregate and disaggregate to support strategic evolution and localized problem solving.* In learning hives, higher-level strategy is customized and enacted at the local level. In the same way that there should be alignment of *strategy* across all levels of the system, there should also be alignment of *measures*. In many cases, measures of higher-level system success (e.g., literacy proficiency rates) will be aggregates of finer-grained local measures. Higher levels of the system will disaggregate data as needed to problem-solve. In contrast, local levels will use disaggregated data (e.g., school, grade-, or classroom-level proficiency; proficiency by race/ethnicity) as a starting point in their monitoring and improvement routines.
- *Align across formal boundaries.* Measurement not only needs to be aligned from top to bottom, but also within and across traditional boundaries and divides (e.g., teams, divisions, schools, agencies) (Bryk et al., 2015). For example, in an effective multi-institution literacy improvement effort, as in Mississippi, each partner uses a shared set of process and outcome measures. State-level departments, districts, schools, and school support partners use a common set of metrics to track implementation and monitor student-level outcomes. This approach may seem self-evident, but it is common for teams, divisions, schools, and agencies in the same system to each develop unique metrics to measure the same services and outcomes, making comparison and learning challenging.
- *Embed in systems, processes, and routines.* Because actors in learning hives are constantly observing their work and that of the system to determine what's working, for whom, and under what conditions, measurement must be integrated into processes and routines to the greatest extent possible. This way, actors do not feel like they are doing two separate jobs: delivering services and measuring service delivery. Rather, measurement becomes part and parcel of service delivery when possible (Austin et al., 2021). For example, to measure team capacity, engagement, and implementation across

CARPE schools, the network's improvement coaches track answers to key assessment questions on a shared measurement document during coaching meetings.

>> Similarly, to measure staff engagement during a team meeting, a facilitator might routinely tally participation at the bottom of their facilitation agenda *during the meeting*. This routine gives the facilitator real-time feedback on engagement that doesn't require an extra measurement step (e.g., returning to meeting notes to tally after the meeting is concluded).

- *Reveal variation (a) in quality or quantity of implementation and results and (b) between expectations and what actually happened.* Employed measures need to be sufficiently sensitive to ensure they detect variability in service provision across contexts and actors and between hypothesized and actual performance (Austin et al., 2021).

Build Structures to Monitor the System as a Whole and as Parts

To ensure measurement serves as a unifying mechanism, leaders organize their hives to embed self-reinforcing measurement structures into broader learning structures, including networked, cross-functional, team-based configurations.

Measurement makes the interrelatedness of system actors and work more visible and more usable. Positional leaders neither operate as auditors who are spatially and temporally distanced from the site of the activity they are measuring, nor as enforcers, who use measurement solely to pass judgment. They use measurement to establish clear definitions of success for both outcomes and process, and to provide rapid alerts when there is a departure from these defined results so that the entire system can refine and generate new knowledge.

Strong alert systems allow anyone in the system to flag problems and opportunities for improvement—large and small—as they occur (Ansell, 2011; Sabel et al., 2011; Spear, 2009). Leaders structure these alarm mechanisms so that they are intuitive, embedded into practice, and consistent across the system.

The technicalities of alert processes look different in each system, but at the highest level, they begin with frequent, collaborative and often cross-functional learning spaces (e.g., huddles) that enable hive members to raise concerns and instances where measurement, including informal observation, reveals that the implementation of strategy is not producing expected results. In many cases, actors present in the learning space are equipped to adapt ground-level strategy and address the challenge immediately. Knowledge brokers tasked with keeping knowledge, support, and resources flowing from one part of the system to another efficiently funnel those "alarms," trigger problem solving, and share surfaced knowledge to those ultimately responsible for updating system strategy (e.g., the strategic planning team, school leaders, a network hub). In cases where additional support is needed, positional leaders mobilize higher-level action; for example, convening a temporary, cross-functional team to problem-solve. In small systems (e.g., a team, a small organization), these structures may be relatively informal. In larger organizations, positional leaders may need to develop processes to consolidate alerts and adaptations funneled from local sites. Whatever the process looks like, most critical is that all hive members are empowered to participate—and that leaders will listen when they do. With full participation, alert systems thwart persistent failure, allowing actors to detect deviations so that they may be addressed instead of perpetually tolerating deviations or generating workarounds.

Toyota's *andon* process, introduced briefly in Chapter 5, is a classic alert system. When a worker notices an issue on the Toyota production line, they activate the *andon* system, pulling a cord that alerts others to the problem and halts the line so it can be immediately addressed. Inspired by Toyota founder Sakichi Toyoda's mother and grandmother's work with hand-powered looms—where an unnoticed defect early in the process could ruin cloth outputs—*andon* means lantern, alluding to workers shining light on problems so they can be resolved and the process improved before they give rise to larger issues (Rother, 2009).

Alert systems have proved similarly successful in the education context, for example, in Finland (Sabel et al., 2011). Finnish students undergo diagnostic testing at the age of 2½ for emergent cognitive conditions that could impact their education. This early testing allows for problems to be flagged before students even enter the educational system, thus allowing their educational experience to be tailored to meet any needs they may have from the very start. By age 6 they have undergone a "rich battery of further tests," which allows teachers and schools to prepare classroom adaptations and support services (Sabel et al., 2011, p. 5). Once students are in school, teachers use low-stakes formative and diagnostic assessments to understand students' progress. When progress lags, teachers "pull the cord," huddling with educators, specialists, family members, and others to diagnose the challenge, develop and implement an intervention plan to support student learning, and monitor the results. Students come into and out of special education, with support plans in place when and for as long they are needed (Sabel et al., 2011). This cycle constitutes the Finnish special education approach, a dynamic, collaborative problem-solving system designed to flexibly meet students' needs—in many ways the opposite of the United States' highly legalized model.

Monitoring the system and its component parts also means monitoring the quality and effect of the hive's own leadership and management model. As with organizational strategy, positional leaders capture their leadership approach as an explicit hypothesis, and set expectations for, observe, and improve their method of designing, structuring, and supporting processes (see Chapter 7). As chief designers and managers of integrated processes, positional leaders rely on timely detection of challenges or flaws at every level of the system so that they might improve structures they put in place. Positional leaders acknowledge that departures from expectations in the system mark a flaw in their leadership and embrace deviations as opportunities to improve.

Focus on Quality

Learning hives recognize that quality of service delivery drives outcomes as much, if not more, than quantity of services. For that reason, they measure how well they work, in addition to how much work they do. Even more, they study and seek to understand and reduce variability in quality of service provision, especially given prevalent and persistent links between sociodemographic factors and service quality.

Measuring quality often requires establishing quality standards, in some cases for both process and outcomes. Done well, these standards are often broad, subjective, flexible, and user-centered (Braithwaite & Braithwaite, 1995; Noonan et al., 2009). They are close, if not exact, statements of how well services should be delivered and of the quality of outcomes sought, they often require engaging with those served to understand the extent to which they are achieved, and their meaning can be elaborated and applied in ways that are contextually relevant. Recall the use of standards in Australian nursing home regulation discussed earlier in this chapter, which set forth quality standards such as creating and maintaining a "homelike environment," enabling "residents to feel secure in their accommodation," and allowing "residents to participate in a wide range of activities appropriate to their interests and capacities" (Braithwaite & Braithwaite, 1995).

An example of this work in the education field comes from New Zealand, one of many systems that utilizes quality standards. Examples include broad, flexible questions such as "how well [schools use information], both formally and informally, to develop programs to meet the needs of individuals and groups of students" and "how well [schools use] available time for the learning purposes" (Ladd, 2010, p. 382).

Set Before-the-Fact Performance Expectations

To avoid hindsight bias, actors set performance expectations in advance (Roese & Vohs, 2012). These expectations capture what should be observed if the strategy is implemented and works as planned, and they set success at a level that increases equity. Detecting deviations between expectation and results triggers the alarm systems described above, allowing hives to respond to the constant influx of new insights generated every time measurement reveals performance gaps. They revise structures, teams, processes, and strategy in light of new learning.

Performance expectations (Austin et al., 2021):

- *Define success.* Expectations state what will be observed if the strategy works as planned.
- *Make equity visible.* Expectations make clear from the outset how strategy might be differentially delivered and received, as well as what variability in outcomes might result. Naming these expectations in advance can help hives set success at a level that increases equity and proactively prompts correction of processes or activities that might reproduce inequities.
- *Motivate action.* Expectations provide a vision of high-quality implementation and goal attainment, while being realistic in what they aim to achieve.
- *Clarify progress.* Expectations reveal whether implemented level or quality of strategy and outcomes is at, below, or above what you expect.

CULTURE AND MINDSETS

Even positional leaders with the most well-designed improvement-driven measurement processes recognize that structures alone are not sufficient for transforming their systems to sustain equity at scale. They acknowledge the need for a strong culture of measurement, one in which people share data freely, approach measurement with an excitement and openness to discovery, and are agile and facile data analysts. The benefits of being open and transparent far outweigh risks conventionally associated with data, measurement, learning, and accountability.

In such a culture, everyone sees and experiences measurement as valuable to their individual and collective goals, feels compelled to share favorable or unfavorable data, and uses measurement to further progress. At every turn positional leaders reinforce a revised definition of success—equity through the pursuit of "ever better"—and build into their systems a sense of collective responsibility to that chief goal, motivating system actors to recognize and interrogate their missteps and to support improvement even in areas in which they are less directly involved.

Demystify Measurement

To drive learning, hives coproduce a measurement system that links measurement across levels and nodes of the operation. Positional leaders—of the hive in its entirety or of component parts—identify the range of actors who need to be engaged to (1) design the measurement approach well, and (2) implement it effectively. They then coproduce the measurement system, ensuring tight linkages between strategy and measures, strong structures to monitor at the aggregate and disaggregated levels, sensitive measures of quality and quantity of work and outcomes, and routines for setting before-the-fact performance expectations. In the process, they make measurement practical, relevant, and participatory, readying actors throughout the organization to engage in measurement and the meaning-making and problem-solving that will be needed when actual performance inevitably deviates from what is expected.

Practice Collective Transparency

Hives foster a culture in which the tangible benefits of sharing data, positive or troubling, far outweigh the risks. This practice starts with foundational work to establish strong, collegial relationships and working norms about how to problem-solve together so that everyone understands the expectation and is ready to discuss the results of their work.

In addition to team building and norm-setting, hives set the foundation for collective transparency by collaboratively setting and explicitly naming shared learning goals. With these goals at the foundation, being open about data becomes easier and more meaningful. Together, hives make explicit what is to be learned through inquiry, how it is to be learned, and in what ways that learning will be distributed throughout the hive. They make clear that everyone has a part to play and that each individual's learning is connected to and depends on that of others. These learning goals link broader aims, showing how learning helps propel the entire hive forward.

In this environment, stigma and fear around data and measurement give way to curiosity and eagerness to tackle shared challenges. Unfavorable data catalyzes inquiry, analysis, and problem solving, not harsh judgment. Positional leaders model this vulnerability and openness by being transparent about and openly sharing measures and results related to their own leadership. Hives discuss results in transparent and straightforward terms, seeking system design flaws to solve rather than blaming individuals for experienced challenges. In so doing, they lessen the need to mask or anonymize the locations of system challenges and results and increase opportunity for collaborative problem solving across teams and other traditional boundaries.

Think Beyond Numbers

Hives design systems that seek out and value measures beyond the quantitative, building user-centered systems capable of capturing the experiences of hive members and those they influence. Hives construct direct communication channels between system actors closest to the ground-level implementation and those further removed so that all levels of the system have access to "street data" (Safir & Dugan, 2021). They value these insights as critical, recognizing that without them, collective understanding remains incomplete and hypotheses flawed. Because positional leaders know that understanding their system is key to transforming it, they think expansively, not narrowly, about the sources of understanding (Spear, 2009). They create space for the messy, the uncomfortable, the honest—conversations and testimonies that round out understandings about how the system is truly functioning. They structure teams to include those closest to implementation and impact, particularly when generating strategies or approaches.

When launching the CARPE College Access network, High Tech High network leaders knew a measurement-friendly culture would be crucial to sustained improvement. In bringing together dozens of schools—each with unique approaches to and systems for measurement—there was, of course, a significant technical hurdle to clear related to streamlining network-related measurement infrastructure. But the larger, more adaptive problem to solve was shifting how members thought and felt about the use of data.

The leadership team understood that *doing*—using real data to solve real problems—would be the quickest route to building capacity in and will for the work. In the first year of the network, looking for a quick win in service of a shared goal, the hub focused early improvement efforts on one primary driver: financial aid completion, a conceptually straightforward metric on which most schools had room for improvement. Leaders hypothesized that a "semi-magical move" would be helping schools start (1) accessing publicly available financial aid completion data and (2) using that data to explicitly target interventions to the students who needed the most support.

Leaders scaffolded that process by anchoring data reflection routines in a networkwide Google Data Studio page that collected and analyzed publicly available data on school and networkwide financial aid completion and displayed results in intuitive data visualizations. Updated weekly, the page provided members with an accurate and consistently refreshed dashboard to support improvement. Inspired by Don Berwick's concept of "lighting up the dots" (i.e., naming the often anonymous institutions and actors represented by "dots" in charts and graphs; Caillier, 2021), the hub made explicit which sites achieved which results. This openness helped normalize transparency—and failure—as key components of learning. Across the network's learning spaces, hub leaders helped members toggle between collective and site-level data, encouraging members to take ownership of both as their own and cultivating a view of the network as a collective.

Throughout this effort, leaders helped participants supplement quantitative outcome data with qualitative process and outcome data surfaced through daily, ground-level implementation (Safir & Dugan, 2021). Providing guidance and protocols for empathy interviews, shadowing exercises, and observations, coaches helped network members analyze these data alongside quantitative outcomes to understand what was working, for whom, and in what ways. Leaders modeled the use of qualitative data in their own work, using the frontline feedback from their interaction with teams during coaching and at convenings—the expression of feelings, observations of practice, and the like—to continuously improve their own efforts.

As CARPE's tireless attention on financial aid spurred demonstrable improvement, participants built positive associations with measurement. One principal noted:

> Getting into the data and getting into the trenches, and looking at the good, the bad, the ugly, the embarrassing, and creating a plan. . . . It just completely changes the way you move forward. . . . It's that true transformational adult learning . . . and you become a believer, like there really is another way to do it. It's not just the way we've been doing it for the last 125 years.

SUMMARY

In this chapter, we explored how hives use measurement as a driver of learning. Hives cocreate measurement systems and structures to ensure they are designed well and implemented effectively. They closely link strategy and measures, monitor both aggregated and disaggregated data, employ measures sensitive to the quality and quantity of implementation and outcomes, and construct routines to set performance expectations before implementing strategy. This tranforms the role of measurement, making it a practical and relevant element of daily improvement and enabling all hive members to participate in system-level innovation and change. Data, harvested purposefully, continuously, and collectively, enable the learning and innovation processes we discussed in Chapter 5.

STARTING THE SHIFT: REFLECT AND ACT

In this section, two activities will help you take stock of your existing measurement efforts and develop an actionable measurement framework.

1. Self-Assessment: Reflect on your current practice, taking stock of your system's current approach to measuring and monitoring strategy.
2. Develop a Measurement Plan: (a) Map your current measurement efforts to your strategy, (b) identify gaps, (c) develop measures to fill those gaps, and (d) plan data collection systems, routines, and tools.

Self-Assessment

To take stock of your current measurement practice, answer the following reflection questions alone, in 1:1 settings, or in larger groups. After documenting your current approach, consider how, when, and why you might evolve your measurement approach to make it more like those of learning hives.

- How does your system use measurement?
- How distributed are measurement practices and responsibilities? How might you restructure measurement so that it is integrated into everyone's daily work?
- What are the most core elements of your strategy? How do you measure them? What measures are prioritized? Do they also align with your core strategy?
- Have you set performance expectations for each measure?

- What alert systems (i.e., *andon* structures) exist in your system? Which alert systems work most reliably? Are there pockets where problems languish unaddressed? As a leader, how might you help set up more sensitive detection apparatuses?
- How widespread is your measurement approach?
- How have you set up measurement to monitor core parts of the system, including your own leadership approach?
- When and why do you measure both process and outcome? When and why do you not? Are there neglected leading indicators that would give you an early read on performance? What are they?
- How are you enabling others to access and make use of data? What obstacles to accessing data could you mitigate?
- Which of your data tools do not work for you or the system? In what ways might you simplify these tools or make them more accessible?

How do you make measurement more than a technical exercise and a part of your culture of discovery and improvement?

- What do you do to ensure you measure what matters most? How do you remind yourself and others of these key measures?
- Have you consistently involved key hive members in designing, implementing, and improving on your measurement system and approach?
- What are system actors' capacity and appetite for engaging in measurement? What capacity building structures have you put in place to support them?
- When and how do you look beyond qualitative data to understand your system? When and how do you collect qualitative data directly from people closest to the problems? How, if at all, have you intentionally included those who have historically been excluded from your system in discussions on measurement and strategy? What opportunities for deepening your understanding of your system and its effects have you missed?

Develop a Measurement Plan

A hive's measurement plan includes measures, tools, performance expectations, and systems for data collection and meaning making, all aligned to and in support of their strategy. Positional leaders might engage the following set of activities with a team to create their measurement system. Though the description of the activities focuses on a small set of in-person coproduction meetings, the number of meetings and the length and complexity of the development process itself will vary depending on a number of team and organizational factors, such as size and measurement capacity. You can use the templates shown as Tables 6.2 and 6.3 to work through your current measurement strategy and plan improvements.

1. Take Stock and Develop Measurement Improvement

Table 6.2 will guide you as you articulate and set measures for a system strategy.

1. Review existing measures and identify gaps.
    a. Identify measures you currently use.
        i. Individually, record measures in use, writing one measure per sticky note.
        ii. As a group, plot current measures in Column 2, placing each measure in the appropriate strategy row and quantitative (2a) or qualitative (2b) subcolumn.

Table 6.2. Measuring Strategy to Fuel Ongoing Learning and Improvement

1. What is our strategy?	2. What do we already measure to know if we implement our strategy as planned and get the anticipated results?		3. What measures might we use in the future to support more effective discovery and improvement?	
	a. Quantitative measures	b. Qualitative measures	a. Quantitative measures	b. Qualitative measures
[Insert Inputs]				
[Insert Actions]				
[Insert Outcomes]				
[Insert Impacts]				

   b. Prioritize measures that are helpful and deprioritize those that are not.
      i. Place a green, yellow, or red dot on each measure to indicate those that are:
         1. Green: Helpful in revealing the efficacy of the strategy and should be used moving forward
         2. Yellow: Somewhat helpful in revealing the efficacy of the strategy and should possibly be used moving forward
         3. Red: Not helpful in revealing the efficacy of the strategy and should be discontinued
      ii. As a group, review and come to tentative agreement on prioritization.
   c. Identify gaps where additional measures are needed.
2. Brainstorm new measures.
   a. Individually brainstorm additional measures to use, writing one measure per sticky note, focusing on identified gaps.
   b. As a group, plot new measures in Column 3 of Table 6.2, placing each measure in the appropriate strategy row and quantitative (3a) or qualitative (3b) subcolumn.
   c. Prioritize brainstormed measures that are helpful and deprioritize those that are not.
      i. Place a green, yellow, or red dot on each measure to indicate those that are:
         1. Green: Helpful in revealing the efficacy of the strategy and should be tested/used moving forward
         2. Yellow: Somewhat helpful in revealing the efficacy of the strategy and should possibly be tested/used moving forward
         3. Red: Not helpful in revealing the efficacy of the strategy and should not be tested/used at this time
   d. Review and come to tentative agreement on measures to try out.

2. Operationalize Measurement Improvements

1. Speak to other teams or organizations engaged in similar work to learn about their measurement approaches, with a particular focus on data collection systems, processes, and tools. Gather

feedback from those teams or organizations on the measures you are considering using.

2. Conduct desktop research about data collection systems, processes, and tools used in analogous work settings or strategy implementation. Use those findings and insights to update your list of draft measures.

3. Populate Table 6.3 with your strategy and draft measures.

4. Brainstorm data collection and analysis systems, routines, and tools.

   a. In small groups organized by strategy element, brainstorm ways of collecting and analyzing the data needed to assess progress on each measure. Discuss questions such as:

      i. What data will you collect?

      ii. How will you gain access to the data you want?

      iii. How will you collect the data? What tools are needed?

      iv. Who will collect the data?

      v. How will the data be shared?

      vi. Who and how will you analyze the data?

   b. In small groups, prioritize systems, routines, and tools for collecting data that embed within everyday work and service delivery.

   c. In small groups, update measures as needed to make data collection and analysis practical.

5. Reach tentative agreement on data collection systems, routines, and tools.

   a. Share ideas from each small group with the whole group, recording ideas on Table 6.3.

   b. Discuss and refine shared ideas.

Table 6.3. Putting Our Measures Into Action

What is our strategy?	What measures will we use to assess our strategy?	What data tools will help us collect and analyze data?	What data collection process will we use and on what timeline?
[Insert Inputs]			
[Insert Actions]			
[Insert Outcomes]			
[Insert Impacts]			

3. Iterate and Finalize

With Phase 2 complete, generate additional feedback on the measurement approach, prototype and test the measures, systems, routines, and tools, and update as needed. Apply the same learning methodology described in Chapter 5 to enhancing the measures used to drive strategy improvements.

CHAPTER 7

Leading the Hive Through Learning

VIGNETTE: NEW YORK CITY CONSORTIUM, INTERNATIONALS, AND OUTWARD BOUND HIGH SCHOOL DISTRICT

The schools in New York City's Consortium, Internationals, and Outward Bound Public High School District (CIOB) are diverse by many metrics—geography, student population, and programmatic focus—but united by a singular vision for learning. Walk into any of the district's 51 schools and a pedagogical throughline is clear. Students collaborate on inquiry-driven projects. Educators engage as codesigners and facilitators of experiential learning. Together they discover and explore within and beyond school walls, treating the city itself as the classroom. All activity evidences a deep belief in student agency, personalization, rigor, reflection, and growth.

This instructional model emerges from the district's learning hive. Over the last five years, Superintendent Alan Cheng and his team have used the community's commitment to experiential learning to reimagine district governance, building a system that collaboratively identifies and solves problems to innovate and improve—in short, a district-wide learning hive that mirrors the experimental, collaborative approach common across its classrooms.

Reflecting on traditional approaches to education governance and leadership during interviews with our team, Cheng notes:

> For a long time, district teams have been built primarily around supervision and accountability—and the innovation and change process is either overprescribed or left up to individual schools. "We'll hold you accountable, but how you get there is up to you."

Cheng's district rejects those more typical approaches, embracing instead coordinated, collaborative experimentation where problem-solving is an expectation and "a constant." As a result, the district has generated and spread a number of improvements. They have surfaced novel approaches to adolescent literacy assessment and support, developed student- and staff-designed AI tools that enable deeper learning and critical thinking, uncovered strategies for career exploration as early as 9th grade, and increased experiential learning opportunities and out-of-school internships. This attention to methodical, system-level improvement has netted stronger outcomes in a number of areas, including graduation rates: Cheng notes that despite serving a diverse group of students, many with specialized needs, the CIOB district has seen tremendous improvement in graduation rates, from 76% in 2019 to 90% in 2023—14 percentage points higher than when Cheng assumed the superintendency and 6 percentage points higher than the citywide average.

These successes result from the district's use of experimentalist governance. Its hive effectuates its vision using (1) an inquiry-based improvement methodology; (2) routines for generating, capturing, sharing, and applying new learning; (3) formative and summative measurement routines; and (4) a dynamic network of learning spaces and teams, including problem-focused learning pods, sustained principal–coach pairings, "critical friend" affinity groups, and school-based improvement teams.

Much of the magic rests with leaders, who act as learners-in-chief. Rather than positioning themselves as know-all, do-all directors—a perspective likely to ruffle feathers in a district that is, by design, full of independent school leaders, teachers, staff, and students—Cheng and his team see their role as animating a learning community capable of discovering how to best serve students. Of this stance and his perspective on good leadership, Cheng notes:

> I think leadership at its very best sometimes can be invisible. A big part of being a leader is to be able to create a particular organizational culture, a sense of belonging, and a sense of belief that we all can make a really big impact in our work—and that it is less about a particular followership and following along the lines of one great person, but is really about the community that a leader is able to create to learn together and grow together.

Having risen to leadership by way of instructional and school leadership roles in the district, Cheng and his team hold themselves accountable to personal and professional improvement. They are humble and have confidence in the capacity of their community, using trusting relationships to seek constant input and feedback. They enact in their own practice principles evident in classrooms across the district, including commitments to big-picture thinking, measured risk-taking, deliberate action, and learning through doing. The district's leaders celebrate when the hive's efforts pay off and are transparent about when their own and the collective's work has fallen short, serving as facilitators, navigators, and "cheerleaders" of learning.

Community members recognize that leadership that powers collective improvement sets the district apart. Melissa De Leon, a CIOB principal, captures this sentiment:

> We are encouraged to gather and grapple with divergent thinking so that we can learn from each other and make positive changes in our school communities. Our district is organized to promote this type of learning, to stretch us into uncomfortable spaces. And this is something that is modeled at all of the levels of the district. The district staff are intensely collaborative. They set up multiple opportunities for us to engage, think about new problems of practice, share our struggles. They model the vulnerability of learning in this very complex role.
>
> Ultimately . . . I feel that I am respected, that I'm treated as an intellectual and a designer and someone capable of continuing to grow and develop. . . . The value of learning as a district community is that it's a reminder that we don't operate in a vacuum. It's not just me and my school and my neighborhood and our students and our families and our teachers. We are part of a larger system. And even though every school has a very unique context, we are actually moving as a unit towards specific goals.

Throughout this book, we've explored how EL systems structure hives, systematize learning, and measure practice to pursue "ever better." As Cheng and his team demonstrate, learning hives require learning leaders who influence the system above, below, and surrounding them for the better and who set the pace for the collective, pushing the group toward transformational, not merely incremental, change (Spear, 2009). By setting their sights both on the day-to-day and beyond, prioritizing learning, and recognizing the limits of their own knowledge, these leaders enable the type of continual innovation, discovery, and change that EL demands.

In this chapter, we'll explore what hive leadership looks like—and how you can start leading through learning.

LEADERSHIP IN PREDOMINANT GOVERNANCE MODELS

Governance doesn't emerge from thin air. Positional leaders decide on, usher in, and sustain these models. If governance forms the logic of systems, leaders form the heart; they embody and bring to life the system's values and priorities (Yohn, 2021). By facilitating the manner, method, and culture of operations, leaders influence how people work and what it feels like to be a part of a system. It will come as no surprise, then, that who is considered a leader, what their role entails, and the norms and values they embody are substantially different across each governance model.

Leaders in Bureaucracy Are Expert Rule Creators and Enforcers

Bureaucratic leaders are expert rule creators and enforcers. Their enforcement power comes from their role atop the system's hierarchy (Kocka, 1981). Meticulous in documenting processes, communications, and policies, they dedicate their time to mastering and demonstrating compliance with rules and ensuring others do the same. Bureaucratic leaders set up myriad structures to help maintain stability, order, and compliance (Liebman et al., 2017). Specialized departments ensure singularity of focus and, by some measures, efficiency (Volti, 2011). Bureaucratic leaders don't foster culture so much as they prescribe it. For example, because hierarchies are documented, they are respected. Formal titles and roles determine the existence and nature of relationships (Volti, 2011). Looming over all interactions is a consciousness of where one sits in relation to power. This consciousness can fuel a desire to please and breed a culture of compulsory deference, silence in the face of mistakes, and fear of being found noncompliant (Liebman et al., 2017; Lipsky, 2010). Bureaucratic leaders prioritize stability in a manner that ultimately discourages change, making it unappealing for others to take risks, innovate, or think critically.

Leaders in Managerialism Are Performance-Driven Strivers

In managerialism, high-stakes, outcomes-focused targets are a primary motivator of improvement and success. Managers act as performance-driven strivers, committed to achieving those centrally identified targets, in some cases, by any means (Aviv, 2014). Their authority derives from their appointed position in the system's hierarchy, which gives them the responsibility and leeway to shift system design, practice, and staffing as necessary (Coglianese & Lazer, 2003).

Managers focus on motivating others to reach targets (Hoopee, 2003). Given latitude to act in accordance with the needs of their contexts so long as they meet specific metrics, managers track and spur individual and group performance (Williamson, 1963). For example, periodic reviews give managers insight into progress toward goals and allow them to intervene with low performers or reward those on track. Public data review meetings—focused on accountability, rather than learning—publicly spotlight those who are doing well while putting on notice those not making expected gains.

Managers foster a culture focused on success above all else, often relying on tenets of pacesetting leadership, modeling in their own practice urgency, intensity, and exceptional performance (Goleman, 2017). In the best cases, this can bring about a shared sense of mission and generate a culture of dogged determination, sharp focus, and creative problem-solving. In the worst cases, the drive for self-preservation may instead take precedence, leading to more controlling, stifling, impersonal tactics like micromanagement, punitive measures, and prioritization of goals over people. This approach to leadership has a tendency to "destroy climate" (Goleman, 2017, p. 36), causing acute stress and overwhelm as staff scramble to accomplish high-stakes targets with little guidance on the individually developed, often tacit strategy to reach them. Without a focus on the process or strategy to reach goals, managers are limited in their ability to coordinate learning across the organization, sparking individualistic competition and desperation to meet targets at any cost.

Leaders in Professionalism and Craft Are Models and Mentors

In professionalism and craft, practitioner expertise and mastery are paramount (Mehta, 2013; Sennett, 2008). Expert practitioners and masters of craft comprise the leadership class and serve as models and mentors. Their authority derives from their membership in the guild, their ability to set the standards by which others are judged, and the power to permit or deny others' entry into the group.

Leaders in professionalism and craft spend their time defining expertise, training others, granting credentials to those who display sufficient mastery, and propagating norms and standards to guide members in their practice (Mehta, 2013; Sennett, 2008). They foster an individualistic culture in which, once admitted, in-group members create their own definition of success and are granted autonomy to determine when they've met the mark. Through their exclusivity about who is "in" and "out," leaders also foster an insular culture, advising members to only trust, follow, and believe in fellow members and to regard outsiders with skepticism.

LEADERSHIP IN THE EL HIVE

If successful leadership in bureaucracy is defined by the maintenance of order and stability through the enforcement of rules, managerialism by the optimization of performance through a relentless focus on high-stakes targets, and craft and professionalism by the development of elite judgment and skill that assures service excellence, EL leadership is defined by something quite different: the orchestration of continuous innovation and improvement through coordinated, participatory problem-solving.

Widespread problem-solving, combined with the tenet that all have and can create and apply knowledge, changes who leads. Whereas in other models, the answer is few, in EL, the answer is all. Leadership in bureaucracy, managerialism, and craft sits neatly with central directors, managers, and professionals. As in real world bee colonies (Seeley, 2011), in EL hives, decision-making authority is distributed across a constellation of empowered actors at various layers of the system, each with their own role to play in advancing organizational change through their daily work and learning (Ansell, 2011; Anyon, 1980; Eckstein, in Allison, 1984).

Still, a group of actors—called positional leaders throughout this book—hold special responsibility for their system's progress toward its shared vision. They motivate innovation, enable democracy, and coordinate ongoing learning. This conception of leadership differentiates EL from both bottom-up and top-down governance models. While local actors retain local discretion and contribute to system-level improvement, a central positional leader (or leaders) has the ultimate responsibility for guiding and advancing system improvement (Ansell, 2011).

In this world, where "learning is the work" (Fullan, 2020, p. 70), even an expert leader's core responsibility is to learn how to lead, striving for ever better approaches to modeling, motivating, incentivizing, coordinating, scaffolding, and clearing the path for innovation, collaboration, and learning. Expert leaders are "stewards of the whole, rather than owners of the parts" (Gerzon, 2006, p. 6), who, holding an understanding of the connections between the work playing out across the full system, organize collective progress toward system goals (Senge et al., 2015).

This adaptive work demands adaptive leaders capable of harnessing—and at times, inciting—disequilibrium to disrupt system dysfunction, while simultaneously providing the steady support hive members need to navigate change. Leaders help the system balance (1) big, creative thinking with methodical improvement, (2) democratic deliberation with urgency, and (3) the alignment necessary for collective learning with the autonomy needed to address local needs.

Across all tasks, leaders take on four key roles. Leaders are:

- *cultivators* who nurture a learning-driven, democratic culture,
- *capacity-builders* who help others acquire the skills and dispositions needed for collaborative problem-solving and cocreation,

- *strategic coordinators* who orchestrate learning and determine when and where participatory processes are most vital to make progress, and
- *architects* who monitor and adapt system structure to enable stronger innovation, learning, and collaboration.

Hive Leaders as Cultivators of Culture

Hives rely on a culture grounded in norms of democratic participation and agential learning and innovation. Leaders live out organizational values through their own actions and set conditions for others to do the same. Rejecting the faulty model of hero leader, leaders empower those they lead to experiment, generate knowledge, and make decisions while building the psychological safety necessary for experimentation, failure, and reflective improvement.

Democratic Culture. To foster a collaborative culture, EL leaders develop competencies discussed in the literature on democratic, participative, and distributed leadership (Khan et al., 2023; Lewin, in Gold, 1999; Likert, 1961; Spillane, 2005; Wang et al., 2022), including a commitment to cocreation, collectivism and mutual support, shared authority and transparency in decision-making, and collective responsibility for progress toward codeveloped goals and standards. The objectives and structures of EL institutionalize and reinforce these behaviors, sustaining them even as leaders transition in and out of the organization.

Leaders shift the balance of power from "power over" to "power with" (Weber, 1993). In the "power over" model, leaders constrain member action; in "power with," leaders distribute decision-making authority and equip hive members to act as agents of improvement who identify, raise, and respond to issues in the system when and where they occur (Follett, 2013/1940; Schimpf et al., 2024).

Of this mindset, Ansell et al. (2024) write:

Fighting the temptation to focus on how to dominate others ("power over") or how to go it alone ("power to") and instead focus on what you can do together as a group of interdependent actors ("power with") presupposes self-efficacy as well as solidarity and the will to move past anger and resistance to nurture hope and transformation. (p.161)

Leaders help their hives embrace "power with" and experience improvement as a necessarily community-driven endeavor, "locating power neither in the hierarchical system nor in empowered individuals, but in the collaborative interaction between relevant and affected actors who aim to solve specific problems based on curiosity, imagination, and experiential learning" (Ansell et al., 2024, p. 161). Superintendent Cheng describes his role in enabling district-wide collaborative improvement work:

> As a district leader, my job is to bring people together and to make sure that we all understand that we're working towards the same purpose and, at the same time, make sure that we are developing the sense of collective ownership and collective efficacy in our work. That means that as an individual principal or an individual teacher, you know that the work that you're doing can make a big difference not only for the students that you're working with, but on behalf of this bigger organization.

To enact this collectivist perspective, leaders verbalize the importance of collective efficacy, toggle between local and system-level data to develop a shared view on progress, and celebrate the emergent outputs of collaborative processes. In efforts to improve their own work, leaders treat each member of the hive as an intellectual equal, seeking out and incorporating feedback into system design and decision-making. In generative spaces, leaders engage as codesigners. They leave room for others to facilitate and participate, ask questions in addition to offering solutions, and contribute knowledge and perspective when relevant, while encouraging dissent and remaining open to having their mind changed (White & Lippitt, 1960). Of enacting this stance in his own practice, Derek Mitchell, Partners in School Innovation's CEO, says:

> It means kind of checking myself and . . . expressing things in a way that lets folks know that if they don't think this is true—challenge it, raise the question! If you were in any meeting at Partners, where I'm facilitating something or demonstrating something or offering some ideas, you're likely to find dissonance. And I'll see it in their faces, and I'll go, "It seems like what I'm saying isn't really jiving with you." And that opens the door.

Physical signaling is powerful, so leaders avoid unnecessarily separating themselves from the group by standing at a podium or sitting at the head of a conference table. Before meetings or interactions with hive members, leaders set intentions for how they will show up and, afterward, seek feedback from participants, reflecting on whether they met their goals, setting explicit improvement targets when they fall short (Aguilar, 2016).

Innovation and Learning Culture. In complex systems, uncertainty and change are constants. To provide effective service, the organization must continuously adapt in large and small ways. But change can be challenging for humans, who, by nature, seek stability and order (Billman, 2020). Positional leaders help the hive harness uncertainty in service of transformative learning by cultivating a problem-solving culture where members respond to ambiguity with curiosity, rather than fear and avoidance. Of this style of learning leadership, Derek Mitchell says:

> Leaders are most powerful when there is uncertainty, when there's no clarity about which the right choices are going to be. They have to own the work of helping folks come to a place where they're going to move forward together—and then own if that movement doesn't get them where they need to go. . . .
>
> And that means embedding into the work times to reflect, to step back and say, "Hey, how did that go? What did you think?" . . . We commit to learning together . . . in community with other people. So sure, we can read things, we can try things on our own, but it's when we have to explain them to other people and, and talk about them in their robust complexities, and problem solve in collaboration with others that the learning becomes much more rich, much more powerful.

At first, this type of leadership can feel jarring, especially for those accustomed to command and control direction. Leaders, too, must reconceptualize their own role, and release "the grip they hold on being seen as knowing" (Nicolaides & Poell, 2020, p. 269).

To this end, leaders cultivate a culture where reflexivity, curiosity, and intrinsic motivation to learn are the norm. This work starts with leaders who embody many of the behaviors associated with constructivist leadership (Lambert, 2002; Lambert, 2009; Walker, 2002), an approach wherein leaders see the process of learning and knowledge development as inherently collaborative. In complex systems, this is a practical choice as much as it is a values-driven one; in contexts of uncertainty, leaders cannot simply direct members toward predetermined solutions because neat fixes do not exist.

This work depends on psychological safety (Edmondson, 1999) that encourages a constitutional curiosity, prompting members to routinely reflect on their own practice and critique organizational common sense, challenging "the way things are done" when it does not serve progress toward a shared strategic vision (Ansell, 2011). As part of their daily practice, members ask, "How can we do better today than we did yesterday?"

In answering this question, members operate from a "we, not they" perspective; they challenge themselves to look inward before assigning blame to others, prioritizing their own role in improving results (Wood, 2022). This practice is motivated by a feeling of cumulative responsibility—a sense of ownership of not just one's own practice, progress, successes, and failures, but of the organization's as well. In a mature hive, nothing is "somebody else's problem" because success is everyone's charge, and the consequences for inaction reverberate far beyond the immediate moment.

Cultivating curiosity and reflexivity can be challenging in education systems, where hierarchical supervision structures and punitive accountability policies have historically discouraged transparency about challenges. To remake these mindsets, leaders first radically redefine what it means to succeed. Rather than relying on traditional definitions of success, like performance (tied to lagging outcomes and compliance with preset rules), learning leaders measure success by a new metric: individual and collective progress toward goals. The system and individuals seek improvement even when high standards are met. Highfliers become those who learn quickly, customize well, and support others in doing the same.

Hive leaders create conditions where it is safe to learn, which can incentivize members to take risks and experiment with changes that move beyond the status quo (Nicolaides & Poell, 2020; Rowe & Boyle, 2005). Leaders frame failure in a new way, positioning it as an expected outcome of innovative work in complex contexts. Leaders take reports of failure seriously but praise messengers and, in most cases, avoid assigning blame, instead working with members to understand why failure occurred and how to redesign processes to ensure it does not persist (Edmondson, 2011; Spear, 2009). In collaborative problem-solving spaces, positional leaders demonstrate systems thinking, framing mistakes as evidence of faulty system design and complex conditions, rather than as poor decision-making by bad actors (Weick et al., 2005). As impotent finger-pointing gives way to productive interrogation of process, hive members are not only more comfortable admitting errors and flagging challenges, but are also more likely to accurately diagnose the systemic roots of these issues and make sense of their own role in solving them. As this work progresses, leaders celebrate and reward staff for taking measured risks during experimentation—as long as failures spur learning.

Superintendent Alan Cheng notes that, in his district, this work is about "principals learning that it's perfectly okay—and in fact highly encouraged—to say 'I know even less than you about this, and we can learn together.'" Cheng and his team encourage members to grow more comfortable digging into learning with others:

Even in principal observations or reviews, we ask them, "Come to this meeting, reflect ahead of time—what's the thing you're struggling *the most* in. *That's* what we're going to focus on. Don't feel like you have to come in here and share all the great things that are going on—there are other pipelines for that. Instead, identify the thing you're struggling with so we can work on improving.

Reflexivity—and failure—is further normalized as positional leaders apply the improvement standards they expect others to use to their own work. They constantly test and improve their practice to achieve desired results, and share their process, successes, and failures with their hive. When community members report challenges, leaders look to their own practice, asking, "What is preventing staff from working according to standards?" (Rother, 2009). Living out this approach requires positional leaders to exhibit authenticity, humility, vulnerability, a constant willingness to learn, and an openness about when and how they have fallen short and where they do not have answers. Anna Zucker, a principal coach coordinator in the CIOB district, reflects on this stance: "I try to be really open about my own learning process and what I don't know . . . I think we all do that. I think Alan does that. And I think that's a big part of the culture of our district."

Through participation, agency, and distributed decision-making, hive leaders support innovation and knowledge generation (Brown et al., 2020; Çoban & Atasoy, 2020; O'Shea, 2021), promote stronger trust in the organization and leaders (Miao et al., 2014; San Antonio, 2008), increase intrinsic motivation to pursue improvement (Fullan, 1994; Somech, 2010), and cultivate a sense of ownership of organizational work at each layer of the hive. In this way, positional leaders cultivate a change-oriented organizational citizenry who consistently contribute to system improvement through their day-to-day work (Bateman & Organ, 1983; Choi, 2007; Podsakoff et al., 2000; Sagnak, 2016).

Hive Leaders as Capacity Builders

Ultimately, a hive leader's goal is to build capacity across their system for independent, collaborative, inquiry-based learning, a task which Fullan (2020) describes as "develop[ing] others to the point that you become dispensable" (p. 60). Chris Thorn, Chief of Partnerships and Strategy at Partners in School Innovation, says of the capacity-building process, "It is an explicit distribution of the most powerful thing you can do in school transformation, which is both give power to and hold accountable adults in the system for their own learning."

The collaborative learning behaviors that enable shared leadership and participation are learned skills. Perhaps unsurprisingly, a preferred method of development in hives is practice through frequent, cross-functional collaboration across various lines of difference and independently driven inquiry to solve emergent challenges.

Building Capacity for Democratic Collaboration. Productive collaborative work and creative interchange does not happen organically, at least initially. Hive leaders "lead through conflict," building members' capacity to "[face] differences honestly and creatively" by establishing routines and ways of working that help mediate and disrupt the hierarchical, adversarial, and competitive stances that derail collaboration (Gerzon, 2006, p. 4).

Orienting collaboration around problems of practice is a useful starting point, as a focus on concrete issues anchors ongoing dialogue to areas of collective uncertainty, shifting actors away from the circular engagement so common in adversarial contexts characterized by rote reiteration and "defense of specific values and positions" (Ansell, 2011). Within these spaces, leaders first support the development of living norms. To ensure norms act as a true foundation for collaborative exchange—avoiding the common situation where norm-creation is treated as a perfunctory exercise—leaders prompt members to get specific about what norms mean and how they show up in practice, keep them visible at each touchpoint, hold the group accountable to following them, and facilitate regular check-in and revision processes (Aguilar, 2016). Rigorously applied agendas and protocols further scaffold discussion and promote voice equity.

In these processes, leaders do not shy away from the conflict natural to collaboration across lines of difference, and, in fact, push participants to practice bringing it into the open. Leaders build hive members' tolerance and skills for navigating the disequilibrium and discomfort of conflict so they can engage in and harness it in service of integrative problem formulations and solutions (Follett, 2013/1940). Through practice, leaders build members' capacity to manage complexity, engage in systems thinking, remain engaged during conflicts, use questioning to understand others' perspectives, engage in conscious conversation and dialogue, and bridge differences—all in service of emergent improvement and innovation (Gerzon, 2006). Leaders monitor, interrupt, and redirect inequitable patterns of exchange, including by drawing in underrepresented voices. They model and provide explicit guidance on how to move from merely "hearing" other's perspectives, to listening skillfully with an open mind (Bartels, 2018; Stivers, 2001), including by providing targeted feedback and coaching those who are not respecting the group's norms. Most of all, leaders think about each interaction as a "round of collaboration" that can be layered atop others to build stronger relationships and participative practice over time (Ansell, 2011, p. 175).

Building Capacity for Innovation and Learning. Sabel and Victor (2022) write that "the only way to move beyond the status quo is to destabilize it, and then learn, quickly, to use the daring and imagination that bubble up in the open space to develop better approaches" (p. 9). Moving to productive solutions from instability is challenging—and uncomfortable—for many. Hive leaders must develop member capacity to inhabit and grow in this space, building skills for problem-solving in much the same way that effective teachers support learning in PK–12 classrooms: by making the processes of and tools to support learning explicit and helping members practice using them.

Effective hive leaders avoid heavy investment in frontloaded training in the organization's learning methodology through sit-and-get professional development or asynchronous learning modules. Instead, they move quickly to in-context application. The problem-solving methodology, routines, and tools discussed in Chapter 5 support learning not because they demand learners neatly follow a set of prescribed rules, but because they help engrain as second nature a problem-solving stance in situations of uncertainty.

As members negotiate real-world inquiry, leaders act as problem-solving mentors (Rother, 2009). They help calibrate the problem space, finding a "sweet spot" in which members encounter complexity but where frustration does not overtake motivation to continue (Kapur & Bielaczyc, 2012). To this end, leaders often work with members to break apart complex problems and sequence tasks appropriately. Recall that CARPE network leaders initiated the network's college access work with FAFSA completion, a challenging but conceptually straightforward problem that allowed members to jump into improvement immediately and focus on practicing the inquiry cycle. Over time, as members grew more proficient with the problem-solving approach, the network moved on to more complex issues like increasing students' sense of collegiate belonging.

As members practice, leaders arm members with available research and information, but avoid advancing a predetermined solution and instead guide members through the "how" of the learning process so they can develop and test sensible hypotheses. For the hive leader, questions like "What do you plan to do?", "What could be a next step?", "How do you know?", and often simply, "Why?" (Rother, 2009, p. 190) are the cornerstone of capacity building, helping guide participants to their own conclusions. In fact, the strength of solutions that learners generate is a critical measure of the quality of learning processes, data that leaders can use to improve and tailor support.

Uncertainty and ambiguity throughout this process, while often uncomfortable for those involved, is a necessary component of personal and organizational growth, maturation, and learning. Of this tension, Murdoch et al. (2020) write:

> This struggle is characterized by the fact that even though one may know that the old ideas and ways of acting no longer suffice, one has not yet found a new way forward; that is, one is struggling to make sense of the difference between old and new. Indeed, in these moments of struggle, one finds oneself in a grey area between knowledge and ignorance, ability and inability, where one asks oneself, "What do I know? What should I do?," and "How can I move on?" Nevertheless, one has not stopped learning; rather, one inhabits an "in-between realm of learning." In this in-between realm, we can describe the activity of the learner as one of being engaged in a quest to understand the discontinuities in his or her experience of the world. (pp. 662–663)

Making progress in this "in-between realm" can be challenging because it requires learners to face up to their own role in organizational challenges and where their existing knowledge falls short. In this space, untrained learners often resort to defensive reasoning, coming up with excuses and evasions that allow them to avoid blame for mistakes and the embarrassment of not knowing (Argyris, 2008). Hive leaders help members learn to navigate this natural instinct and redirect it toward more productive patterns. This begins with rigorous coaching during the learning process. Leaders are honest about where they see issues with how learners are working through problems, avoiding the instinct to "benevolent[ly]" protect them from guilt and shame by failing to raise concerns (Argyris, 1994, p. 81). When hive leaders see faulty practice, they name it, emphasizing the learning process as much as its outcomes. Critically, leaders are equally open to feedback about their own thinking and mentorship, modeling reflexivity and building trust in their approach to facilitation.

Throughout this process, leaders help members surface and make explicit their feelings about learning, guiding progress through the natural discomfort that emerges when the limits of knowledge are reached (Dewey, 1916/2024). By naming and helping members make sense of this experience, leaders prepare them to more independently navigate future learning. This agential approach, wherein learners shape and are shaped by problems and inquiry, is critical to the cultivation of independent, critical thinkers who can challenge the norms of the status quo.

Superintendent Alan Cheng and his team have applied this method to help CIOB district members build muscle for collaborative learning. In an effort to more strongly network district learning efforts, the district leadership team has developed a user-friendly learning methodology informed heavily by continuous improvement. Given schools' inquiry-driven pedagogical practice, the approach is in some ways intuitive but has also required members to apply to learning a more methodical and collaborative technique than they have used in the past. Rather than frontloading training on improvement concepts and tools, district leaders have redesigned existing learning spaces to allow principals to build collaborative improvement capacity primarily through doing.

Repurposing a citywide mandate for the creation of strategic plans as a learning tool, district leaders supported principals in developing year-long learning arcs that prompted principals to ask, in a structured fashion, "What do I need to know as a principal to support better instruction and practice at my school?" Two structures—collaborative professional learning pods and, in some schools, principal coaching—have allowed principals to practice using various improvement tools to test and improve these plans, as well as to contribute to improvement in district practice around key priorities. Of this effort, Deputy Superintendent Tom Rochowicz notes, "It's two initiatives, both trying to build the same capacity around two key questions: How's it going? And how do you know?" In these spaces, the district leadership team has introduced and helped principals practice each step of the learning process in turn (e.g., problem identification, root cause analysis, inquiry cycles) as they tackle challenges related to attendance, literacy, and out-of-school time learning. The capacity building process has been its own feedback loop: As school leaders experiment with the learning methodology and tools, district leaders have observed their own ability to lead learning, adapting their methodology, tools, facilitation, and support in response to feedback.

Hive Leaders as Strategic Coordinators

While all hive members contribute to system improvement in their own domain of influence, positional leaders hold special responsibility for ensuring the system as a whole is progressing toward its vision, goals, and learning priorities. Part of that role is developing with members an organizational plan for learning, orchestrating people and efforts across the system, and drawing out and weaving together emerging insight to advance toward shared goals. In this way, positional leadership teams are like command centers (McCannon & Margiotta, 2015), tasked with coordinating the complex web of learning across the hive.

Coordinating Democratic Participation. Hives practice democracy (Ansell, 2011; Bachtiger et al., 2018; Woods, 2005) in that each member plays a meaningful role in problem-solving, the generation of new knowledge, and the cocreation of strategy and practice. Participation occurs in many ways, including through joint experimentation, daily adaptation of strategy, and robust feedback loops between layers of the system. Moving beyond the symbolic participation so often practiced in bureaucracies (Souza & Neto, 2018), democracy serves a practical purpose: activating the rich expertise and resources distributed across each layer of the organization in service of collective improvement. Yet, in practice, a tension exists, because even as hives embed democratic processes in their work, they must also be agile in their response to ever-changing conditions—a characteristic not often associated with the deliberate pace of participatory processes. This site of tension is where EL shines. Hives effectively mobilize collective know-how in service of transformative change precisely because they retain a strong role for central leadership, even as the functional responsibilities of those leaders change. No longer expected to provide all the answers to organizational challenges, leaders become participation strategists, using their system-level perspective to orchestrate, foster, engage, and guide the hive through complex democratic learning and change processes (Jing et al., 2017).

Leaders help coordinate participation by being strategic about when and where it is necessary to advance collective progress toward goals; in hives, problems abound, and time is a precious resource. Thinking backward from the application of new knowledge, they assess the locus of problems and the implications that participation has on the uptake of solutions. As they identify and tap members, leaders are as thoughtful about the politics of participation as they are about drawing in specialized and experiential expertise, considering when and how the exclusion of particular groups and perspectives might sow distrust—and where inclusion might spur ownership and stronger uptake of solutions. As problem-solving and cocreation progress, leaders support nimble adaptation of the membership of problem-solving groups to bring in fresh perspectives at different stages of the work as understandings of problems and potential solutions evolve (Ansell et al., 2024). At times, this requires drawing in partners from beyond the formal boundaries of the system who can support efforts to tackle the roots of challenges that extend beyond the immediate purview of a single department or organization. Mississippi's success in literacy relied on leaders who built a bigger hive—looking far beyond their immediate organizations and the walls of PK–12 classrooms to work alongside, for instance, state legislators and institutions of higher education to retrain faculty, refresh teaching training programs, and develop new preservice exam requirements.

Leaders may opt to participate more or less actively in various cocreation and problem-solving spaces but remain a consistent motivating presence, ensuring that deliberation processes do not stagnate in attempts to reach consensus or craft perfect strategy. Leaders consistently emphasize the iterative nature of decision-making in hives, and at times, help make tough calls when problem-solving is stalled. Throughout this work, leaders ensure that processes remain transparent and open to feedback from the larger system.

Coordinating Innovation and Learning. To make the most of learning constantly emerging from local efforts, leaders maintain a system-level view of learning efforts across the hive. As ground-level staff drive learning processes aligned to shared system-level theory and aims, leaders:

- promote the hive's shared vision and ensure continued alignment between local learning and system level learning priorities;
- explicitly map and monitor learning efforts, using both regular touchpoints with members and measurement systems to track progress and bright spots;
- connect members working on similar issues, formally or informally linking parallel learning happening across the system to accelerate improvement;
- work with teams to resolve barriers to learning,
- help hive members determine when learning is "good enough" and support movement to new challenges, and
- shift system-level strategy and priorities in response to new learning.

This coordination work happens constantly *as learning occurs,* not merely at prescribed, infrequent step-backs (e.g., annual reviews). Hive leaders are able to do this because they build real-time feedback loops, in part by toggling between a command center view and deep engagement on the ground (Heifetz, 1994), including through structures like membership on cross-functional problem solving teams, formal and informal coaching relationships, and regular site walk-throughs. It is this purposeful balance between maintaining a strategic and operational focus that allows leaders to coordinate meaningful system-level improvement.

Hive Leaders as Architects

As the primary designers of participatory learning structures—including the system's knowledge management infrastructure, communication pipelines, measurement and alert systems, and learning and problem-solving spaces—leaders hold a special responsibility for assessing, maintaining, and improving these structures. To do so, they apply the same EL principles and learning methodology used to improve strategy and practice across the organization: Build a clear vision of the outcomes of an optimally functioning system and the theory that can get you there; actively measure the implementation of this hypothesis, and track where expectations are diverging from results; and engage in collaborative problem-solving when expected results are not achieved.

Democratic Participation Structures. As they seek to improve system structures, leaders attend particularly to the quality of democratic structures, assessing, for example, the breadth and depth of participation, the degree to which each constituency has real decisional capital, and process transparency. When issues become clear, hive leaders use EL to understand the roots of those challenges and test changes in real time. They do not hew to the status quo and instead use the inherent dynamism of the hive's organizational schema to adjust teaming structures and membership to tackle new dimensions of each challenge.

In the High Tech High CARPE network, for example, positional leaders flagged robust, authentic student participation as a missing element of their efforts to engage those closest to the work in knowledge generation, analysis, and decision-making. "The adults were doing really great work," network leader Sofía Tannenhaus notes, "but we were also realizing we need to talk to those that we're seeking to serve because there's a lot of *doing for* and we were wanting to do more *improving with*." In collaboration with a handful of network schools, CARPE piloted a student fellowship program that ran parallel to the network's adult improvement efforts. Throughout the year, the high school fellows met monthly to conceive of and execute a project addressing a challenge felt acutely across their school contexts: inadequate early access to information about the college application process before senior year. The fellowship was successful: Students surfaced and implemented new ideas that influenced network practice, including a a well attended, youth led college access workshop for middle and high school peers.

This first attempt at working with students helped CARPE's leaders understand how they could more robustly and authentically integrate young people into the network, moving beyond important but limited touchpoints like empathy interviews. In response, they fundamentally altered network team membership, asking all school improvement teams to include students as full members. As students had to balance participation in the network with the academic demands of high school, network leaders were thoughtful about when and where participation was most critical, and identified the learning meetings, convening sessions, and coaching calls students should attend. They adapted improvement protocols to promote voice equity and monitored implementation to ensure that students were not tokenized or sidelined in those conversations.

Student membership strengthened the network's performance. Students contributed ideas for innovations and flagged foundational issues with proposed interventions even before they were implemented. For example, as one team discussed announcements to remind students of the FAFSA completion deadline, a student member pointed out a flaw with the proposed solution: English language learners in her classes could not always understand the school-wide morning announcements. The team immediately adapted the intervention, instead tasking classroom teachers with providing the FAFSA reminders. Through this work, students contributed meaningfully to improvements in college access outcomes and, together, the network learned how to successfully enact intergenerational democratic improvement.

Learning Structures. Ted Sizer, a founder of the Essential Schools Movement, wrote that "you can tell everything you need to know about a school's priorities by the way it allocates adult and student time and resources" (Riordan & Caillier, 2019, p. 127). Hive leaders are attentive to creating what one Partners in School Innovation staff member calls "a spaciousness for learning," or protected time for the pursuit of individual and shared improvement. In service of this goal, leaders treat learning as a core function of each role, adjusting and aligning schedules to create space for shared learning, appropriating and redesigning existing meeting agendas, and deliberately accounting for learning time in each member's role description. Leaders leverage their perspective as a central actor in the system to monitor various learning spaces and ensure that each structure is purposeful and high-value for participants, to streamline overlapping learning meetings and processes, and to routinely shear away vestigial structures. In practice, this often means finding resources—including appropriate funding—for this type of functional reorganization. Derek Mitchell says of the leaders' role in these efforts:

> I think it's really important for organizations to commit time for the organization's learning. And that means from a CEO's perspective resourcing

that time. In fact, a lot of my colleagues have asked me, "How is it you can afford to do this?", and it means raising the resources that we need to be able to commit that time for that learning.

Perhaps most of all, leaders understand that the primary time and space for learning is time spent doing: leading, teaching, counseling, and coaching. Michael Fullan (2020) writes:

> When learning is confined to workshops, training, performance, appraisals, and the like, we see the intended learning as one or more steps removed from actually doing the work. . . . In successful organizations, the culture is based on daily learning built into daily interaction. Think of it this way: it is what happens in between meetings or workshops that counts. (p. 70)

Leaders make sure that learning tasks like measurement and individual and collective sensemaking are streamlined and integrated into daily doing so that learning doesn't feel like an add-on task to "real" work. Leaders are as attentive to protecting time and space for their own learning routines as they are for others. Seeing their own improvement as a model for and linchpin of system-level progress, leaders challenge themselves to constantly interrogate their own practice, using protected individual and collective working time to seek feedback and problem-solve. Hive leaders do this by applying the same learning mindsets and tools used in system-level problem solving to their own work. Partners' Derek Mitchell and his team often describe this as "eating their own cooking." Mitchell says:

> Education leaders, writ large, are often talking about and advocating for practices and tools that they themselves aren't using. That's not how Partners operates. Any tool or process that you see us facilitating with or walking team members along through or even advocating for are all tools that we, [as organizational leaders], use ourselves. And part of the reason for that is that there's no better way to learn something than by doing it.

Just as teams build theories of improvement to outline their hypotheses for problem solving, leaders create "theories of leadership," that outline their own role in designing, guiding, and participating in system learning and improvement. Argyris (2008) writes:

> Everyone develops a theory of action—a set of rules that individuals use to design and implement their own behavior as well as to understand the behavior of others. Usually these theories of action become so taken for granted

that people don't even realize they are using them. One of the paradoxes of human behavior, however, is that the master program people actually use is rarely the one they think they use. Ask people in an interview or question-naire to articulate the rules they use to govern their actions and they will give you what I call their "espoused" theory of action. But observe these same people's behavior and you will quickly see that this espoused theory has very little to do with how they actually behave. (p. 10)

To counter this tendency, leaders explicitly articulate their espoused the-ory and test and iterate on it as they carry out their work. For example, in a parallel process to school-level strategic planning, CIOB Superintendent Alan Cheng and all members of his leadership team developed district-level plans that outlined their own role in system-level improvement. Cheng describes this process:

[We] chart out this causal chain—what are some of the district priorities in which we want to see improvements? If we're going to get there, what does student behavior look like? What does student learning look like? What are some of the things that teachers, assistant principals, principals might need to do in the school? *And then, what are the things that we need to do to help them do that?*

While the demands on system leaders are many, leaders take their learning work seriously and safeguard time for ongoing study of their own behavior, rather than relying on retrospective review. Derek Mitchell talks about this practice in his own work:

You really have to manage your time effectively as a leader if you want to be a leader focused on both personal and professional improvement. The coin of the realm for any leader is really time, how they manage time. And so I make a point of creating the space in every one of my days to be in a reflective space. I've forged space between every meeting—usually it's 20 minutes, sometimes it can be more—for me to reflect on what I just experienced, what commitments that I make, how am I going to deliver on those? And if I was scheduled back to back, there'd be no time for that.

In the case of the New York City CIOB district, throughout the year, the team consistently enacted a number of learning structures, including a se-ries of formal meetings with various configurations of the district-level leadership team, that allowed leaders to make sense of feedback and data received as they implemented their leadership-level theories of leadership and adjust them in real time.

SUMMARY

In this chapter, we explored leadership in evolutionary learning, focusing on how leaders orchestrate innovation, collaboration, and continuous learning. Rather than operating as know-all directors, leaders understand themselves as culture cultivators, capacity builders, coordinators, and architects. To do this work well, hive leaders maintain a dual perspective—one in touch with frontline work while holding a strategic systems view to support alignment of those efforts with system-level goals. Acknowledging the link between themselves and their systems, hive leaders are explicit about and deliberate in improving their own leadership. They resist the comfort of the status quo, using conflict and disruption to fuel collaborative problem-solving and innovation. They model and foster in others reflexivity and fruitful conflict, which accelerates communal learning and improvement.

STARTING THE SHIFT: REFLECT AND ACT

In this section, you'll have the opportunity to articulate the effect of your leadership.

1. Define Your Leadership Metaphor: Find a metaphor that illustrates your personal model of leadership.
2. Create a Theory of Leadership: Capture your approach to leadership in a logic model that describes the causal relationship between your leadership actions and short and long-term goals.

Define Your Leadership Metaphor (adapted from Pietruszka & Randall, 2023)

1. With a partner or partners in your organization, consider the following question.
   a. When I am at my best as a leader and problem-solver, I am
   _____.
2. Write and describe your metaphor. Draw a picture, symbol or graphic representation of your metaphor.

3. Share your metaphor with a partner.
    a. Request feedback from your partner leader.
        i. What did you hear?
            1. What do you perceive as strengths of the
               metaphor?
            2. What do you perceive as weaknesses or challenges of
               the metaphor?
    b. Consider and share with your partner what resonates with you
       about the feedback.

Build a Theory of Leadership

As a leader, how you design, organize, set the conditions for, and participate in learning across your system—while measuring your success in
driving progress toward the outcomes you care about—will either obstruct
or open the path toward learning and transformative change. While most
leaders operate with a tacit leadership approach in mind, articulating an
explicit theory allows leaders to capture, measure, and improve their own
practice over time, as well as share their approach with others within or
beyond their organization.

Your theory of leadership can be captured in a logic model that describes the causal relationship between leadership actions and short and
long-term goals. By ensuring that your articulated actions and goals are explicit, and therefore measurable, you can treat your leadership approach as
a hypothesis, testing and refining it over time; strengthening the relationship between your leadership and the behaviors, mindsets, and conditions in your system; and rising to meet new challenges and opportunities.

The following steps will guide you through the development of your own,
high-level theory of leadership. You may choose to use the Theory of Action
template at Figure 4.3 (page 77) to structure your theory, or you might opt for
something less formal—choose whatever format works best for you.

1. Draft a shared, high-level vision—a theory of action—for your
   leadership approach.
    a. Start with impacts, articulating no more than three long-term
       goals. As you craft these statements, think about what your
       organization hopes to achieve 3 to 5 years from now, including
       shifts in student outcomes.
    b. Develop three to four Outcome statements. These should be
       the shorter-term results of your leadership approach—think
       changes in behaviors, mindsets, and early results in your
       organization that will lead, over time, to your impacts.

    c. Draft up to five If statements that articulate the high-level actions you and other leaders in the organization will take to enable the outlined outcomes and impacts. Note that your actions do not need to line up 1:1 with your Outcomes or Impacts.

    d. Assess your Theory of Action as a whole, using the following questions to guide refinements in language and content.

        i. Is your language clear, precise, and accessible?

        ii. Will the theory, as written, easily communicate your vision with various hive members?

        iii. Is there a clear logic between your Actions, Outcomes, and Impacts?

        iv. Is the Theory feasible to achieve in the timeframe you have outlined?

        v. Is the Theory inspirational? Will it motivate action?

    e. Test your Theory with hive members and advisors, refining as needed.

2. Articulate a list of 3–4 action steps you'll commit to test improvements in your own leadership.

CHAPTER 8

Get Buzzing!

Effective public schools are essential to advancing and maintaining our democracy. At their best, they prepare children to thrive and adapt in a quickly changing world. They inspire young minds and help a diverse people cross lines of difference and live, play, work, and create together. They are hubs for community and political engagement, acting as many people's first and most formative experience in participatory citizenship.

We can't realize public schools' too often unfulfilled promise by tinkering around the edges, solving for out-of-school time, or scaling silver bullets. We've tried that, and it hasn't worked.

What will it require? Transforming the way the system works—its approach to governance; its democracy. A hundred years ago, progressives used bureaucracy to scale a standard approach to schooling across the country. With schoolhouses and institutions in place to serve our 74 million kids, it is past time to adopt a model that shifts the focus from serving all kids to serving all kids *well*.

Evolutionary Learning offers that model. It is an approach to governance and democracy designed to function in complex, dynamic systems facing complex, dynamic problems. EL hives pursue equity by acknowledging that the diversity of needs and contexts in public education requires constant learning and adaptation. EL systems mobilize the power of the collective to identify and tackle challenges using a shared democratic and collaborative framework that guides not just daily, ground-level experimentation, but broader discovery and improvement. Each member of the hive has the agency—and responsibility—to adapt strategy and relay what is learned from each to all—from the individual and the local to the system levels. Measurement provides a learning tool that holds members of the hive accountable to each other, to those served, and to their shared goals. Leaders facilitate, rather dictate, their own and others' learning, shifting from top-down direction to coordinated discovery and application of knowledge in service of forward progress.

But where to start? The change process can feel daunting, in part because the strength of many formal organizations is their stability, which often stems from structural inertia and resistance to change (Hannan & Freeman, 1984). EL disrupts this rigidity, using experimentalist governance to find a balance between flexibility (learning, innovation) and consistency.

Enacting this vision is no mean feat. In this final chapter, we briefly discuss how you can get started with others in using the ideas and exercises throughout this book to effect governance change in your own system, large or small. The good news is that you're already on your way; systems that evolve into hives begin by understanding the essential, if often hidden, deficiencies and impact of their existing governance and leadership models. You've begun that work by reading this book.

You've also laid the foundation for a second key capacity, using EL not only as the governance approach to which your system is shifting but as also the way to manage the shift. After diagnosing their current model, aspiring hives generate a vision for what they will achieve and a provisional strategy for getting there.

Mindset shifts accompany and emerge from system and practice change. Table 8.1 makes explicit the shifts that have been addressed throughout the book. First is to reframe equity, from treating all alike to an acknowledgment of and response to difference so all thrive. Second is to replace the presumption that central experts alone possess the knowledge needed to pursue equity with respect for the expertise collectively held by the hive, including its leaders, frontline staff, students, families, and community, requiring a new division of labor from discrete and siloed jobs to collaborative and cross-functional teams. Third is to reject the understanding of authority as top-down and conferred and to make it multidirectional and earned. Fourth is to recognize that knowledge cannot be communicated effectively through top-down rules and instead must be shared as standards, adjusted as needed through constant feedback loops. Fifth is to recognize that outcomes, not compliance, define success, allowing actors across the system to value local adaptation over rote reproduction of mandated practices. And sixth is to relinquish siloed, command-and-control approaches to decision-making and implementation in favor of collaborative, democratic learning processes. As a system transitions to EL governance, these mindsets act as foundational standards that guide the implementation of exceptionally complex transition work.

RIGHT-SIZE YOUR HIVE'S AMBITION AND VISION

We have yet to meet a system or organization that can operate as a bureaucracy (or any other governance model) one day and a hive the next.

Table 8.1. Shifts in Mindset Necessary in Transition

	Feature	From Bureaucracy	To Evolutionary Learning
1	What is the definition of equity?	Treat all alike	Provide each with what is needed so all can thrive
2	Who is assumed to have knowledge? How then is labor distributed?	Central experts based on synoptic understanding and perspective / Discrete, hierarchical jobs	Everyone, including those served, frontline staff, system leaders, and actors outside the organization (e.g., researchers) / Collaborative, cross-functional teams
3	How is authority defined and exercised?	Conferred, top down	Earned, multi-directionally
4	How is knowledge about effective practice communicated?	Rules, from the top, requiring reproduction of mandated practices	Standards, developed multidirectionally through feedback loops, allowing customization of actions to local conditions
5	What is the definition of success?	Compliance with prescribed rules and protocols	Progress toward desired outcomes
6	How does democracy operate?	Interest-group politics; decision-focused; weakly participatory and deliberative	Problem-solving politics; decision and implementation-focused; robustly participatory and deliberative

Just as hives learn by doing with respect to strategy development and implementation, aspiring hives learn by doing to change governance.

Having decided to pursue EL, your next steps are to assess your context, your role in it, and what you want to achieve. Are you looking to transform the way a team, department, or division operates? Or is your goal to motivate governance shifts across your entire system or organization? How do your near-term goals differ from your longer-term ones? For some systems, their deeply entrenched bureaucratic starting point, size, maturity, or other contextual factors make immediate, organization-wide transformation unrealistic. Others may be well on their way to Evolutionary Learning.

There is no one-size-fits-all model for transition. There are, however, several change-process typologies, which fall into four categories:

1. *Whole hive*: System-level leaders initiate and support intensive shifts in governance across the whole organization, from top to bottom and inside out, all at once.
2. *Strategically dispersed to hive*: System-level leaders initiate and support shifts in governance in several strategically selected teams or units at various layers of the organization. Leaders gradually intensify and scale shifts, so that, over time, the whole organization practices EL.
3. *Solo*: One or more ground-level actors, departments, teams, or units across the organization initiate shifts in the subunit of the larger system within which they have authority, without a goal of scaling local transformation to the full organization in the near-term.
4. *Ground-level to hive*: Ground-level actors, departments, teams, or units initiate shifts in their local context with a goal of, over time, scaling EL practices across the organization.

Choosing the typology that makes most sense for you and your organization requires consideration of (1) your own sphere of influence and (2) your organization's readiness for change.

1. Reflect on your sphere of influence.
    » What is your role in the organization? Where can you influence change? Consider your formal authority and the earned influence you have in your system and the scale at which you can realistically motivate change.
    » Who else may champion transition and who may challenge it? Think of people you work with laterally, those you supervise, and those with authority over or influence on your work. Consider who is satisfied with the current model, as well as who has tried EL before, and to what effect.
2. Consider your organization's readiness for change.
    » How big is your organization? Transition becomes more complex as the size of an organization grows.
    » How mature and established is your organization? Older, more established organizations tend to have entrenched values and approaches to governance and democracy that take time to dislodge.
    » What is your dominant governance model? To what degree do values, mindsets, and existing structures in your organization align or operate at odds with key EL principles (see Table 8.1)? Consider, for example, the degree to which your organization is open to data and explicit practice sharing

and has other structures, cultural attributes, and leadership behaviors that underlie a learning stance.

» How interconnected are your teams and divisions? Regardless of your current governance model, if your system is ordered and includes collaborative structures that could be appropriated to support co-creation, your organization may be more ready for change than a less ordered, less interconnected system.

» What is the source of motivation to serve children better? Consider whether and which various actors within the system are primarily motivated to change and improve outcomes by external pressures or internal inclinations (internal to individuals, groups of colleagues, or schools). Change can build on both motivations, but ultimately the more internal the motivations, the greater their impact.

» To what degree is there a strong and dispersed motivation to change? Both shocks to the system (i.e., external and internal disruptions) and gradual shifts in mindset can induce strong, widely-distributed openness to change.

» How aligned with and sympathetic to EL principles and practice are current organizational leaders? If organization leaders are open to EL mindsets and methods, transition at the organizational level may be more straightforward.

» How ready are you to effect change? Consider the extent to which you and others in the organization have internalized and begun to integrate into your own practice the shifts in mindset articulated in Table 8.1. Leading governance change will require you and allies to communicate and model these mindsets.

In answering these questions, determine how narrow to wide is your sphere of influence in the organization or system you are interested in changing, and how low to high is the organization or system's readiness for change. Plotting those on a matrix (see Figure 8.1) suggests which approach might be best used when selecting a course of action.

Consider which model might be best suited to your change goals and system conditions. Because the end-state itself never stops changing and improving, note that the transition will not have a clear end-point and will gradually merge into the EL system's ongoing improvement process. In many cases, the transition process itself might progress in phases, with the use of one typology setting up the organization for another in later stages of the work.

Figure 8.1. Transition Typologies Matrix

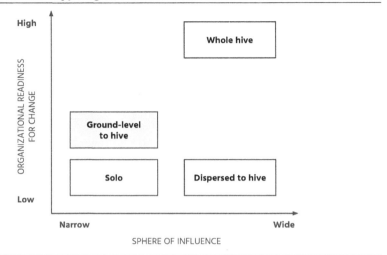

1. Whole Hive (Wider Sphere of Influence + Higher Organizational Readiness for Change)

If you have organization-wide authority and influence and think your organization is ready for full-scale governance change, conditions may be ripe for systemwide, intensive transition toward Evolutionary Learning. This course of change is characterized by intensity, often inspired by internal or external disruption that shocks the system and spurs openness to institutional shifts in practice that diverge from the status quo (Ansell, 2011). In this model, system leaders catalyze relatively rapid, large-scale progress toward a hive model using tactics that require enough positional authority on the part of change makers to drive and coordinate shifts in structure and culture, mobilize resources, motivate participation, support coherence and consistency, and sustain change over time.

Although this model uses positional authority to enact transformation, it supplants traditional top-down with EL principles in the design and execution of the change strategy. Each move in the direction of change is treated as a hypothesis, subject to reflection, revision, or rejection. Refusing the false narrative of a linear path to transformation, leaders measure and adapt implementation of the change strategy over time. Throughout this process, leaders democratically engage, learn from, and empower as change agents actors at each layer of their system—its client populations and communities included—understanding that without broad buy-in and coordinated activity, transformation will fail.

That said, an EL-driven approach to change does not preclude organizational leaders from applying bureaucratic, managerialist, and craft tactics in the shorter term to achieve broader uptake of EL in the longer term. A mandate—for example, requiring that all educators and schools in a district co-develop then use shared curricular materials to improve literacy instruction—can powerfully communicate priorities and catalyze change. Treating such tactics as one tool in a larger toolbox and applying EL principles to their development and use can vastly expand your options for propelling change.

Consider the transition of Aldine Public Schools, a large public school district just north of Houston, from a largely craft model of governing teaching and learning to one of EL. In response to student outcome data that suggested the system had critical issues in literacy and numeracy—recalled by late Superintendent Nadine Kujawa as "the shock our system needed to wake up" (Childress et al., 2011)—Kujawa used her positional authority as the then deputy superintendent and the district's existing craft-oriented empowerment of teachers to accelerate its readiness for broad "whole hive" transformation.

Kujawa began what she described as a "difficult" but ultimately successful transition by retracting schools' and teachers' previous freedom to design their own curriculum, scopes and sequence, and assessment practices and mandating district-wide learning standards, a standards-aligned uniform curriculum for each grade, a strict pacing guide, and standard unit tests (Zavadsky, 2009, p. 28).

These actions may call to mind bureaucracy, but the model and tactics Kujawa used to get there exhibit many hallmarks of EL. First, she empowered teachers themselves—drawing on their prior power to formulate their own standards, curricula, and pacing to develop ones for the district as a whole. Kujawa organized (and paid) vertical teams of teachers and discipline-specific program directors to collaboratively design curriculum for each subject, starting with feedback from every teacher in the district on content and sequencing. Bridge teams of teachers from each and the following grade level then worked to assure that each grade's standards aligned and that curriculum prepared students for the next grade's learning. While the transition initially encountered resistance, particularly from high school teachers, this approach garnered buy-in by honoring teacher expertise while helping educators cooperatively turn tacit beliefs about successful instruction to explicit, testable standards and materials (Zavadsky, 2009).

A newly developed curriculum served as the default, but schools and educators retained considerable influence in implementation and even modified the default upon a showing of need. Each school, for example, developed its own strategic plan, setting tailored aims that aligned with the district-wide strategic and instructional framework. Each teacher or group of them developed its own lesson plans to enact shared curriculum, meet standards, and advance the school's plan and aims—in all cases applying the shared strategy in ways most appropriate for each context.

The Aldine central office concurrently shifted toward an EL-driven measurement strategy that enabled continuous learning and improvement. District leaders continued to set broad goals regarding learning progress in certain subjects and asked schools to articulate how they planned to make progress toward those goals. Leaders then regularly conducted walk-throughs to assess rigor relative to peer schools, understand how instruction was designed to meet expectations, and whether schools were making progress toward their own goals. When curriculum and local implementation strategies did not yield improvements, educator inquiry teams, supported by central office facilitators, used structured problem-solving to hypothesize causes and solutions, test the latter, and generate improvements to both the school's strategic plan and daily lesson plans. Critically, based on what was learned, inquiry teams also proposed changes to the district's default standards, curriculum, and pacing guide, which district-wide teacher teams revised each summer based on teacher feedback (Zavadsky, 2009).

2. Strategically Dispersed to Hive (Wider Sphere of Influence + Lower Organizational Readiness for Change)

When whole system transformation is a long-term goal, but the viability of high-intensity change across the system is low, organizations may opt for a longer runway and a more dispersed process for transition. In this approach, those with influence and authority—typically positional leaders—act gradually, strategically testing shifts in governance in teams or units at various layers of the organization and using those dispersed efforts to accelerate the expansion of learnings from those experiments over time. In this approach, leaders empower and organize a cohort of questioning, disgruntled, or innovative central and frontline staff who have already demonstrated a desire for change to try out new EL operating structures (Ansell, 2011; Nadelstern, 2013). Over time, changes in governance are intensified, adapted, and tested in new contexts. As the new values that underlie changes are put into practice, they permeate culture and shift operations across the system.

To spur organizational transformation using this model, leaders must maintain momentum. Early progress depends on producing and celebrating small wins (Weick, 1984) that convince both current and potential participants of the value of the EL approach. In our experience, this reality leads systems to start with lower-hanging fruit, for example, encouraging empowered first movers to begin by applying a continuous improvement learning methodology to a straightforward technical challenge. But an early focus on exclusively technical challenges risks stranding change at the level of superficial transformation—and leaving the disgruntled only more so. The most effective change leaders are ambitious; they take up both technical *and* adaptive challenges, breaking them into smaller steps that allow for early success while working—and empowering ambitious first-movers—to keep the system on track for transformative change.

The transition story of the High Tech High charter school network exemplifies this gradual, multilevel transition. High Tech High was founded as a craft organization designed to give teachers—possessed of experientially driven, tacit expertise—the power to run their classrooms based on their independent, expert judgment. Yet as the organization grew, a nagging question plagued a number of leaders and teachers: Was craft's heterogeneity of practice assuring student learning, collective improvement, and progress toward equity *across* the network's schools? The moral imperative generated by impressionistic evidence of a negative answer to that question catalyzed organizational leaders to initiate a shift toward more disciplined EL-driven learning and improvement structures that would honor the organization's foundational values while allowing for more methodical adult learning practice.

Change began through close relationships between High Tech High's K–12 and graduate school leaders, who identified key challenges and then sought out training to build their own capacity to lead improvement. Soon after, they initiated a college access network and a school-based administrative pilot focused on absenteeism that allowed them to test out new governance and learning structures. When those efforts demonstrated strong results, the leadership team looked for ways to scale the practices tested through the network and pilot, identifying and working on complex, adaptive problems of practice with school-based champions: teachers who had already begun to question craft governance practices. Throughout this effort, positional leaders honored the organization's craft roots, leveraging the natural alignments between High Tech High's core values and features of the hive model—experimentation, learning by doing, democratic participation, and collaboration—to motivate transition. There was never a mandate for governance change from above: Leaders built buy-in slowly and organically, adapting their strategy for scale based on feedback from the ground—for example, taking teachers' advice to simplify the language and routines associated with continuous improvement and align them with High Tech High's distinctive organizational culture. Though some staff remain skeptical of elements of continuous learning, interest in participation has grown as the initial teams demonstrate progress, and today, EL has scaled across many of High Tech High's constellation of graduate divisions, K–12 schools, and networked improvement communities.

3. Solo (Narrower Sphere of Influence + Lower Organizational Readiness for Change)

Even when system-wide governance transformation is not viable in the short or medium term, teams and actors within the broader organization may opt to implement EL within their subsystem (e.g., a community district within a citywide district, a school within a district, a division within an organization, a team within a department). Without the expectation of near-or medium-term, systemwide change or scale, those leading the transition can invest resources in localized transition, rather than diffusing them to influence larger change beyond the boundaries of local leaders' authority. Mirroring Model 1 or 2, local leaders and staff initiate localized intensive or gradual transition depending on the readiness for change within their subsystem. At times, the local system may collaborate with and bring in actors from lateral teams.

This model requires local leaders to manage dissonance between subsystem governance and that of the broader system, navigating differing and sometimes conflicting expectations and norms. For example, when working within bureaucratic systems, local leaders of subsystem hives may comply with broader mandates while interpreting and implementing those directives more flexibly.

Consider the utility of this model for a community school district or school within a large urban school system. Local leaders of subdistricts may opt to facilitate their own hive within the broader district's prevailing and hard-to-change model. In these cases, local leaders—spanning from local superintendents, to principals, to school-level staff—play a role in managing the transition process. Take New York City Public Schools (NYC PS), for example. Like most public school systems, NYC PS employs several governance models to effectuate its mission, with bureaucracy being most prominent. Within this broader system sit dozens of community and citywide school districts. In each of these districts, local leadership teams have the autonomy to lead their subsystems using alternative forms of governance, provided they comply with system-wide directives. For example, when Superintendent Alan Cheng assumed the leadership of the Consortium, Internationals, and Outward Bound high school district, the district had already begun working within the broader bureaucracy to incorporate elements of a craft-driven governance model that empowered schools to tailor local instruction and support to diverse contexts and community needs. Cheng and his team, however, recognized that continued improvement and consistent delivery of high-quality, context-dependent services as a district would require more intentional and coherent collaborative learning *across* schools, and so, over the past 5 years, they have guided CIOB's transition from this hybrid bureaucracy-craft model toward EL governance.

Continuous learning, improvement, and innovation had long been part of Cheng's leadership approach, but a citywide reorganization that expanded the CIOB district team from 7 to 25 members catalyzed a shift in the district's governance model. First, Cheng collaborated with new team members and partners to build and socialize a previously tacit vision of the role of district staff: Facilitating principal, school, and teacher improvement, rather than demanding those subordinates' compliance. With this vision as a North Star, the district team mapped a provisional strategy for the expansion and formalization of district-wide learning structures. Appropriating existing cross-school meeting spaces, the district, in collaboration with various partners, designed learning pods focused on using continuous improvement to more collaboratively address and share knowledge about collective problems of practice, including adolescent literacy, competency-based education practices, and work-based learning. Concurrently, the district built out a principal coaching initiative to provide context-specific, ongoing learning support for schools. Cheng and his team moved quickly from planning to action, launching both structures—and cross-district continuous improvement training—at the start of the 2022–2023 school year.

Paired with a strong learning leadership approach and rigorous measurement systems, CIOB has worked with the district community—including principals, teachers, and external partners—to refine the strategy and design of EL learning structures across the district. In contrast to the gradual transition plan used in the High Tech High transformation in Model 2, CIOB has opted for a relatively intensive transition, with schools across CIOB experiencing and shaping shifts at once, as a collective. Pivotal to the district's progress has been the application of EL to the transition process itself. The district has treated each design decision as a hypothesis, captured in a shared theory of action and monitored using an aligned measurement framework. Through application and frequent leadership-level learning routines, the CIOB team tests and refines that theory throughout each school year and from year to year—leading it, for example, to adapt the cadence of learning meetings, the structure and facilitation of cross-school collaboration, the topics around which cross-district learning are organized, and the support offered for the development of strategic plans.

Reflecting on this transition (which is still ongoing as this book goes to press), Cheng notes:

> The thing we're most proud of is being able to move from a collection of schools that, whether for convenience or for political expediency or for financial reasons are clustered together under one superintendent into a real, deep sense that we belong to this greater district, this greater system, and we're here to learn together.

Over time, shifts toward EL have allowed the CIOB to cultivate stronger instructional and strategic coherence, a culture of mutual accountability, and collective learning across schools, while maintaining and respecting the collective's existing, deeply held value of local autonomy. Key to the district's early success is the bounded aim of the work; Cheng's team has not invested its finite resources in bids to transform NYC Public Schools' massive network of governance structures from the ground up. Instead, they have shifted practice within their own, admittedly large, locus of influence, nurturing local innovation and consistent application of effective practice within the broader frame of the city schools' bureaucracy. Members of CIOB do, of course, have ambitions to act as change agents in the broader ecosystem, influencing practice and policy across New York City and beyond, but their primary aim, at this time, is to shift *governance* practice within the CIOB district, rather than throughout the system at large.

4. Ground-level to Hive (Narrower Sphere of Influence + Lower Organizational Readiness for Change)

A final change typology proposes catalyzing system-level governance change from the ground up. In this model, as in Model 3, ground-level leaders and staff initiate local governance shifts. As this work proceeds, the local system catalyzes shifts in governance outside of ground-level leaders' immediate sphere of influence, in part by capturing the attention of system-level leaders using demonstrated results, inspiring those leaders to, over time, pursue larger-scale, system-level governance change.

While this is a compelling vision—and one we have experimented with ourselves—proceed with caution. In our experience, this bottom-up model is often very difficult to execute successfully. Without the early support of system leaders, incentives for maintaining the status quo are strong, often leading to initiatives that engage in a superficial approach to EL practices or stall out in ground-level change that never translates to larger-scale shifts in governance practice. Making this model work requires rigorous planning on how to capture the attention of and draw in system-level. The investment of resources required for this type of effort is typically high, especially in contexts that experience leadership churn. As a result, across many systems, and particularly in large, mature institutions like school districts, we have seen exciting ground-level change initiatives flounder using this model.

Consider, for example, a common approach to governance change: an organizational working group, composed of cross-functional mid-level leaders and frontline staff, is brought together to work on a common problem of practice. To kick off the process, they receive coaching or training on EL or continuous improvement. Teams try out new improvement practices, working together to find the root causes of the problem of practice and test solutions, often making quick progress toward a shared aim. In Phase 2 of this approach, each member of the original working group endeavors to spread EL-aligned behaviors, structures, routines, and norms to new teams (e.g., their home team, a new working group), pollinating EL governance practices to a broader swath of the organization. Theoretically, this process is replicated over time as newly converted members scale EL to more and more teams and actors across the organization. While this approach sounds promising, inevitably, the limited authority of members driving scale efforts—and the absence of strategic coordination, condition setting, and support from organizational leaders—nearly always dooms it to failure, despite often promising early results. Although this approach is difficult to pull off as the sole method of system-wide governance transformation, it can be useful as a means of laying the groundwork for future transformation, for example if new leadership takes on whole system redesign. In those cases, the ground-level-to-hive effort can generate readiness for Whole Hive transformation, both because previous (failed) transformation efforts can (1) birth champions of change and groundlevel mindset and practice shifts and (2) reveal insights about how best to manage a more robust transition process moving forward. This approach exemplifies the way systems apply EL to the transition process in addition to end-state governance.

IDENTIFY A COURSE OF ACTION

As you read this book, you may have begun experimenting with tools introduced in prior chapters. But to embark on *system* change, you will need to plan, implement, and learn alongside others. Achieving real shifts in governance requires setting your sights on impact from the first stages of your change effort. Here are some helpful steps:

Step 1: Build Your Team. Identify the people within and beyond your community who you anticipate will be critical partners at various stages of your effort, inviting a cross section of those hive members to join or advise a steering committee. Use the questions below to consider whom you might tap for that team, keeping in mind that as you progress through transition, you will inevitably adjust team composition and draw in other members of your hive in various ways. Consider:

- Who has insight, expertise, and essential skills?

To map your system and understand potential contributors and road-blocks to transformation, you'll need people with a deep understanding of the culture and practices of the local systems (e.g., communities, classrooms, schools, teams, departments) you hope to change. Selecting representatives from early sites of change—the schools, teams, and divisions where you will pilot new governance structures—can help shape a strategy more attuned to local needs. The inclusion of those most impacted by changes, including students, families, communities, and frontline staff, is critical. It can also be helpful to tap team members with expertise in relevant topics like governance, adult learning, democratic collaboration, continuous im-provement, and systems change. Finally, among your most important tasks is recruiting a team member with strong project management skills who can help maintain momentum toward deadlines and goals.

- Who has authority and influence?

People who have the power to allocate resources (time, people, fund-ing) and initiate shifts in structure (e.g., changes in meeting times, changes in staff roles and responsibilities) are essential allies in any governance transition. Keep in mind that you are not looking for the people with the most authority broadly but for the people with the most authority in the systems you are trying to change. For example, if you are pursuing Model 3 in a large school support organization, you might include on your plan-ning committee team-level directors who have discretion over staff time and department budget, rather than tapping the organization's executive director.

- Who are your champions and challengers?

A successful change effort is always ready to include those enthusias-tic about the vision for change (McCannon & Margiotta, 2015). Tapping potential champions early on, particularly those with a gift for communica-tion and influence among peers, can build momentum and excitement for your effort.

On the other hand, every change effort faces challengers, people with a deep understanding of the shifts you mean to make but who hold reservations that will prevent or slow their own and others' uptake of new practices and mindsets. Here, think of those teachers hesitant to move away from craft in Aldine or the staff slow to warm to continuous improvement at High Tech High. Rather than sidelining these viewpoints, learn from them. Incorporating challengers into your planning team—and taking seriously their often legitimate concerns and feedback—can help expose flaws in your initial logic and support the construction of stronger strategy during every stage of your transition. As important, including challengers early in the development of change can build their buy-in to change efforts.

- Who could support change from outside the formal boundaries of the organization?

EL systems are most effective when they look beyond traditional organizational boundaries and include those outside the system who offer fresh ideas and open new avenues of influence. Consider which actors outside of your immediate system might help innovate, scale practices, and bring new resources to the table.

Step 2: Map Your Governance Practices. Once you have convened an initial team, it's time to get started! Use the exercises throughout this book to discuss and map out your existing governance practices—including those related to hive structure (Chapter 4), problem-solving and knowledge management (Chapter 5), measurement (Chapter 6), and leadership (Chapter 7).

Step 3: Develop a Vision. Take time to discuss and map your ideal end-state organizational governance vision, customizing the vision presented in this book to your local context.

Step 4: Create a Theory of Change. Use that vision and the transition typologies articulated in this chapter to develop both a high-level and detailed theory of action (Chapter 4) that details a provisional hypothesis on how you will pursue transition. Include in that theory key measures you will use to track progress (Chapter 7). Take time to ensure the logic of your theory is strong, but do not belabor consensus, remembering that the best way to refine your theory is through its application. Be sure to pressure test and refine your theory based on feedback from representatives of all groups who will implement and be affected by governance transition before communicating it more broadly.

Step 5: Choose a Place to Start. There will be no perfect moment to get started. Pick a place to start and get going! Again, apply EL to your transition. Use shared time with your planning team to consistently return to three familiar learning questions:

1. What are we trying to do, and what will success look like?
2. Is what we are doing working as expected?
3. How might we improve what we are doing?

Build check-in and measurement structures that allow you to answer question 2, keeping an eye on where leading outcomes are diverging from expectations and local implementation from planned strategy—and mining those challenge areas for insight. Cultivate strong relationships and alert structures that allow hive members to flag when and where problems are occurring and trust them to take action to address them. Be flexible about who is involved in your efforts and what their roles are, forming problem-solving teams, adjusting planning team membership, and bringing in actors with expertise from inside and outside the system. And above all, seek and model constant improvement—of strategy, implementation, and your own leadership of this initiative.

GET BUZZING!

Sometimes, it feels impossible to change the systems we are part of. Our public institutions seem huge, complex, labyrinthine, and immovable. Even as an organizational leader, it's easy to think: What influence do I have? How much can I really change?

Our answer? A lot.

In the first chapter of this book, we posed three questions:

- What if instead of searching for the right policy for all contexts, we search for good ways to identify and improve policies for each context?
- What if instead of constant triage to address challenges, we alter our organizational structures so that we can get to and solve the roots of these challenges?
- And what if instead of relying on central leaders to have all the answers, we engage everyone—system and local leaders, frontline staff, students, families, communities—in embracing uncertainty as they learn together?

In the rest of the book, we presented a vision in response to these questions. When governance is well matched to the goals and context of public education, our public school systems become innovative and nimble. Actors throughout the system face up to and address education's most deeply entrenched problems and tackle new ones as they inevitably arise. Public schools become engines of learning, adapting to provide better education for more students, produce stronger outcomes, and support thriving communities.

We owe it to every child we serve to do whatever we can to bring this vision to life in each school, district, and community. With Evolutionary Learning, this task is less intimidating. By attacking the roots of some of our biggest challenges—the *how* of what we do—we build capacity to take on new problems and learn, adapt, and innovate better.

In a hive, this work need not be lonely because it's "we," not "I." *We* are taking on big problems. *We* are discovering how to improve our own and collective practice. *We* are changing the status quo. *We* are discovering how to be better, together.

If you take one thing away from this book, we hope it's a predilection for action: a willingness to think and dream big—and then jump in with others, experiment, and learn as you go. So let's get buzzing and build public schools that do better for our kids and communities, every day.

References

Aghina, W., Ahlback, K., De Smet, A., Lackey, G., Lurie, M., Murarka, M., & Handscomb, C. (2018, January 22). *The five trademarks of agile organizations*. McKinsey & Company. https://www.mckinsey.com/business-functions /people-and-organizational-performance/our-insights/the-five-trademarks -of-agile-organizations

Aguilar, E. (2016). *The art of coaching teams: Building resilient communities that transform schools.* John Wiley & Sons.

Alavi, M., & Leidner, D. E. (2001). Knowledge management and knowledge management systems: Conceptual foundations and research issues. *MIS Quarterly, 1*(10), 107–136.

Aldrich, H., & Herker, D. (1977). Boundary spanning roles and organization structure. *Academy of Management Review, 2*(2), 217–230.

Allison, E. (1984). Otto Eckstein: Contributions in education. *The Review of Economics and Statistics, 66*(4), 543–546. http://www.jstor.org/stable/1935977

Alvarado, A. (1998). Professional development is the job. *American Educator, 22*(4), 18–23. https://www.aft.org/ae/winter1998/alvarado

American Bar Association. (2024). *ABA profile of the legal profession 2024.* https://www.americanbar.org/news/profile-legal-profession/demographics

Ansell, C. (2011). *Pragmatist democracy: Evolutionary Learning as public philosophy.* Oxford University Press.

Ansell, C., & Gash, A. (2008). Collaborative governance in theory and practice. *Journal of Public Administration Research and Theory, 18*(4), 543–571.

Ansell, C., Sørensen, E., & Torfing, J. (2024). The democratic quality of co-creation: A theoretical exploration. *Public Policy and Administration, 39*(2), 149–170.

Anyon, J. (1980). Social class and the hidden curriculum of work. *Journal of Education, 162*(1), 67–92.

Argyris, C. (1977). Double loop learning in organizations. *Harvard Business Review, 55*(5), 115–125.

Argyris, C. (1994). Good communication that blocks learning. *Harvard Business Review, 72*(4), 77–85.

Argyris, C. (2008). *Teaching smart people how to learn.* Harvard Business Review Press.

Arnstein, S. R. (1969). A ladder of citizen participation. *Journal of the American Institute of Planners, 35*(4), 216–224.

Associated Press. (2023). "Mississippi miracle": Kids' reading scores have soared in Deep South states. *U.S. News.* https://www.usnews.com/news/best-states /louisiana/articles/2023-05-17/mississippi-miracle-kids-reading-scores -have-soared-in-deep-south-states

Association of American Medical Colleges. (2020). *Physician specialty data report: Active physicians with a U.S. doctor of medicine (U.S. medical degree) by specialty, 2019.* https://www.aamc.org/data-reports/workforce/data/active-physicians -us-doctor-medicine-us-md-degree-specialty-2019

Austin, K., Cahn, A., Chu, E., Clay, A., & Liebman, J. (2021). *Leading through learning: Using evolutionary learning to develop, implement, and improve strategic initiatives* [Report]. Center for Public Research and Leadership, Columbia University. https://cprl.law.columbia.edu/sites/default/files/content/EL%20 Toolkit/CPRL-Leading-Through-Learning-FINAL.pdf

Aviv, R. (2014, July 14). Wrong answer. *The New Yorker.* https://www.newyorker .com/magazine/2014/07/21/wrong-answer

Bachtiger, A., Dryzek, J., Mansbridge, J., & Warren, M. (2018). *The Oxford handbook of deliberative democracy.* Oxford University Press.

Bandura, A. (1977). Self-efficacy: Toward a unifying theory of behavioral change. *Psychological Review, 84*(2), 191–215. https://doi.org/10.1037/0033 -295X.84.2.191

Bandura, A. (1993). Perceived self-efficacy in cognitive development and functioning. *Educational Psychologist, 28*(2), 117–148.

Bandura, A. (2000). Exercise of human agency through collective efficacy. *Current Directions in Psychological Science, 9*(3), 75–78.

Barksdale Reading Institute. (n.d.) *Barksdale Reading Institute: The Mississippi story* [Video]. https://readinguniverse.org/about/who-we-are#barksdale

Barksdale Reading Institute. (2010, March-April). *Mississippi Magazine, 28*(4), 84. Retrieved January 30, 2025, from https://link-gale-com.ezproxy.cul.columbia.edu /apps/doc/A221902347/ITOF?u=columbiau&sid=summon&xid=5ad8e36a

Barnum, M. (2023, July 18). Mississippi made big test score gains: Here's what to make of them. *Chalkbeat.* https://www.chalkbeat.org/2023/7/18/23799124 /mississippi-miracle-test-scores-naep-early-literacy-grade-retention-reading -phonics/

Bartels, K. P. (2018). Encounters with an open mind: A relational grounding for neighborhood governance. In M. Stout (Ed.), *From austerity to abundance? Creative approaches to coordinating the common good* (pp. 181–200). Emerald Publishing Limited.

Bateman, T. S., & Organ, D. W. (1983). Job satisfaction and the good soldier: The relationship between affect and employee "citizenship." *Academy of Management Journal, 26*(4), 587–595.

Bellamy, G. T., Crawford, L., Marshall, L. H., & Coulter, G. A. (2005). The fail-safe schools challenge: Leadership possibilities from high reliability organizations. *Educational Administration Quarterly, 41*(3), 383–412.

Bens, I. (2017). *Facilitating with ease!: Core skills for facilitators, team leaders and members, managers, consultants, and trainers.* John Wiley & Sons.

Berwick, D. M. (2009). What 'patient-centered' should mean: Confessions of an extremist. *Health Affairs, 28*(4), w555–w565.

Bianchi, C. (2021). Fostering sustainable community outcomes through policy networks: a dynamic performance governance approach. In J. W. Meek (Ed.), *Handbook of Collaborative Public Management* (pp. 349–372). Edward Elgar Publishing Limited. https://doi.org/10.4337/9781789901917.00036

Billman, G. (2020). Homeostasis: The underappreciated and far too often ignored central organizing principle of physiology. *Frontiers in Physiology, 11.* https://doi.org/10.3389/fphys.2020.00200

Blagg, K., Chingos, M., Luetmer, G., Rosenboom, V., Recht, H., Baird, C., Chartoff, B., & Tilsley, A. (2020). *America's gradebook: How does your state stack up?* Urban Institute. https://apps.urban.org/features/naep/

Bowles, S., & Gintis, H. (1976). *Schooling in capitalist America: Educational reform and the contradictions of economic life.* Basic Books.

Braithwaite, J., & Braithwaite, V. (1995). The politics of legalism: rules versus standards in nursing-home regulation. *Social & Legal Studies, 4,* 307–341.

Bray, L. E., & Russell, J. L. (2016). Going off script: Structure and agency in individualized education program meetings. *American Journal of Education, 122*(3), 367–398.

Brown, C., MacGregor, S., & Flood, J. (2020). Can models of distributed leadership be used to mobilise networked generated innovation in schools? A case study from England. *Teaching and Teacher Education, 94,* 103101. https://doi.org/10.1016/j.tate.2020.103101

Bryk, A., Gomez, L., Grunow, A., & LeMahieu, P. (2015). *Learning to improve: How America's schools can get better at getting better.* Harvard Education Press.

Burk, K. (2020). The perfect storm: Mississippi's momentum for improving reading achievement. *The Reading League Journal, 1*(2), 33–47. https://excelined.org/wp-content/uploads/2020/09/TheReadingJournal.ThePerfectStorm.KymyonaBurk.May2020.pdf

Burk, K. (2022). *How Mississippi reformed reading instruction.* The Catalyst. https://www.bushcenter.org/catalyst/how-to-improve-our-schools/how-mississippi-reformed-reading-instruction

Butler, K. (2024, May/June). The long view of literacy in Mississippi: Major components that contributed to reading achievement in Mississippi . . . and beyond! *The Reading League Journal, 5*(2), 51–59. https://www.thereadingleague.org/wp-content/uploads/2024/10/Changing-Course-Article-for-EAC.pdf

Caillier, S. (Host). (2021). Don Berwick on building courageous networks. [Audio podcast episode]. In *HTH UNBOXED.* HTH Graduate School of Education. https://hthunboxed.org/podcasts/s02e22-don-berwick-on-building-courageous-networks/

Cannon, M. D., & Edmondson, A. C. (2005). Failing to learn and learning to fail (intelligently): How great organizations put failure to work to innovate and improve. *Long Range Planning, 38*(3), 299–319.

Catone, W. V., & Brady, S. A. (2005) The inadequacy of individual educational program (IEP) goals for high school students with word-level reading difficulties. *Annals of Dyslexia, 55*, 53–78. https://doi.org/10.1007/s11881-005 -0004-9

Chabran, M., & Norman, J. (2018, April 4). *Measurement for improvement* [Presentation]. Carnegie Foundation for the Advancement of Teaching. http:// summit.carnegiefoundation.org/session_materials/C1.%20Measurement%20 for%20Improvement/C1_JNorman_MeasurementforImprovementPPT.pdf

Childress, S. M., Grossman, A. S., & King, C. (2011). *Meeting new challenges at the Aldine Independent School District.* Public Education Leadership Project at Harvard University. https://projects.iq.harvard.edu/files/pelp/files/pel030p2 -1.pdf

Choi, J. N. (2007). Change-oriented organizational citizenship behavior: Effects of work environment characteristics and intervening psychological processes. *Journal of Organizational Behavior: The International Journal of Industrial, Occupational and Organizational Psychology and Behavior, 28*(4), 467–484.

Chu, E., Gurny, M., McCarty, G., & Turchin, S. (2024). *Curriculum implementation change framework.* Center for Public Research and Leadership, Columbia University.

Churcher, M., & Talbot, D. (2020). The corporatisation of education: Bureaucracy, boredom, and transformative possibilities. *New Formations,* (100–101), 28–42. https://www.researchgate.net/publication/343156800_The_Corporatisation _of_Education_Bureaucracy_boredom_and_Transformative_Possibilities

Clarke, T., Cook, K., Gopal, S., Kajenthira, A., & Preskill, H. (2017). *Systems thinking toolkit: Putting systems thinking into practice in your organization* [Resource]. FSG. https://www.fsg.org/tools-and-resources/systems-thinking -toolkit-0

Çoban, Ö., & Atasoy, R. (2020). Relationship between distributed leadership, teacher collaboration and organizational innovativeness. *International Journal of Evaluation and Research in Education, 9*(4), 903–911.

Coglianese, C., & Lazer, D. (2003). Management-based regulation: Using private management to achieve public goals. *Law & Society Review, 37*(4), 691–730. https://doi.org/10.1046/j.0023-9216.2003.03703001.x

Cole, S. M., Murphy, H. R., Frisby, M. B., Grossi, T. A., & Bolte, H. R. (2021). The relationship of special education placement and student academic outcomes. *The Journal of Special Education, 54*(4), 217–227. https://doi.org/10.1177 /0022466920925033

Collins, T. (2022, January 6). *Student retention and third-grade reading: It's about the adults.* Thomas Fordham Institute. https://fordhaminstitute.org/national /commentary/student-retention-and-third-grade-reading-its-about-adults

Collins, T. (2023, February 24). *The Mississippi reading model continues to shine.* Thomas Fordham Institute. https://fordhaminstitute.org/national/commentary/mississippi-reading-model-continues-shine

Cooper, E. (2016, May 19). The Atlanta cheating scandal: Students were the victims, but the school system suffers too. *Huffpost.* https://www.huffpost.com/entry/the-atlanta-cheating-scan_b_7309084

Coston, L. (2011). *The Atlanta Public Schools cheating scandal.* Georgia Public Policy Foundation. https://www.georgiapolicy.org/news/the-atlanta-public-schools-cheating-scandal/

Crosswaite, C., & Curtice, L. (1994). Disseminating research results—the challenge of bridging the gap between health research and health action. *Health Promotion International, 9*(4), 289–296.

Data tools state profiles: Mississippi [Data set]. (n.d.). *The Nation's Report Card.* https://www.nationsreportcard.gov/profiles/stateprofile/overview/MS?cti=PgTab_OT&chort=1&sub=MAT&sj=MS&fs=Grade&st=MN&year=2022R3&sg=Gender:%20Male%20vs.%20Female&sgv=Difference&ts=Single%20Year&sfj=NP

Dewey, J. (1899). *The school and society: Being three lectures.* University of Chicago Press.

Dewey, J. (2012). *The public and its problems: An essay in political inquiry* (M. L. Rogers, Ed.). Penn State University Press. http://www.jstor.org/stable/10.5325/j.ctt7v1gh (Original work published 1927)

Dewey, J. (2024). *Democracy and education.* Columbia University Press. (Original work published 1916)

Drucker, P. F. (1993). The rise of the knowledge society. *The Wilson Quarterly, 17*(2), 52–72.

Edmondson, A. C. (1999). Psychological safety and learning behavior in work teams. *Administrative Science Quarterly, 44*(2), 350–383. https://doi.org/10.2307%2F2666999

Edmondson, A. C. (2011). Strategies for learning from failure. *Harvard Business Review, 89*(4), 48–55.

Edmondson, A. C., & Verdin, P. J. (2017, November 09). Your strategy should be a hypothesis you constantly adjust. *Harvard Business Review.* https://hbr.org/2017/11/your-strategy-should-be-a-hypothesis-you-constantly-adjust

Elmore, R, & Burney, D. (1997). School variation and systemic instructional improvement in Community School District #2, New York City. *Office of Educational Research and Improvement.* https://files.eric.ed.gov/fulltext/ED429264.pdf

Elmore, R., & Burney, D. (1998, December). Continuous improvement in Community District #2, New York City. *Inter-American Development Bank.* http://dx.doi.org/10.18235/0011020

Feicke, K. (2007, Fall). Protocols in practice—whose voice? *Connections: The Journal of the National School Reform Faculty, Fall 2007, 4,* 17–18. https://www.nsrfharmony.org/wp-content/uploads/2017/10/2007.Fall_.Connections.ProtocolsInPracticeWhoseVoice.pdf

Follett, M. P. (1919). Community is a process. *Philosophical Review, 28*(6), 576–588. https://www.jstor.org/stable/2178307

Follett, M. P. (2013). Constructive conflict. In H. Metcalf & L. Urwick (Eds.), *Dynamic administration: The collected papers of Mary Parker Follett* (pp. 30–49). Routledge. (Original work published 1940)

Folsom, J., Smith, K., Burk, K., & Oakley, N. (2017). *Educator outcomes associated with implementation of Mississippi's K–3 early literacy professional development initiative.* U.S. Department of Education, National Center for Education Evaluation and Regional Assistance, Regional Educational Laboratory Southeast. https://files.eric.ed.gov/fulltext/ED573545.pdf

Freire, P. (1996). *Pedagogy of the oppressed* (rev. ed.). Continuum.

Fullan, M. (1994). *Change forces.* Falmer.

Fullan, M. (2020). *Leading in a culture of change* (2nd ed.). John Wiley & Sons.

Fullan, M. G., & Miles, M. B. (1992). Getting reform right: What works and what doesn't. *Phi Delta Kappan, 73,* 744–752.

Gagnon, M. L. (2011). Moving knowledge to action through dissemination and exchange. *Journal of Clinical Epidemiology, 64*(1), 25–31.

Garda, R., & O'Neill, P. (2020). Charter schools and special education: Ensuring legal compliance and effectiveness through capacity building. *The University of Memphis Law Review, 50*(4), 947–994. https://www.proquest.com/scholarly-journals/charter-schools-special-education-ensuring-legal/docview/2621174152/se-2

Gerzon, M. (2006). *Leading through conflict: How successful leaders transform differences into opportunities.* Harvard Business Review Press.

Giroux, H., & Penna, A. (1979). Social education in the classroom: The dynamics of the hidden curriculum. *Theory and Research in Social Education, 7*(1), 21–42.

Glicken, J. (2000). Getting stakeholder participation 'right': A discussion of participatory processes and possible pitfalls. *Environmental Science & Policy, 3*(6), 305–310.

Goddard, R. D., Hoy, W. K., & Hoy, A. W. (2000). Collective teacher efficacy: Its meaning, measure, and impact on student achievement. *American Educational Research Journal, 37*(2), 479–507.

Gold, M. (Ed.). (1999). *The complete social scientist: A Kurt Lewin reader.* American Psychological Association. https://doi.org/1037/10319-000

Goleman, D. (2017). *Leadership that gets results.* Harvard Business Review Classics; Harvard Business Review Press.

González, R. (2019). The spectrum of community engagement to ownership. *Facilitating Power.* https://d3n8a8pro7vhmx.cloudfront.net/facilitatingpower/pages/53/attachments/original/1596746165/CE2O_SPECTRUM_2020.pdf?159674616

Gowdey, L. (2015). Disabling discipline: Locating a right to representation of students with disabilities in the Americans with Disabilities Act. *SSRN.* http://dx.doi.org/10.2139/ssrn.2566022

Greene, G. (2018). The emperor has no clothes: Improving the quality and compliance of ITPs. *Career Development and Transition for Exceptional Individuals, 41*(3), 146–155. https://doi.org/10.1177/2165143417707205

Grindal, T., Schifter, L. A., Schwartz, G., & Hehir, T. (2019). Racial differences in special education identification and placement: Evidence across three states. *Harvard Educational Review, 89*(4).

Grissom, J. A., Kern, E. C., & Rodriguez, L. A. (2015). The "representative bureaucracy" in education: Educator workforce diversity, policy outputs, and outcomes for disadvantaged students. *Educational Researcher, 44*(3), 185–192. http://www.jstor.org/stable/24571254

Gully, S. M., Incalcaterra, K. A., Joshi, A., & Beaubien, J. M. (2002). A meta-analysis of team-efficacy, potency, and performance: Interdependence and level of analysis as moderators of observed relationships. *Journal of Applied Psychology, 87*(5), 819.

Hall, G. E., & Hord, S. M. (2006). *Implementing change: Patterns, principles, and potholes*. Pearson.

Hanford, E. (2018). Hard words: Why aren't kids being taught to read? *APM Reports*. https://www.apmreports.org/episode/2018/09/10/hard-words-why-american-kids-arent-being-taught-to-read

Hannan, M. T., & Freeman, J. (1984). Structural inertia and organizational change. *American Sociological Review, 49*(2), 149–164.

Harris, B. (2019). Fighting for Mississippi's struggling 5-year-olds, one student at a time. *The Hechinger Report*. https://hechingerreport.org/fighting-for-mississippis-struggling-5-year-olds-one-student-at-a-time/

Harris, D. (2020). *Charter school city: What the end of traditional public schools in New Orleans means for American education*. University of Chicago Press.

Hattie, J. (2012). *Visible learning for teachers: Maximizing impact on learning*. Routledge.

Heifetz, R. A. (1994). *Leadership without easy answers*. Belknap Press.

Heifetz, R. A., Grashow, A., & Linsky, M. (2009). *The practice of adaptive leadership: Tools and tactics for changing your organization and the world*. Harvard Business Press.

Heifetz, R. A., & Linsky, M. (2002). *Leadership on the line: Staying alive through the dangers of leading*. Harvard Business School Press.

Henderson, A. T., Kressley, K. G., & Frankel, S. (2016). *Capturing the ripple effect: Developing a theory of change for evaluating parent leadership initiatives* [Report]. Annenberg Institute for School Reform, Brown University. https://annenberg.brown.edu/sites/default/files/capturingtherippleeffectreportweb.pdf

Henig, J., Gold, E., Orr, M., Silander, M., & Simon, E. (2011). Parent and community engagement in New York City and the sustainability challenge for urban education reform. In O'Day, J., Bitter, C., & Gomez, L., (Eds.) *Education reform in New York City: Ambitious change in the nation's most complex school system* (pp. 33–55). Harvard Education Press.

Heubeck, E. (2023). Mississippi students surged in reading over the last decade: Here's how schools got them there. *Education Week.* https://www.edweek .org/teaching-learning/mississippi-students-surged-in-reading-over-the -last-decade-heres-how-schools-got-them-there/2023/06

Hoopee, J. (2003). Managerialism: Its history and dangers. *Historically Speaking, 5*(1), 6–8. https://doi.org/10/1353/hsp.2003/0051

High Tech High Graduate School of Education. (n.d.). *Resource library: Protocols, tools, and media for learning, leading, and teaching improvement for equity.* https://hthgse.edu/research-center/resource-library/

Hyatt, S. K. (1989). The remedies gap: Compensation and implementation under the Education for All Handicapped Children Act. *NYU Review of Law & Social Change, 17*(689).

Individuals with Disabilities Education Act, 20 U.S.C. § 1400 (2004). https:// www.congress.gov/bill/108th-congress/house-bill/1350/text

Innes, J. E., & Booher, D. E. (2016). Collaborative rationality as a strategy for working with wicked problems. *Landscape and Urban Planning, 154,* 8–10.

Jing, Z., Jianshi, G., Jinlian, L., & Yao, T. (2017). A case study of the promoting strategies for innovation contest within a company. *Science Research Management, 38*(11), 57.

Justice, B., & Meares, T. (2014). How the criminal justice system educates citizens. *The ANNALS of the American Academy of Political and Social Science, 651*(1), 159–177. https://doi.org/10.1177/0002716213502929

Kapur, M. (2008). Productive failure. *Cognition and Instruction, 26*(3), 379–424.

Kapur, M., & Bielaczyc, K. (2012). Designing for productive failure. *Journal of the Learning Sciences, 21*(*1*), 45–83.

Khan, M.A.S., Jianguo, D., Du, J., Jin, S., Saeed, M., & Khalid, A. (2023). Participative leadership and service recovery performance: A moderated mediation model. *Journal of Service Theory and Practice, 33*(4), 537–555. https://doi .org/10.1108/JSTP-07-2022-0146

Kim, M., & Shin, Y. (2015). Collective efficacy as a mediator between cooperative group norms and group positive affect and team creativity. *Asia Pacific Journal of Management, 32*(3), 693–716.

Kini, T., & Podolsky, A., (2016). *Does teaching experience increase teacher effectiveness?: A review of the research.* Learning Policy Institute. https://learningpolicyinstitute .org/sites/default/files/product-files/Teaching_Experience_Report_June _2016.pdf

Kinlaw, A., Snyder, M., Chu, E., Lau, M., Lee, S., & Nagarajan, P. (2020). *Managing for change: Achieving systemic reform through effective implementation of networks for school improvement.* Center for Public Research and Leadership.

Kleinfeld, R. (2023, September 5). *Polarization, democracy, and political violence in the United States: What the research says.* Carnegie Endowment for International Peace. https://carnegieendowment.org/research/2023/09/polarization -democracy-and-political-violence-in-the-united-states-what-the-research -says?lang=en

Kocka, J. (1981). Capitalism and bureaucracy in German industrialization before 1914. *The Economic History Review, 34*(3), 453–468.

Kramarczuk Voulgarides, C., Aylward, A., Tefera, A., Artiles, A. J., Alvarado, S. L., & Noguera, P. (2021). Unpacking the logic of compliance in special education: Contextual influences on discipline racial disparities in suburban schools. *Sociology of Education, 94*(3), 208–226. https://doi.org/10.1177/00380407211013322

Kurtz, C. F., & Snowden, D. J. (2003). The new dynamics of strategy: Sensemaking in a complex and complicated world. *IBM Systems Journal, 42*(3), 462–483.

La Prad, J. (2016). The Coalition of Essential Schools in rural educational reform. *The Rural Educator, 36*(3). https://doi.org/10.35608/ruraled.v36i3.319

Labaree, D. F. (1997). Public goods, private goods: The American struggle over educational goals. *American Educational Research Journal, 34*(1), 39–81.

Lacy, J., & Stark, C.E.L. (2013). The neuroscience of memory: Implications for the courtroom. *National Review of Neuroscience, 14*(9), 649–658. https://doi.org/10.1038/nrn3563

Ladd, H. (2010). Education inspectorate systems in New Zealand and the Netherlands. *Education Finance and Policy, 5*(3), 378–392. https://doi.org/10.1162/EDFP_a_00005

Lagemann, E. (2000). *An elusive science: The troubling history of education research.* University of Chicago Press.

Lambert, L. (2002). *The constructivist leader* (2nd ed.). Teachers College Press.

Lambert, L. (2009). Constructivist leadership. In B. Davies (Ed.), *The essentials of school leadership* (2nd ed., pp. 112–132). Sage Publications.

Langley, G. J., Moen, R. D., Nolan, K. M., Nolan, T. W., Norman, C. L., & Provost, L. P. (2009). *The improvement guide: A practical approach to enhancing organizational performance* (2nd ed.). John Wiley & Sons.

The Learning Accelerator. (n.d.). *Activity: Conduct empathy interviews with stakeholders.* https://practices.learningaccelerator.org/strategies/activity-conduct-empathy-interviews-with-stakeholders

The Learning Pit. (2018). *Hattie: Collective efficacy [video].* Vimeo. https://vimeo.com/267382804

Lenzi, M., Vieno, A., Sharkey, J., Mayworm, A., Scacchi, L., Pastore, M., & Santinello, M. (2014). How school can teach civic engagement besides civic education: The role of democratic school climate. *American Journal of Community Psychology, 54*, 251–261.

Liebman, J., Cruikshank, E., & Ma, C. (2017). Governance of steel and kryptonite politics in contemporary public education reform. *Florida Law Review, 69*(2), 365–374.

Liebman, J. & Sabel, C. (2003). A public laboratory Dewey barely imagined: The emerging model of school governance and legal reform. *New York University Review of Law and Social Change, 28*, 183–304.

Likert, R. (1961). *New Patterns of Management.* McGraw-Hill Book Company.

Lipsky, M. (2010). Street-level bureaucrats as policy makers. In *Street-level bureaucracy: Dilemmas of the individual in public services* (30th anniversary expanded ed.) Russell Sage Foundation.

Liu, J., Chen, J., & Tao, Y. (2015). Innovation performance in new product development teams in China's technology ventures: The role of behavioral integration dimensions and collective efficacy. *Journal of Product Innovation Management, 32*(1), 29–44.

Long, J. C., Cunningham, F. C., & Braithwaite, J. (2013). Bridges, brokers and boundary spanners in collaborative networks: A systematic review. *BMC Health Services Research,* 13, 1–13.

Luscombe, B. (2022). Inside the massive effort to change the way kids are taught to read. *Time Magazine.* https://time.com/6205084/phonics-science-of-reading-teachers/

Mahnken, K. (2022, June 20). After steering Mississippi's unlikely learning miracle, Carey Wright steps down. *The 74 Million.* https://www.the74million.org/article/after-steering-mississippis-unlikely-learning-miracle-carey-wright-steps-down/

McBride, M. (2021). A statewide journey toward structured literacy instruction. *Perspectives on Language and Literacy, 47*(2), 11–18.

McCannon, J., & Margiotta, B. K. (2015). Inside the command center. *Stanford Social Innovation Review.* https://doi.org/10.48558/D008-8B19

McCormick, R., Fox, A., Carmichael, P., & Procter, R. (2011). *Researching and understanding educational networks.* Routledge.

McQuillan, P. J. (2008). Small-school reform through the lens of complexity theory: It's "good to think with." *Teachers College Record, 110*(9), 1772–1801.

McQuillan, P. J., & Muncey, D. E. (1994). "Change takes time": A look at the growth and development of the Coalition of Essential Schools. *Journal of Curriculum Studies, 26*(3), 265–279.

Mehta, J. (2013). From bureaucracy to profession: Remaking the educational sector for the twenty-first century. *Harvard Educational Review, 83*(3), 463–543.

Mehta, J., & Fine, S. (2019). In *search of deeper learning: The quest to remake the American high school.* Harvard University Press.

Mehta, J., Yurkofsky, M., & Frumin, K. (2022). Linking continuous improvement and adaptive leadership. *Educational Leadership, 79*(6), 36–41.

Meyer, M. (2010). The rise of the knowledge broker. *Science Communication, 32*(1), 118–127.

Miao, Q., Newman, A., & Huang, X. (2014). The impact of participative leadership on job performance and organizational citizenship behavior: Distinguishing between the mediating effects of affective and cognitive trust. *International Journal of Human Resource Management, 25*(20), 2796–2810. https://doi.org/10.1080/09585192.2014.934890

Miesner, H. (2022). Dynamic and static working conditions: Examining the work of special education teachers. *Educational Forum, 86*(2), 125–137. http://dx.doi.org/10.1080/00131725.2020.1861146

Milgram, S. (1967). The small world problem. *Psychology Today, 2*(1), 60–67.

Mississippi Department of Education. (n.d.). *Mississippi Comprehensive Literacy Plan.* https://www.mdek12.org/sites/default/files/documents/OAE/Literacy/mclp-7-16-2017_final-(1).pdf

Mississippi Department of Education. (2023) *Superintendent's annual report: Mississippi marathon 2022–2023.* https://www.mdek12.org/sites/default/files/Offices/MDE/SSE/2023-AnnRep/mde_annual_report_2023_web_0.pdf

Mississippi Literacy-Based Promotion Act, Miss. Code Ann. § 37-177-1 (2013). Retrieved from https://legiscan.com/MS/text/SB2347/id/818137

Murdoch, D., English, A. R., Hintz, A., & Tyson, K. (2020). Feeling heard: Inclusive education, transformative learning, and productive struggle. *Educational Theory, 70*(5), 653–679.

Nadelstern, E. (2013). *10 lessons from New York City schools: What really works to improve education.* Teachers College Press.

National Center for Education Statistics. (2023). *Condition of education: Characteristics of traditional public, public charter, and private school teachers.* U.S. Department of Education, Institute of Education Sciences. https://nces.ed.gov/programs/coe/indicator/sld

National Center for Education Statistics. (2024). Racial/ethnic enrollment in U.S. public schools. *Condition of Education.* U.S. Department of Education, Institute of Education Sciences. https://nces.ed.gov/programs/coe/indicator/cge

National Center for Learning Disabilities. (2023, July 14). *Significant disproportionality in special education: Current trends and actions for impact* [Report]. https://ncld.org/wp-content/uploads/2023/07/2020-NCLD-Disproportionality_Trends-and-Actions-for-Impact_FINAL-1.pdf

National Reading Panel. (2000). *Teaching children to read: An evidence-based assessment of the scientific research literature on reading and its implications for reading instruction: Reports of the subgroups.* National Institute of Child Health and Human Development, National Institutes of Health. https://www.nichd.nih.gov/sites/default/files/publications/pubs/nrp/Documents/report.pdf

New York City Department of Health. (2024, April 2). *Window guards save lives* [Press release]. https://www.nyc.gov/site/doh/about/press/pr2024/window-guards-save-lives.page

New York City Public Schools. (n.d.). *The IEP process.* https://www.schools.nyc.gov/learning/special-education/the-iep-process

Nicolaides, A., & Poell, R. F. (2020). "The only option is failure": Growing safe to fail workplaces for critical reflection. *Advances in Developing Human Resources, 22*(3), 264–277.

Nonaka, I. (1994). A dynamic theory of organizational knowledge creation. *Organization Science, 5*(1), 14–37.

Nonaka, I., & Takeuchi, H. (1995). *The knowledge-creating company.* Oxford University Press.

Noonan, K., Sabel, C., Simon, W., (2009). Legal accountability in the service-based welfare state: Lessons from child welfare reform. *Law & Social Inquiry 34*(3), 523–569.

O'Dell, C., & Grayson, C. J. (1998). If only we knew what we know: Identification and transfer of internal best practices. *California Management Review, 40*(3), 154–174.

Office for Civil Rights. (2015, April). *Protecting civil rights, advancing equity: Report to the President and Secretary of Education*. U.S. Department of Education. https://www.ed.gov/sites/ed/files/about/reports/annual/ocr/report-to -president-and-secretary-of-education-2013-14.pdf

Ong-Dean, C. (2009). *Distinguishing disability: Parents, privilege, and special education*. University of Chicago Press.

O'Shea, C. (2021). Distributed leadership and innovative teaching practices. *International Journal of Educational Research Open, 2*, 100088. https://doi.org/10 .1016/j.ijedro.2021.100088

Park, S. (2021). Politics or bureaucratic failures: Understanding the dynamics of policy failures in democratic governance. *Journal of Policy Studies, 36*(3), 25–36.

Pellegrini, M., Lake, C., Inns, A., & Slavin, R. (2018, September 10). *Hard words: Why aren't kids being taught to read*? American Public Media (APM). https:// www.apmreports.org/episode/2018/09/10/hard-words-why-american -kids-arent-being-taught-to-read

Perry, J. (2009, October). Are drastic swings in CRCT scores valid? *The Atlanta Journal-Constitution*. https://www.ajc.com/news/local/are-drastic-swings -crct-scores-valid/1uNxbbiLUZjvYQx6gMkyyN/

Pietruszka, L. J., & Randall, J. (2023, October 24). *Leadership Identity* [Conference presentation]. Networks for School Improvement Community of Practice, Chicago, IL.

Podsakoff, P. M., MacKenzie, S. B., Paine, J. B., & Bachrach, D. G. (2000). Organizational citizenship behaviors: A critical review of the theoretical and empirical literature and suggestions for future research. *Journal of Management, 26*(3), 513–563.

Pourdehnad, J., Warren, B., Wright, M., & Mairano, J. (2006, June). Unlearning/learning organizations—The role of mindset. *Proceedings of the 50th Annual Meeting of the ISSS-2006, Sonoma, CA, USA*. https://journals.isss.org/index .php/proceedings50th/article/view/326

powell, j. a. (2019). Bridging or breaking? The stories we tell will create the future we inhabit. *Nonprofit Quarterly, 26*(4). https://nonprofitquarterly.org /bridging-or-breaking-the-stories-we-tell-will-create-the-future-we-inhabit/

Preskill, H., Gopal, S., Mack, K., & Cook, J. (2014). *Evaluating complexity: Propositions for improving practice* [Report]. FSG. https://www.fsg.org/publications /evaluating-complexity

Proctor, A., & Lupiani, J. (2024, June 25). *Atlanta Public Schools cheating scandal: Remaining defendants make deals to avoid prison*. Fox 5 Atlanta. https://www .fox5atlanta.com/news/atlanta-public-schools-cheating-scandal-defendants -court

Raj, C. S. (2021). Rights to nowhere: The IDEA's inadequacy in high-poverty schools. *Columbia Human Rights Law Review, 53*(2), 409–466.

Raymond, L. (2006). Cooperation without trust: Overcoming collective action barriers to endangered species protection. *Policy Studies Journal, 34*(1), 37–57.

Reading Universe. (2023, July 18). B*arksdale Reading Institute: The Mississippi story* [Video]. https://readinguniverse.org/about/partner-organizations#barksdale

Riordan, R., & Caillier, S. (2019). Schools as equitable communities of inquiry. In J. W. Cook (Ed.), *Sustainability, human well-being, and the future of education* (pp. 121–160). Palgrave Macmillan Cham. https://doi.org/10.1007/978-3-319-78580-6_4

Riser-Kositsky, M. (2019). Education statistics: Facts about American schools. *Education Week.* https://www.edweek.org/leadership/education-statistics-facts-about-american-schools/2019/01

Rittel, H. W., & Webber, M. M. (1973). Dilemmas in a general theory of planning. *Policy Sciences, 4*(2), 155–169.

RMC Research Corporation. (2019). *Mississippi's Literacy-Based Promotion Act: An inside look.* Excel in Ed. https://www.excelined.org/wp-content/uploads/2019/03/ExcelinEd.MSGatewaytoSuccess.March2019.pdf

Roberts, S. (2024). Anthony J. Alvarado, former New York City Schools Chancellor, dies at 81. *The New York Times.* https://www.nytimes.com/2024/01/05/nyregion/anthony-j-alvarado-dead.html

Roese, N. J., & Vohs, K. D. (2012). Hindsight bias. *Perspectives on Psychological Science, 7*(5), 411–426.

Rother, M. (2009). *Toyota Kata: Managing people for improvement, adaptiveness, and superior results.* McGraw-Hill Professional Publishing.

Rowe, P., & Boyle, M. (2005). Constraints to organizational learning during major change at a mental health services facility. *Journal of Change Management, 5*(1), 109–117. https://doi.org/10.1080/14697010500036320

Russell, J. L., Bryk, A. S., Peurach, D., LeMahieu, P. G., Shearer, D., Sherer, J., & Hannan, M. (2019). *The social structure of networked improvement communities: Cultivating the emergence of a scientific-professional learning community* [Report]. Carnegie Foundation for the Advancement of Teaching. https://www.carnegiefoundation.org/resources/publications/the-social-structure-of-networked-improvement-communities/

Saad, L. (2023, July 6). *Historically low faith in U.S. institutions continues.* Gallup. https://news.gallup.com/poll/508169/historically-low-faith-institutions-continues.aspx

Sabel, C., Saxenian, A., Miettinen, R., Hull Kristensen, P., & Hautamäki, J. (2011). Individualized service provision in the new welfare state: Lessons from special education in Finland. *Sitra Studies, 62.* SITRA and the Ministry of Employment and the Economy. https://researchportal.helsinki.fi/en/publications/individualized-service-provision-in-the-new-welfare-state-lessons

Sabel, C. F., & Victor, D. G. (2022). *Fixing the climate: Strategies for an uncertain world.* Princeton University Press.

Safir, S., & Dugan, J. (2021). *Street data: A next-generation model for equity, pedagogy, and school transformation.* Corwin.

Sagnak, M. (2016). Participative leadership and change-oriented organizational citizenship: The mediating effect of intrinsic motivation. *Eurasian Journal of Educational Research, 16*(62), 181–194. http://dx.doi.org/10.14689/ejer.2016 .62.11

Salmen, K., Ermark, F.K.G., & Fiedler, K. (2023). Pragmatic, constructive, and reconstructive memory influences on the hindsight bias. *Psychonomic Bulletin & Review, 30*, 331–340. https://doi.org/10.3758/s13423-022-02158-1

San Antonio, D. M. (2008). Creating better schools through democratic school leadership. *International Journal of Leadership in Education, 11*(1), 43–62.

Satell, G. (2015, June 8). Organizational restructuring: What makes an organization "networked"? *Harvard Business Review.* https://hbr.org/2015/06 /what-makes-an-organization-networked

Schein, E. H. (1993). On dialogue, culture, and organizational learning. *Organizational Dynamics, 22*(2), 40–51.

Schimpf, C., Swenson, J., & Burris, C. (2024, July). Power over and power with: Integrating the concept of power into design team and stakeholder interactions. *Frontiers in Education, 9.* https://doi.org/10.3389/feduc.2024 .1371216

Schwartz, S. (2024, November 5). Which states have passed "Science of Reading" laws? What's in them? *Education Week.* https://www.edweek.org /teaching-learning/which-states-have-passed-science-of-reading-laws -whats-in-them/2022/07

Seeley, T. D. (2011). *Honeybee democracy.* Princeton University Press.

Senge, P., Hamilton, H., & Kania, J. (2014). The dawn of system leadership. *Stanford Social Innovation Review, 13*(1), 27–33. https://doi.org/10.48558/YTE7 -XT62

Sennett, R. (2008). *The craftsman.* Yale University Press.

Sizer, T. R. (1986). Rebuilding: First steps by the coalition of essential schools. *The Phi Delta Kappan, 68*(1), 38–42. http://www.jstor.org/stable/20403257.

Sizer, T. R. (2004). *Horace's compromise: the dilemma of the American high school.* Harper Paperbacks.

Skrtic, T. (1991). The special education paradox: Equity as the way to excellence. *Harvard Educational Review, 61* (2), 148–207. https://doi.org/10.17763/haer .61.2.0q702751580h0617

Snowden, D. (2002a). Complex acts of knowing: Paradox and descriptive self-awareness. *Journal of Knowledge Management, 6*(2), 100–111.

Snowden, D. (2002b, January). *Conversations with David Snowden* [Interview]. Association of Knowledgework Star Series. https://web.archive.org/web /20080723221440/http://www.kwork.org/Stars/snowden_part1.html

Snowden, D. (2003). Innovation as an objective of knowledge management. Part I: The landscape of management. *Knowledge Management Research & Practice, 1*(2), 113–119.

Snowden, D. (2008, October 10). *Rendering knowledge.* The Cynefin Co. https:// thecynefin.co/rendering-knowledge/

Snowden, D. (2012). The social ecology of knowledge management. In C. Despres & D. Chauvel (Eds.), *Knowledge Horizons* (pp. 237–265). Routledge.

Snowden, D. (2024). As through a glass darkly: A complex systems approach to futures. In R. Poli (Ed.), *Handbook of futures studies* (pp. 48–65). Edward Elgar Publishing.

Snowden, D., & Boone, M. E. (2007). A leader's framework for decision making. *Harvard Business Review, 85*(11), 68–76.

Snowden, D., Pauleen, D. J., & van Vuuren, S. J. (2011). Knowledge management and the individual: It's nothing personal. In D. J. Pauleen & G. E. Gorman (Eds.), *Personal knowledge management: Individual, organizational and social perspectives* (pp.115–128). Routledge.

Somech, A. (2010). Participative decision making in schools: A mediating-moderating analytical framework for understanding school and teacher outcomes. *Educational Administration Quarterly, 46*(2), 174–209.

Souza, V. B., & Neto, L. M. (2018). A typology of coproduction: Emphasizing shared power. In M. Stout (Ed.), *From Austerity to Abundance?: Creative approaches to coordinating the common good* (pp. 117–139). Emerald Publishing Limited.

Sparrow, M. K. (2000). *The regulatory craft: Controlling risks, solving problems, and managing compliance.* Brookings Institution.

Spear, S. J. (2009). *The high-velocity edge: How market leaders leverage operational excellence to beat the competition.* McGraw-Hill.

Spillane, J. P. (2005, June). Distributed leadership. *The Educational Forum, 69*(2), 143–150.

Stivers, C. (2001). The listening bureaucrat: Responsiveness in public administration. In C. Stivers (Ed.), *Democracy, bureaucracy, and the study of administration* (pp. 222–234). Routledge.

Strauss, V. (2015). How and why convicted Atlanta teachers cheated on standardized tests. *The Washington Post.* https://www.washingtonpost.com/news/answer-sheet/wp/2015/04/01/how-and-why-convicted-atlanta-teachers-cheated-on-standardized-tests/

Taketa, K. (2023, August 13). Which San Diego school districts send the most kids to college, and how well do they prepare them? Here's what the data show. *The San Diego Union Tribune.* https://www.sandiegouniontribune.com/2023/08/10/which-san-diego-school-districts-send-the-most-kids-to-college-and-how-well-do-they-prepare-them-heres-what-the-data-show/

Taylor, J. R., & Van Every, E. J. (1999). *The emergent organization: Communication as its site and surface.* Routledge.

Toprani, A., Robinson, M., Middleton, J. K., III, Hamade, A., & Merrill, T. (2018). New York City's window guard policy: Four decades of success. *Injury Prevention, 24* (Suppl. 1), i14–i18. https://doi.org/10.1136/injuryprev-2017-042649

Tyack, D. B. (1974). *The one best system: A history of American urban education.* Harvard University Press.

Tyack, D. B., & Cuban, L. (1997). *Tinkering toward utopia: A century of public school reform*. Harvard University Press.

Turnage, L. (2020). Out of sight, out of mind: Rural special education and the limitations of the IDEA. *Columbia Journal of Law & Social Problems, 54*(1), 1–47.

Uzzi, B., Amaral, L. A., & Reed-Tsochas, F. (2007). Small-world networks and management science research: A review. *European Management Review, 4*(2), 77–9.

Vaughan, D. (2016). *The Challenger launch decision: Risky technology, culture, and deviance at NASA* (Expanded ed.). University of Chicago Press.

Volti, R. (2011). *An introduction to the sociology of work and occupations* (2nd ed.). Sage Publications.

Von Krogh, G., Ichijo, K., & Nonaka, I. (2000). *Enabling knowledge creation: How to unlock the mystery of tacit knowledge and release the power of innovation*. Oxford University Press.

Walker, D. (2002). The preparation of constructivist leaders. In L. Lambert (Ed.), *The constructivist leader* (2nd ed., pp. 204–239). Teachers College Press.

Wang, Q., Hou, H., & Li, Z. (2022). Participative leadership: A literature review and prospects for future research. *Frontiers in Psychology, 13*, 924357. http://doi.org/10.3389/fpsyg.2022.924357

Weber, M. (1993). Power, domination, and legitimacy. In M. E. Olsen, M. N. Marger, & V. Fonseca (Eds.), *Power in modern societies* (pp. 37–47). Routledge.

Weick, K. E. (1984). Small wins: Redefining the scale of social problems. *American Psychologist, 39*(1), 40.

Weick, K. E. (1995). *Sensemaking in organizations*. Sage Publications.

Weick, K. E., & Sutcliffe, K. M. (2015). *Managing the unexpected: Resilient performance in an age of uncertainty* (3rd ed.). Wiley.

Weick, K. E., Sutcliffe, K. M., & Obstfeld, D. (2005). Organizing and the process of sensemaking. *Organization science, 16*(4), 409–421.

White, R. K., & Lippitt, R. O. (1960). *Autocracy and democracy: An experimental inquiry*. Harper & Brothers.

Wicks, A. (2023). *Mississippi's reading revolution*. The Catalyst. https://www.bushcenter.org/catalyst/the-fix/mississippis-reading-revolution

Will, M. (2020, January 27). More teacher-preparation programs are teaching the "Science of Reading," review finds. *Education Week*. https://www.edweek.org/teaching-learning/more-teacher-preparation-programs-are-teaching-the-science-of-reading-review-finds/2020/01

Williamson, O. (1963). Managerial discretion and business behavior. *The American Economic Review, 53*(5), 1032–1057. http://www.jstor.org/stable/1812047

Wilson, A. (2000, July 24). The gift of literacy: Sally and Jim Barksdale. *Time*. https://time.com/archive/6741807/the-gift-of-literacy-sally-and-jim-barksdale/

Wilson, R. E., Bowers, M. J., & Hyde, R. L. (2011). *Special investigation into test tampering in Atlanta's school system*. Georgia Bureau of Investigation.

https://archive.org/details/215252-special-investigation-into-test-tampering
-in/mode/1up

Wood, L. (2022). *We, not they* [Video]. High Tech High Unboxed. https://
hthunboxed.org/videos/we-not-they/

Woods, P. A. (2005, February 3). Democratic leadership in education. SAGE
Publications.

Yackee, J. W., & Yackee, S. W. (2006). A bias towards business? Assessing interest
group influence on the U.S. bureaucracy. *The Journal of Politics, 68*(1), 128–139.
https://doi.org/10.1111/j.1468-2508.2006.00375.x

Yeager, D., Bryk, A., Muhich, J., Hausman, H., & Morales, L. (2013). *Practical
measurement* [Unpublished manuscript]. Carnegie Foundation for the Advancement of Teaching.

Yohn, D. L. (2021, February 28). Company culture is everyone's responsibility. *Harvard Business Review.* https://hbr.org/2021/02/company-culture-is
-everyones-responsibility

Zavadsky, H. (2009). *Bringing school reform to scale: Five award-winning urban districts.* Harvard Education Press.

Index

About the Authors

Elizabeth Chu is the executive director of the Center for Public Research and Leadership and Senior Research Scholar and Lecturer of Law at Columbia Law School. Her ideas and research have appeared in numerous publications including *American Journal of Education, Columbia Human Rights Law Review, Teachers College Record, Education Week, Learning Forward,* and *Forbes.* Before joining CPRL, Elizabeth was an assistant professor of practice at Relay Graduate School of Education, where she taught general pedagogy courses, designed and managed internal data collection systems, and performed research on school discipline, teacher preparation, and social-emotional learning. Elizabeth began her career in education as a middle and high school English teacher in the South Bronx. She earned her PhD in education policy from Columbia University, an MS in teaching secondary English from Pace University, and a BA in English language arts and literature from Yale University.

Andrea Clay is a director of legal strategy and policy at CPRL. In this role, she provides policy advice and leads student teams on projects on topics including high-quality instructional materials and teacher professional development to use those materials, the use of continuous improvement methodologies to improve instructional practice, and restructuring work to include meaningful stakeholder participation. Prior to joining CPRL, Andrea worked at various organizations in the education sector, including community-based organizations, legal services groups, and schools. She is also a former middle school English teacher, having taught in Newark, New Jersey. She earned a JD from Harvard Law School and an AB in English from Princeton University.

Ayeola Kinlaw is a project director at CPRL. She provides research, organizational strategy and development, and philanthropic advising services to nonprofit organizations and foundations. At CPRL, she has developed strategic plans and measurement frameworks, designed and conducted a formative evaluation of improvement networks, and facilitated trainings on Evolutionary Learning. Prior to launching her consulting practice, Ayeola served as a senior program officer at the Wallace Foundation focused on school and district leadership and was the founding director of the 100Kin10 Funders Collaborative where she supported the strategic philanthropy of more than 34 national, regional, and corporate funders. Ayeola has a BA from Duke University and an MS from Harvard Graduate School of Education.

Meghan Snyder is a director of research strategy and policy at CPRL. In this role, she works with partners on a range of topics related to governance and system design, knowledge management, networked improvement, and deliberative democracy. Prior to joining CPRL, Meghan worked with adult learners at Academy of Hope Adult Public Charter School, the Borough of Manhattan Community College, and the Caledonian School in Prague, where she taught and developed social studies, reading, and writing curriculum. Meghan earned a MA in sociology and education from Teachers College, Columbia University and a BA in international studies from American University's School of International Service.